praise for *slow democracy*

"This is a truly important book: it explains, with copious example and lots of common sense, why democracy works better close to home. If you've begun to think the carrot from the farmers' market tastes better, this volume will lead you (liberal or conservative) down the logical path toward a working society."
—Bill McKibben, author of *Deep Economy:*
The Wealth of Communities and the Durable Future

"*Slow Democracy* just may be the best thing happening in America today. Connecting in a meaningful way with our community and reclaiming our power as citizens is both powerful and possible. Read this book and consider how this movement can revitalize the communities you care about!"
—Joan Blades, cofounder, MoveOn.org

"Great stories about democracy—showing us that democracy is not what we have but what we do. So if you've been 'looking for hope in all the wrong places,' now you've found one that's right! Enjoy."
—Frances Moore Lappé, author of *EcoMind:*
Changing the Way We Think to Create the World We Want

"It is all too easy to be cynical about the contemporary democratic process. Clark and Teachout provide a roadmap for turning that cynicism into the sort of regionalized action that can improve lives and transform communities. Don't give up on democracy: Read this book and get to work!"
—Ben Hewitt, author of *The Town that Food Saved*
and *Making Supper Safe*

"*Slow Democracy* is a lively and significant book. Clark and Teachout use a broad array of stories to illustrate how our democracy is changing, and how we can capitalize on the pressures and opportunities we face in our communities. They describe how carefully structured public engagement can lead, ironically, to faster, better solutions to public problems. Finally, they show how improving local democracy, one place at a time, can add up quickly to much larger national and global impacts."

—Matt Leighninger, executive director,
Deliberative Democracy Consortium

"The time is exactly right for a book that takes democracy seriously, and knows where to look for it. Clark and Teachout recognize that representative democracy must be rooted in the fertile soil of face-to-face, local, problem-solving democracy. With engaging storytelling skills, they remind us of how vibrant these civic roots still are, and they encourage us to give this democratic garden even greater care and attention, and to enjoy its fruits while we're at it."

—Daniel Kemmis, former mayor of Missoula, Montana;
author of *Community and the Politics of Place*

"The 'slow' in *Slow Democracy* doesn't mean decision making needs to take longer. It's an acknowledgment that investing in inclusive, deliberative, and empowered local decision making is worth the time. Here are community stories that will fill you with hope for American politics."

—Sandy Heierbacher, director,
National Coalition for Dialogue & Deliberation

"Slow democracy is the only kind that can take root, because it answers our deepest longings for connection, community, and voice. Clark and Teachout provide compelling examples and guiding principles for nurturing inclusive, participatory communities that work for everyone. Read this book, and then put it into action!"

—Martha McCoy, executive director, Everyday Democracy

slow
democracy

slow
democracy

Rediscovering Community,
Bringing Decision Making Back Home

SUSAN CLARK *and* WODEN TEACHOUT

CHELSEA GREEN PUBLISHING
WHITE RIVER JUNCTION, VERMONT

Editor: Joni Praded
Project Manager: Bill Bokermann
Designer: Melissa Jacobson
Copy Editor: Nancy Ringer
Proofreader: Helen Walden
Indexer: Margaret Holloway

Printed in the United States of America
First printing September 2012
10 9 8 7 6 5 4 3 2 1   12 13 14 15 16

Chelsea Green Publishing is committed to preserving ancient forests and natural resources. We elected to print this title on 30-percent postconsumer recycled paper, processed chlorine-free. As a result, for this printing, we have saved:

14 Trees (40' tall and 6-8" diameter)
6 Million BTUs of Total Energy
1,247 Pounds of Greenhouse Gases
6,762 Gallons of Wastewater
453 Pounds of Solid Waste

Chelsea Green Publishing made this paper choice because we and our printer, Thomson-Shore, Inc., are members of the Green Press Initiative, a nonprofit program dedicated to supporting authors, publishers, and suppliers in their efforts to reduce their use of fiber obtained from endangered forests. For more information, visit: www.greenpressinitiative.org.

Environmental impact estimates were made using the Environmental Defense Paper Calculator. For more information visit: www.papercalculator.org.

Our Commitment to Green Publishing

Chelsea Green sees publishing as a tool for cultural change and ecological stewardship. We strive to align our book manufacturing practices with our editorial mission and to reduce the impact of our business enterprise in the environment. We print our books and catalogs on chlorine-free recycled paper, using vegetable-based inks whenever possible. This book may cost slightly more because it was printed on paper that contains recycled fiber, and we hope you'll agree that it's worth it. Chelsea Green is a member of the Green Press Initiative (www.greenpressinitiative.org), a nonprofit coalition of publishers, manufacturers, and authors working to protect the world's endangered forests and conserve natural resources. *Slow Democracy: Rediscovering Community, Bringing Decision Making Back Home* was printed on FSC®-certified paper supplied by Thomson-Shore that contains at least 30% postconsumer recycled fiber.

Library of Congress Cataloging-in-Publication Data
Clark, Susan.
  Slow democracy : rediscovering community, bringing decision making back home / Susan Clark and Woden Teachout.
      p. cm.
  ISBN 978-1-60358-413-5 (pbk.) — ISBN 978-1-60358-414-2 (ebook)
  1. Democracy—Decision making. 2. Deliberative democracy. I. Teachout, Woden. II. Title.

JC423.C583 2012
321.8—dc23
                                    2012025228

Chelsea Green Publishing
85 North Main Street, Suite 120
White River Junction, VT 05001
(802) 295-6300
www.chelseagreen.com

contents

foreword   vii

preface   xiii

introduction   xxi

PART I: Slow Democracy: Why Do We Need It?

one: "Town Halls" from Hell, and Other Stories   1

two: The Rise of Experts and the Decline of Local Decision Making   20

three: Communities Taking Action in a Big World   38

PART II: Slow Democracy: Why Now?

four: The Time Is Right   61

five: Cultural Cognition and Slow Democracy   82

PART III: A Recipe for Slow Democracy

six: The Promise of Local   107

seven: Inclusion   116

eight: Dialogue and Building Understanding   130

nine: Deliberation   143

ten: Power   163

PART IV: Reflections on Slow Democracy

eleven: The Jury, Town Meeting, and Slow Democracy   177

twelve: When Advocacy Meets Slow Democracy   186

epilogue: Closing Thoughts: The Ecology of Slow Democracy   203

appendix a: Slow Democracy Rules   205

appendix b: Slow Democracy Resource List   209

acknowledgments   212

notes   215

index   234

foreword

What is understood . . . in the United States is the slow and quiet action of society upon itself. It is a regular state of things really founded upon the enlightened will of the people. It is a conciliatory government, under which resolutions are allowed time to ripen, and in which they are deliberately discussed, and are executed only when mature."

—Alexis de Tocqueville

The decline of democracy in America is best marked by the decay of its very definition. Calling America a democracy is like calling football tennis. In truth democracy is a construct so thin that its meaning has been reduced to flagrant ambiguity. Like love, its meaning has become wholly dependent on its adjectives.

Worse, the word "democracy," in one form or another, has migrated into strange oxymorons. Consider, as in America's case, "democratic republic." Oxymorons like "Fox News" (found inside the locket on Sarah Palin's neck) and "voluntary mandate" (found inside President Obama's health care law) can be funny. But like "democratic republic," they may cry warning: mischief is afoot; disaster awaits. This book has no definitional ambiguity. It is about face-to-face deliberative democracy.

Postmodern culture, says the French philosopher Pascal Bruckner, is increasingly caught up in disasters. In his recent book, he calls this the "ideology of catastrophe." Fueled by a capitalist media that sells doomsday scenarios with impunity, the ideology of catastrophe has itself become catastrophic. Hyperactive fear leads not to reasoned action but to paralysis, writes Bruckner. It shuts off oxygen to the brain. I tend to agree with this unfortunate diagnosis but would add a friendly (and age-old) amendment: The greatest danger of apocalypse baiting may have been forewarned in the fifth century B.C. by a Greek slave named Aesop. Sometimes the wolf is real. What then?

Trust me. It is with appropriate humility and extreme deference to both Bruckner and Aesop that I now cry warning: The American center is collapsing. It is nearly brain-dead. The Republic, so resplendent in hope and promise a mere century past, now gasps for air, its parts panting along but its heart (a mosaic of local democracies throughout the land—Jefferson's "schoolhouses" of democracy) beating ever fainter. The sound of democratic oxygen beating upward to sustain our national citizenship has become but a whisper. This accelerating calamity is made more tragic still by the presence of a solution that lies right under our noses. Why can't we see it? Why can't we embrace it?

Fortunately, Susan Clark and Woden Teachout can and have. Even better, they chose to share it. You have their blueprint for an American redemption in your hands.

Their prescription calls for oxygen, and the oxygen of our representative Republic is and has always been *democracy*—real, face-to-face democracy. Even the "father of representation," John Stuart Mill, recognized the essential role democracy plays in sustaining the kind of government he so wisely envisioned as the solution to the fall of monarchy. Mill proffered not the oxymoron he eschewed (a democratic republic) but a representative republic *sustained* by democracy—by democrats reared and trained as citizens in human-scale communities. Mill's genius is in part found in his recognition that the presence of homegrown democrats is essential to the proper functioning of a distant representative republic. "All politics," a famous New England Democrat once said, is "local." Tip O'Neill, the congressman from Massachusetts, might well have added: "That is why all democracy is local, too—or at least it had better be."

Bottom line? Face-to-face *democracy* in the parts is essential to a *representative* republic for the whole. It is because the latter—our splendid Republic—is so critical to us (and to the world) that a renaissance of what the authors of this book call "slow" democracy is now so critical. We need to take back our localities, reacquaint democracy with place (and vice versa), and, by governing these places ourselves, give the center the space to breathe again. By doing this, three good things will happen. First, much of our public policy (both left and right now agree) will be much better designed and (thus) much better implemented. Second, the Nation will be freed to do those things it must do much better. Third (and most importantly), democracy will be restored—where it belongs. Representation will be dramatically improved because those who represent and those who are represented will be trained in the art of democracy, the product of face-to-face tutorials in deliberative and humane decision making.

Briefly: how did we get into this mess and what are the chances we can pull off the fundamental changes needed to get out of it? In truth we need not be hard on ourselves. America came of age in the teeth of the urban-industrial revolution. We were captivated by it—body and mind. Hierarchy, authority, symmetry, and centralism were more than the natural outcroppings of the machine age. They were causal. That our social and political institutions followed suit is neither surprising nor actionable in the jurisprudence of history.

The world has changed but (quite understandably) our behavior has not. We, and our political leadership, are still trapped in the vacuum of purpose created when new behavioral opportunities (and in some cases mandates) are caught in the reverse momentum, the ebb tide, of a bygone age. Our collective behavior still is drawn backward by the *habits* of hierarchical rigidity.

What is needed now is a smart, holistic, and most importantly courageous reassessment of the options available to us in terms of governance. The potential for such a new calculus of democracy is immensely enhanced by the passing of the second-wave urban-industrial model, driven by steam and then gasoline. In its place we find the ascendance of a third wave—a new paradigm—for today's electronic age. It's a paradigm that is nonhierarchical, community centered, and fundamentally (and uniquely) democratic in character. At its core one axiom prevails: the third wave is as centrifugal as the second wave was centripetal.

This new model has been recognized and indeed explored for some time. In fact, it dominates marketplace culture and is thus rapidly transforming the way we live, the way we think, the way we buy and sell, the way we read and educate and play and dream. Only one constellation of human activity seems relatively untouched: the way we govern. Worse still, to the extent that the electronic revolution (especially the information and communication technology associated with it) has informed our politics, it has driven us further into the morass of enhanced *second-wave* behavior. Our political system has become faster, more centralized, more homogeneous, more predictable. Thus it has become more inhumane. As for our more and more centralized (thus counter-paradigmatic) representative "democracy," it grows thinner, ever thinner. And it grows dumber, meaner, and, yes, more and more abhorrent.

Everywhere we need smart, young, creative scholars and activists who are unattached to the old framework and brave enough to commit their precious personal resources to a postmodern democracy project. We need a new generation of democrats who look at the times into which they were born and say: We can fashion a fresh, unique world of human-scale politics and reinstate the citizen as the center of a humane republic of democratic governance.

Enter Clark and Teachout.

They have several things going for them. One is that they are gutsy. They are willing to look both liberal and conservative mantras straight in the eye and call them to account. Mind you, they know their audience. Still, they don't flinch. They've seen enough of the "buy local," "sell local," "think local," and "be local" along with "Vote Obama" bumper stickers and seem to be just itching to sneak up and slap on a "govern local" bumper sticker for good measure—if only to call a bluff or two. They are democrats, you see. Real democrats. Their brand of "slow democracy" is perfectly situated on the nexus where traditional "local control" conservatives and newer "small is beautiful" liberals meet. In today's America, with the marketplace capitalist/social-conservative Republicans and the mega-state/centralized-planning Democrats soiling themselves and each other with their incessant, inane yapping, Clark and Teachout are a breath of fresh air.

They are also in sync with a new and hopeful movement in academe—and on the ground in communities across the nation—that uses real-time application of deliberative democracy as both a laboratory *for* and a means of disseminating the results *of* deliberative democracy. Deliberative democrats argue that face-to-face interaction is of critical value in a democracy for its *own sake*. The authors of *Slow Democracy* are in many ways, therefore, radical decentralists.

Some argue that citizens can be drawn from a national pool to participate in face-to-face deliberation, the results of which are then ratcheted upward to inform national policy. Others prefer to concentrate on enhancing face-to-face deliberation in more natural settings, such as local deliberative forums or even formal institutions like councils and boards, with the results to be used for the immediate purpose of influencing local jurisdictions directly. But most significant is the existence (at last!) of a cadre of thinkers and doers at large in the country who truly believe in *democracy*. It is this last group who might find the authors' provocative vision most intriguing.

Moreover, Clark and Teachout are, to borrow a phrase from *Megatrends* author John Naisbitt, "riding the horse of history in the direction history is going." Americans are (and have been for some time) returning home again. The ascendant techno-electronic paradigm is making this journey both natural and easy.

Finally, the politics are lining up in a way favorable to slow democracy. We have known for some time that the dehumanizing effects of centralization, hierarchy, and authority have been bending the extremes of the classic left-right ideological continuum downward and inward toward an inevitable rendezvous with a new dichotomy. The right (properly) fears big government. The left (properly) fears big business. The shift began with Eisenhower, who saw danger in the creation of a new and all-too-powerful "military-industrial" establishment. It took shape slowly for the next half century, gaining momentum in the last decade. Most recently it appeared in the congruence—which seemed at first a bit weird—between the Tea Party and the Occupy Wall Street protesters. But more and more, we are realizing that the commonality is not weird at all. The "sector"—public (government) or private (industry)—matters less than the dynamic. The undemocratic, indeed the antidemocratic imperative of both traditional sectors was centralism, hierarchy, and authority. Now it has become (blessedly) apparent that the fact that one is somehow "public" and the other is somehow "private" matters not.

Slow Democracy is a book apart. Its courage permits it to be honest. Its honesty compels us to think of community and democracy as one—inseparable in concept as well as practice. Its vision commands us to make good on our professed faith in each other by practicing collective action face-to-face. Its hope is that we can learn to accept that properly understood, democracy needs no adjectives, that the title of the book, while perfect for the authors' generation, becomes a redundancy for the future. Its wisdom suggests that their hope will be fulfilled.

As for the rest of us, we should join in that hope. The future of the Republic depends on it.

FRANK M. BRYAN
MAY 2012

preface

In *Slow Democracy*, we've drawn on the values of slow food as an inspiration for community decision making. Our book is a collaboration of two authors who have, in different but complementary ways, been working to keep community interests alive in government. Here are our stories.

Susan's Story

Appropriately enough, the idea for this book began in the garden. Mind you, if gardening were only about producing food, I would have thrown in the trowel long ago; if I got paid minimum wage for all of the inept hours I spend in the garden, my zucchinis would cost twenty-five bucks each. Still, I am out there with my hands in the dirt every chance I get. As a person who deals with community conflicts and political decision making on a regular basis, I find there is no better place to relax than in the sunshine with a good audiobook playing in my earbuds.

I was thinning carrots one weekend while listening to Michael Pollan's *The Omnivore's Dilemma* when it hit me: the work I had been doing in community development was perfectly aligned with the efforts of the Slow Food movement. The metaphor was inspiring, and it brought a wave of fresh, exciting ideas to mind. Slow Democracy!

I ran inside and tested the idea out on my husband. He seemed impressed at first, saying enthusiastically, "Slow Democracy? Great idea! Hey, I bet you could even get the domain name—SlowDemocracy.org!"

Then I noticed the twinkle in his eye as he added, in deadpan, "While you're at it, why not see if you can get PainfulDentistry.org too?"

Okay, he had a point. Who wants their democracy to be slow?

Still, despite my husband's teasing (believe me, I'm used to it), I remained convinced that "slow democracy" was a concept that should be part of the public conversation. And I even found a co-conspirator.

I don't recall where Woden and I first crossed paths. I'd like to say it was when I was teaching at Woodbury College in Montpelier, Vermont, where she was a department head, and we had an insightful exchange on some key policy issue. However, it's probably more likely we met at the local elementary school that our kids attend. My rear end was probably sticking out of the supply closet as I tried to find the squirrel puppets for the nature lesson I'd volunteered for in my son's classroom.

And if it was a school encounter, that would have been fitting. Because at Rumney Memorial School (named after the farmer whose land the school was built on), there's a strong sense of volunteerism. When parents' fannies aren't sticking out of closets, their smiling faces are being welcomed into the classrooms by friendly teachers. I've pitched in on science studies, led songs in the kindergarten, helped backstage in theater productions, and frosted more bake-sale cupcakes than I really like to think about.

It's not only the teachers who welcome participation. Where I really remember working with Woden was at Rumney school board meetings—and neither of us was actually *on* the school board. Woden and I were among the parents who attended these meetings to speak out in favor of our town retaining our school and our school board.

The alarm bell had rung loudly for both Woden and me when Vermont lawmakers passed a law encouraging school consolidation. The law offered incentives for school districts to merge—incentives that, we knew, would ultimately cause communities to reduce the number of school boards and probably close small schools. I know that most of the legislators who voted for this bill just hoped it would save money. But they also, either mindfully or out of neglect, were diminishing local democratic infrastructure and opportunities for parents and neighbors to engage in decisions about their children's education.

Many people assume that given Vermont's town meeting tradition—combined with the fact that Vermont is small and almost insanely liberal—surely we make all of our decisions locally, by consensus, perhaps over crunchy-topped apple crumble at potluck suppers. But you'd be surprised. We have at least our share, maybe more than our share, of top-down, state-centralizing policies on the books, and more are coming. While citizens have been happily focused at our annual town meetings on making decisions about potholes and road salt, power on larger issues has slowly but surely been siphoned away from towns. Sometimes it goes to the state level, sometimes to the federal level, but either way, with it goes the much of the inspiration for community involvement.

The law encouraging school consolidation was just one more step in an erosion of local democratic infrastructure that I was already painfully familiar with. In my research for a book on Vermont town meetings, I had traveled all over the state interviewing citizens and community leaders about local democracy. In community after community, I had heard stories of how deeply residents valued the give-and-take of town-meeting decision making. And yet, as power has become more and more centralized, towns have had the ability to take binding action on fewer and fewer issues. As Vermont's town population size has risen and we have lost connections with our neighbors, fewer people have been attending town meetings. Between commuting, screen time, and working extra jobs in a tough economy, we allocate less time for local democracy. Every year, it seems, another Vermont town has gotten rid of its town meeting altogether and switched to ballot voting.

The Rumney school board was preparing to take a key vote on whether to move forward on the school consolidation idea. The night of that meeting, I had written a letter to the board with my concerns. I showed up at the meeting feeling nervous to the point of mild nausea. Why had I gone out on this limb? What difference could our voices make?

When I arrived at the meeting, someone had taken the trouble to make copies of my letter and put them on people's chairs. When it came time to discuss the issues, school board members referred to my letter directly and discussed which parts they agreed with, which they didn't, and how they would take action.

In my career, I have spoken before audiences of hundreds of people, given radio and television interviews, and testified many times before the state legislature. But I have never felt more validated than when my local school board paid attention to my opinion.

Why did they pay attention to me? Because they are my neighbors. They knew I had a right to speak. They'd seen my rear end sticking out of that closet enough times to know my heart was here, too.

My school board doesn't see parents as a "they," and Woden and I don't see the school board as a "they." *We* all know *we* are in this together. While I don't expect always to see eye-to-eye with my local officials, I know at least my voice, along with the voices of my fellow community members, can be heard.

This is the beauty of slow democracy. It is inclusive, it is deliberative, it is empowered, and it's local. At this level, we have access to our leaders, and they have access to us.

I am tired of apologizing for the time democracy takes. I'm changing my strategy. No more apologies—only celebration. Yes, local democracy and strengthening community takes time; so enjoy it. I challenge anyone to find a better investment of those hours. You can do it at school board meetings, but you can also do it while you're on the sidelines of a soccer game, working with friends to insulate a community building, or savoring a delicious dinner shared with neighbors. When it takes place at a human scale and a humane pace, democracy can offer the profound satisfaction of a job well done. As Slow Food founder Carlo Petrini describes his movement, it is "a responsible, knowing form of pleasure."

Slow democracy can work in many different ways in many different places—and in the pages that follow we explain a wide range of approaches. It isn't perfect. But I have yet to encounter a system that works better. Especially today, local, slow democracy offers lessons that America profoundly needs to hear.

Woden's Story

Recently a friend who lives in Detroit told me that she'd never been to the Detroit city hall. Her comment shocked me, especially when I realized that her experience was probably more typical than mine. I am constantly running off to school board meetings, and at least every two months I drop in at the town offices to pay taxes or pick up forms or leave something for my neighbor, who happens to be the town clerk.

Vermont is a small state, and local government feels more than accessible. In most Vermont towns, you can walk into a public meeting and everyone will call you by your name. School board and selectboard meetings are held in the evenings, in empty rooms with fluorescent lights, and they are generally delighted to have visitors. Often, you can propose changes and—as long as they are within town powers—see them instituted in a matter of several meetings. In fact, getting recruited for town office is a common occurrence. For most of these positions, politics is less a matter of ambition and more a matter of taking your turn—with some wily neighbors throwing flattery your way to get you to *want* to do it.

Even our statehouse feels welcoming. There are no security measures, no velvet cordons keeping you off the marble floors: you just walk right in. You can watch the action on the floor of the House or Senate, or go up and walk into the committee rooms to hear testimony. And because the state is so small, it's not unusual for an ordinary citizen to know people wandering around the halls—legislators, reporters, lobbyists. Last year I was looking for a public hearing, opened the wrong door, and came face-to-face with Susan, who happened to be giving a talk to high school students at that very moment.

I often think about the hearings leading up to Vermont's civil-union law, which was enacted in 2000. The state was polarized over the issue of whether gay residents should have benefits parallel to those of marriage. It was an intense time, full of angry rhetoric and righteous feelings. I remember going with a friend to the statehouse on a January night, flooding in with hundreds of others, stamping the snow off our boots. Downstairs, we passed people from both sides handing out stickers from long rolls: white ones reading "'Don't Mock Marriage" and pink ones saying "I Support the Freedom to Marry." Upstairs, the green-and-gold House chamber was already full, and the balcony was overflowing, so about thirty of us crowded into the small anteroom off the balcony. There were no chairs, so we sat on the floor: shoulder to shoulder, legs outstretched, pink stickers next to white stickers next to none at all.

We couldn't hear what was being said, but someone had brought a battery-powered radio, so we listened by broadcast to the testimony being given in the next room. It was quieting to hear the stories citizens told the committee; across the political spectrum, they were all deeply rooted in personal experience and demanded a quality of attention that is rare in politics. This was no kumbaya moment—the gay-rights activists and the evangelicals still eyed each other warily—but it was civil. We all knew that evening was historic, watching our state poised to do something that no other state had done. And the effect, when the state passed the law, was profound. Our small state's action led to the passage of real marriage-equality acts in a number of other states—acts that have had concrete effects on tens of thousands of lives and a profound impact on our culture. I still feel a deep sense of pride in that law, and it is a pride that is weirdly personal, because of having been there.

Living in Vermont, with experiences like that, has shaped my approach to local government in a way that is increasingly inconceivable to friends who live elsewhere. Here, getting involved seems self-evident, rather than alien. To a large degree, Vermont already *does* slow democracy. It's not that we do it better than other places; as you'll read in these pages, local communities from the Atlantic to the Pacific are claiming their power and building their own democratic processes. But living here—where even state government is arguably "local"—has hit me over the head with the fact that it can and should be done.

Because of this, running up against national and corporate power in my home state has come as a shock. The Vermont Yankee nuclear plant is forty years old and counting; it has exceeded the life span it was designed for, and there are constant news reports of tritium leaks and cooling-tower break-downs. Most Vermonters want it shut down, and the legislature voted not to renew its license. But the Nuclear Regulatory Commission and federal judges have combined to force a renewal. The situation is infuriating to me. Why should the NRC, with its entrenched pro-industry interests, make decisions that Vermonters should be making for themselves?

So it has been clear to me all along why "local" is an important part of slow democracy. While national politics roils on, there is so much we can do on the local level to create real change. I get fired up when I read about counties in California banning GMOs and tiny towns in Pennsylvania fighting back against fracking. I'm thrilled that our state is working toward a single-payer health care system. The reason I was initially drawn to this project was to highlight those issues, and the exciting things that can be done on the local level.

But Susan has been insistent that slow democracy is not just about advocacy on the local level, but rather about creating processes that foster relationships. At first I wrinkled my eyebrows and thought, "That's Susan." For her, watching communities in conversation is a heart-and-soul experience. As the moderator of our town meeting, she loves standing in the school gym, watching everyone shuffle in—the lawyers and the farmers and the nurses and the road commissioner and the teachers, all in their parkas and boots. She loves helping people discuss issues that matter to them and spending the long hours it may take to find answers they can live with.

I'm not like that. I dread meetings: the scraping of chairs and the lights and the drone of people endlessly talking. I wish they'd stop expressing themselves and just get to the point. I'd prefer to be washing dishes, hauling wood, even cleaning out the oddments that have accumulated in the silverware drawer—anything not to be in that room. A professor once told me never to go to a meeting unless my presence makes a difference, and I try to live by that rule. I go only if some real change is likely to result. The same process that warms Susan leaves me cold: I'd rather quit talking and get up and *do* something.

I also love advocacy. Give me a fight any day, preferably of the David and Goliath variety, in which I can battle against an opponent in power. I love the sense of working for ordinary people against corporate interests or government intrusions. The strategies, the alliances, the fact gathering, the crafting of rhetoric to resonate with people's values in the service of a worthy cause—all that turns me on. And yes, I enjoy the feeling of being right. Experience has shown me that, on whatever side of an issue, I'm not alone in that.

So while I was fully convinced of the importance of local democratic action, I wasn't sure about all this communities-coming-together business. Some issues are about right and wrong, about protecting civil rights and the environment, about fighting real intrusions from big business and big government. Those tend to be the ones I care about, and it is hard to see how a touchy-feely conversation was going to change the underlying power dynamics.

Two things really convinced me. The first was realizing that there is a place for advocacy and a place for slow democracy—something we'll talk about in chapter 12. The second was seeing how specific communities have used slow democracy techniques to create workable solutions to local problems. Because even more than the win-lose tactics of advocacy, the thing that excites me about local government is the opportunity for problem solving.

I was especially struck by how the problem-solving techniques we describe in this book cut through ideological divisions and allowed communities to frame their own questions. This was brought home to me when our school was thinking about combining with the smaller school in the next town. I dug into the research on consolidation, downloading scholarly articles in my living room at midnight and figuring out what the issues were. As it was presented in the literature, the issues were stark: you were either pro-consolidation or anti-consolidation, and given my values, I knew where I stood.

But then Susan told me about the example of Portsmouth, New Hampshire. Faced with a similar question, they had used the techniques we outline here. Instead of stepping into roles in an ideological debate about consolidation, they had sidestepped that debate and figured out how to shift a small group of children from school to school, in a way that worked for everyone. Their situation was different—an urban redistricting question instead of a rural consolidation one—but their solution suggested possibilities that hadn't been slotted into a national conversation.

This was an epiphany for me. As our discussion of cultural cognition in chapter 5 shows, Americans have a tendency to accept a polarized framing of hot issues. I know I'm guilty. But we don't have to do that, certainly not at the local level. There is a real empowerment in rejecting the way that issues have been framed for us—often by national parties and coalitions—and deciding what our own questions and values are. As citizens, we need to be able to define our own agendas and have the power to implement them.

Yes, this is a longer process than I would like, and yes, it involves meetings, but I'm convinced. The time for slow democracy has come.

SUSAN CLARK AND WODEN TEACHOUT
MAY 2012

introduction

The protestors stood on the Piazza di Spagna in Rome, brandishing bowls of penne pasta. Above them rose the wide marble staircase of the Spanish Steps; nearby, turquoise water spilled from the square's iconic marble fountain, just as it had for centuries. But on the far end of the plaza, just south of these defining Roman landmarks, was a new and alien symbol: the Golden Arches.

The year was 1986, and the just-opened McDonald's was the world's largest to date. Many Romans had protested in outrage: in a country renowned for its artisanal cheeses, native herbs, and traditional long-simmered tomato sauces, mass-produced hamburgers were sacrilege.[1] But the government had allowed the franchise to open, and now the demonstrators stood in the Piazza on opening day, handing out bowls of penne and marinara sauce. Their offering was an expression of values—simple, traditional, and local—and they underscored it with the chant, "We don't want fast food! We want slow food!"

Three years later, in 1989, representatives from fifteen countries gathered in Paris to sign the Slow Food Manifesto, articulating a critique of fast food that resonated far beyond Italy. The manifesto argued that regional cooking and leisurely, sensual meals were a value unto themselves, necessary to "preserve us from the contagion of the multitude who mistake frenzy with efficiency":

> Our century, which began and has developed under the insignia of industrial civilization, first invented the machine and then took it as its life model. We are enslaved by speed and have all succumbed to the same insidious virus: *Fast Life*. . . . In the name of productivity, *Fast Life* has changed our way of being and threatens our environment and our landscapes.[2]

Since then, the Slow Food movement has expanded its mission: no longer primarily about food appreciation, it is dedicated to the creation of a just, sustainable food system. In the name of slow food, over 100,000 official members and untold thousands of additional supporters are organizing farmers' markets, lobbying for sustainable agricultural policies, and preserving heirloom varieties of fruit and vegetable seeds. Others start gardening programs in schools and prisons, and still others support local growers in struggling countries. Even more important than these individual projects has been the ripple effect in the larger culture, as "slow" and "local" have become explicit values. As one organizer recently commented, "[Slow food] links the pleasure of food with a commitment to the community."[3]

Indeed, to many, "slow" has come to mean a way to live one's life. If I am what I eat, then I will choose food that supports local growers instead of industrial agriculture; I'll support diffusion rather than centralization. I'll support sustainable practices over short-term profits. I prefer community networking to distant power structures, variety to homogeneity; adaptability rather than uniformity; authenticity over hype. Perhaps most importantly, slow has come to mean local. And yet slow food doesn't mean we will eat only food from our own backyards; it is a celebration of everyone's backyard. Wine makers call it *terroir*—the one-of-a-kind flavor that the soils and traditions of a place impart.

From Slow Food to Slow Democracy

Slow democracy, in turn, is an invitation to bring the advantages of "slow" to our community decision making. Paralleling slow food's push for authenticity in what we eat, slow democracy calls for firsthand knowledge of the local decisions that matter to us. Just as slow food encourages chefs and eaters to become more intimately involved with the production of local food, slow democracy encourages us to govern ourselves locally with processes that are inclusive, deliberative, and citizen powered. Reconnecting with the sources of decisions that affect us, and with the processes of democracy itself, is at the heart of twenty-first-century sustainable communities.

Slow food celebrates diversity and local traditions: briny seafood from Maine, wild rice from the shores of Lake Superior, artichokes from the dry, hot hills of California. Similarly, slow democracy applauds the range of regional democratic practices. New England town meetings don't need to be spread like frosting across American townscapes. Other, very different examples of slow democracy have taken root from Oregon to Georgia, and from downtown Chicago to coastal New Hampshire—each with its own regional flavor. Slow democracy celebrates the *terroir* of community process.

"Slow" is a wise, almost tongue-in-cheek term—a raised eyebrow at what "fast" has come to mean. It's not that slow food advocates like waiting around. Indeed, plucking a sun-warmed heirloom tomato from the garden and savoring it out of hand is about as "fast" as food gets. But this grazing is arguably a slow food experience, because it encompasses your handling of the tiny seed, your careful transplanting of the slim seedlings into the garden bed, and the hot afternoons of weeding and watering. Admittedly, with all of that satisfyingly in mind and the taste on your tongue, you might linger a moment with pleasure—but that's a matter of choice.

Similarly, slow democracy is not a call for longer meetings or more time between decisions. Instead, it is a reminder of the care needed for full-blooded, empowered community decision making.

Slow food has shown that in the interest of efficiency and cheap food, policies often are skewed toward corporate agriculture and consolidation, resulting in food and food systems that are unnatural and unhealthy. Similarly, slow democracy observes that we have moved increasingly toward centralization and privatization of public resources and decision making. In the name of efficiency, we often give only lip service to citizens' wisdom, and as a result, we wind up with unrepresentative, unsustainable decisions and a discouraged, democratically anemic citizenry.

Over the past twenty years, scholars and practitioners in the emerging field of dialogue and deliberation have discovered a pent-up demand for authentic community interaction, in which citizens can have their voices heard locally and make a difference. Americans are eager for a return to community service; in one recent poll, nearly 90% of respondents said that they valued being involved in their communities.[4] And with a new generation of technological tools at our command, we are more skilled in self-organizing than at any other point in our past. We have the ability to make choices that are more ecologically, economically, and socially sustainable, and the will to implement them. The message from slow democracy's grassroots is clear: it may take time, but it's worth it.

If we're going to take the time to slow down, we want quality. Slow democracy doesn't mean we have to attend every poorly advertised, badly run city council meeting. What slow democracy *can* help us do is learn to identify authentic, healthy processes; participate judiciously and with the patient confidence that real change takes time; and support the people who engage us in meaningful decision making, so they'll do it some more. Inclusive, well-run deliberations with effective follow-through can make an enormous difference in the life of a community.

Slow food advocates know that a sustainable food system must offer healthy food in an ecologically viable way, but there's more. As journalist Ben Hewitt describes in *The Town That Food Saved*, "It must feed the locals." Just as slow food cannot only feed the rich and elite, slow democracy must be open to all. The people, or *demos* in Greek, are at the heart of the word "democracy."

Finding a place in the life of the already overburdened and underprivileged—such as single working parents, or low-wage workers who string together two or three jobs—is one of the greatest challenges of slow democracy. But these are the populations most often shut out of the democratic process, and most in need of what it has to offer. Slow democracy incorporates people from all walks of life and the full range of the human condition: from talkers to doers, from those who value charts and graphs to those who love chatting over coffee. It makes room for those who like to talk at microphones but also celebrates the vast majority of us who would, frankly, rather die than make a speech. It builds on the already-existing web of relationships that form a community, recognizing that some of our best ideas come while taking a walk with a neighbor. And it forges new relationships, introducing us to people we might have avoided but come to appreciate.

Slow democracy says to parents who want to understand local school spending and be able to influence it: we need your expertise. Slow democracy says to landowners who care about their property values and the decisions that affect them: you are not alone.

Slow democracy gives a vocabulary to people who would like more decisions to be made with, not by, their leaders. It gives confidence to policy makers who have a hunch that citizens have valuable wisdom and skills to share. And it offers a checklist to those who wonder whether their community's democratic process is all it should be.

Slow Is on the Rise

The slow food movement has spawned slow movements of other kinds. Most notably, the "slow money" movement urges economic support for local, sustainable endeavors and an understanding that quick profit should not be the only criterion for investment. Slow democracy takes its inspiration from these other movements. They are invigorating citizens to take back power from centralized institutions, and we seek a parallel understanding for our towns, schools, and communities.

Slow democracy presents a paradigm shift: instead of seeing politics as something that is national, Washington-based, and out of reach, we can see the real possibilities at home. Communities have the ability to address fundamental issues and create real change. Many of them have already done so.

We think the greatest promise of modern democracy lies right in our local communities. And our goal is twofold: to expand the power of those places where democracy is most vital, and to ensure that those citizens have the tools to govern themselves in the most inclusive, democratic, empowered, and effective ways possible.

We recognize that there is always a gap between democracy (the political ideal) and government (the administrative apparatus that enforces laws and regulations).[5] But that gap varies in size. Right now, on our national level, it is a chasm. It is hard to look at Washington and see anything that looks remotely radical or thrilling. But there are places—local places that many of us call home—where that gap is, or can be, much smaller.

If our future holds an increased focus on local food, local energy, and local economy, then surely we will need to improve our skills at local governance. Many of the local/slow activism books (for example, Michael Pollan's *The Omnivore's Dilemma*, Carlo Petrini's *Slow Food*, and Woody Tasch's *Inquiries into the Nature of Slow Money*) and those that sound the alarm (Bill McKibben's *Eaarth*) emphasize the need for everyone to come together to make change. But what will that "coming together" look like? With *Slow Democracy* we are taking that next step, proposing a shift in the way we think about community and democratic engagement.

Does *every* democratic process need to be "slow"—in other words, must we talk about *everything*, and include and empower *every*one, *all* the time? Clearly, that would be not only impractical but enough to drive us mad. As political scholar Benjamin Barber argues, a strong democracy is not one where everyone participates all the time, nor where some people participate all the time, but where everyone participates some of the time.[6] Or, as the slow money movement says, "We must slow our money down—not all of it, of course, but enough to matter."[7]

The Slow Democracy Alternative

Slow democracy offers broad principles, tools, and vocabulary that citizens can use to create a healthy local democracy. And slow democracy *is* local—happening in the communities and towns that we all live in, whose processes we can be part of. It weaves together three key elements of democratic decision making:

- **Inclusion**—ensuring broad, diverse public participation
- **Deliberation**—defining problems and weighing solutions through a public process based on sound information and respectful relationships
- **Power**—defining a clear connection between citizen participation, public decisions, and action.

These principles are inspired by the emergence of new ways of thinking, new fields of inquiry, and the exciting real-time experiments that are happening in communities right now. Across the country and the world, citizens and local governments are feeling their way toward self-government and better decision making. Some are addressing painful issues like racism and crime; others are taking on the too-hot-to-handle concerns—like local budget cuts and planning controversies—that often rend communities or go unaddressed because of lack of political will. Most aren't thinking about paradigm shifts; they are simply trying to solve real problems by using their community assets. But what they are doing is slow democracy:

- In Austin, Texas, residents use a technique called "meeting in a box" to gather with friends and neighbors in hundreds of locations around the city, from community centers to living rooms, to offer their ideas on key city priorities like housing. Meeting results are sent directly to city staff members who use them to shape the city's comprehensive plan for the future.
- In districts of New York City and Chicago, and under consideration in a growing number of communities, a new participatory budgeting process means that local residents develop ideas for projects that would most improve their daily lives, on issues like street resurfacing and lighting, bike lanes, and parks and playgrounds. Then it's the citizens, not representatives, who make the binding decisions on how to spend funds.
- In Portsmouth, New Hampshire, citizens have used a community dialogue and deliberation approach to find creative solutions to school

redistricting, sustainable development, planning, race relations, and other complex issues.

- In downtown Chicago, the police department has been working directly with residents to identify priorities and solve problems for nearly twenty years; their approach has reduced crime rates and transformed their relationship with residents of many tougher neighborhoods.
- In coastal Maine, a town that was ravaged by a Walmart battle is using a community planning process, with input from over a thousand residents, to save the town's historic downtown and encourage economic development.
- In seven northwestern states, inclusive community conversations have helped citizens of poor towns and reservations identify the poverty issues that affect them, envision solutions, and create local businesses and institutions to bring new life to their communities.

Democracy—Fact and Fiction

Much of what we know about democracy we have learned from "watching the show" at the national level. But what may be true about national democracy is not necessarily true in our towns and neighborhoods. So if we're going to engage politically at the local level, many of us will need to relearn what democracy means. Too many people have turned away from the political process because of widely held ideas and myths that don't hold true at the local level. Let's address some of the more common ones.

"Democracy is about fighting."

There is a time for advocacy; but it's not *all* the time. We can struggle to find the best answer; but that doesn't always mean we have to fight *each other.* Media reports might make us think that if there's no controversy, then nothing is happening. But with creativity and respectful deliberation, citizens are often able to find workable solutions at the community level. Significant transformations can happen locally and spread outward from there.

"Democracy is about winning."

Our national two-party system is set up to create winners and losers—and to keep all other perspectives out of the equation. At the local level, democracy can look much different. With careful work, we can help reduce that left-right dynamic and create new cross-community connections. Instead of being about "winning," local democracy can actually be about making the best decision. Then, in the long run, everyone wins.

"Local government is something to get around, not something to work with."
When we lose faith in our local government, we turn our backs on one of the most valuable allies we can have. We need to make our local government a "we" and not a "they." This will open doors to resources, power, and the natural flow of ideas that comes from a functioning democracy.

"Talking about things only makes things worse."
The person who coined the phrase "a camel is a horse designed by a committee" had obviously endured a torturous group process. We're going to highlight some of the breakthrough processes now being used at the local level; these aren't your grandfather's budget meetings. You'll see how they're helping communities make thoughtful decisions and how you can make them happen in your community.

"Problems are becoming too complex for citizens to understand."
Yes, many of today's issues are complicated. But local people are smart and invested—with access to national resources that can help them figure out the intricacies. That's all the more reason to seek out local wisdom and creativity.

"We should leave difficult problems to the experts."
Slow democracy doesn't mean we don't need outside experts. It only means that we should use them as consultants, rather than handing our power over to them. No one knows more about living in your community than you and your neighbors. In today's interconnected world, communities are finding myriad new creative arrangements to tap citizen energy, talents, and, yes, expertise.

"Public participation takes too long."
Citizen involvement takes time. But with democracy, we get to choose: Do we want citizen participation up front, which comes with the side benefits of local wisdom and buy-in? Or do we prefer to take a gamble on making speedy decisions and spending even more time cleaning up afterward,

in a firestorm of cynicism, backlash, and protest? Slow democracy gives communities the wisdom to identify which public questions are most ripe for public engagement, and the skills to take them on.

"Government is too slow already."
We agree. Gridlock is destroying us at the national level. That's why we need to get things moving at the local level. Communities are making progress on budget decisions, race and social conflicts, and finding creative environmental solutions that our national leaders can only dream about.

The Politics of Slow Democracy

So whose side is slow democracy on? Is slow democracy a left-wing Occupation to wrest power from corporations? Or is it a right-wing move to shrink government down to the size where we can drown in a Tea Party teapot?

We know that slow food has a leftie reputation. And we'll admit it from the beginning: as coauthors, on most issues we're over there on the left ourselves. But we want to be clear. Slow democracy is not about the left talking among themselves. Nor is it about strengthening a uniquely progressive agenda—unless you believe that getting more people engaged in local decision making is purely a left-wing enterprise.

Instead, slow democracy is about dropping the left-right labels and trying to find real-world solutions to real-world problems. While this presents an enormous challenge on a national level, it is remarkably doable on a local level.

"Freedom and Unity" is the motto of our home state of Vermont, and at times we are awed by the wisdom of that balancing framework. We can't help but notice that our motto doesn't give us the choice of "Freedom *or* Unity"; but then again, we never found the motto of our good neighbors in New Hampshire, "Live Free or Die," very practical. We each must have the freedom to pursue happiness, but each of us also has some responsibility for the common good.

Adopted in 1788, back before Vermont was even a state, "Freedom and Unity" has held us together through extraordinary deliberations, from whether to join the cause of the Civil War to whether women should be able to vote to whether to allow civil unions and gay marriage.

The motto offers us guidance only, not answers. As historian Joseph Ellis noted, even America's founders knew they could never create a constitution or governance structure full of *answers*; instead, their legacy to us is much more valuable: "a framework in which the salient *questions* could continue to be debated."[8] The founders' gift to us is a structure—slow, perhaps, but astonishingly durable up until now—for finding the right balance, on each issue, between freedom and unity.

Freedom: when we arrive at the table, we'll argue the merits of our various economic, environmental, and social concerns. Unity: we will put our heads together to find the best possible balance of those priorities. Freedom *and* unity: with every decision we make, we'll also weigh whether we are strengthening or weakening our democratic structure. Even as we engage in democracy, we must simultaneously keep an eye on protecting that democracy. Reaching for the fastest, cheapest, or most "efficient" answer, if it bypasses the democratic process, will exact a lasting price.

Working on the local level, with a balance of freedom and unity, we see the possibility of reinventing government in our own times.

The Promise of *Slow Democracy*

Slow Democracy is a call to turn toward our local communities and the ways we can govern ourselves right here, right now. The book offers broad principles that citizens can use to create a healthy local democracy. Some public meetings are satisfying and productive; too many are infuriating, at best a waste of time and at worst disempowering, leaving everyone hot-faced and angry. *Slow Democracy* offers the tools and vocabulary to identify what went wrong in those cases—and to ensure that we can do it better the next time.

Part 1 explores the need for slow democracy. It highlights the surprising parallels between our current democracy and industrial food production: the ways in which they both centralize and privatize their operations, removing control from the local level. It describes the decline of local decision making and the rise of a model of expertise that effectively disenfranchises citizens. And it looks at the ways in which communities are fighting back, taking action to regain power that has been usurped by state and national entities.

In part 2, we show how our twenty-first-century world is uniquely suited to slow democracy. It is the top-down, expert-driven thinking of the twentieth century that is now passé; today's decision making can be flexible and democratic. Society's ability to organize no longer belongs solely to large institutions and governments; electronic communication tools allow for unprecedented networking and collective action. At the same time, insights from new fields can help us improve our self-governance and problem solving. Cultural cognition explores the ways in which people make sense of a complex world; it helps explain how our existing political structures, particularly at the national level, funnel citizens into opposing camps and shut down possibilities for creative thinking. The field of dialogue and deliberation explores the ways in which people can create that much-needed communication, offering inspiration and techniques to help us transform traditional top-down processes into engaging, citizen-based conversations.

Part 3 draws on these new developments to identify the elements that are essential to slow democracy. First, slow democracy must be local, with direct connection between citizens and the issues that can and should be decided in the community itself. Second, it should be inclusive, drawing on participation from across the community. Third, it should be deliberative: a process that requires a foundation of trust and that calls for citizens to define the problems, trade-offs, and solutions. And fourth, it must be empowered, giving people the political, economic, and social tools to follow through on their decisions.

Part 4 offers reflections on the historic role of slow democracy in our country through an exploration of two long-standing American institutions, the jury and the New England town meeting. And we explore the question of when to use slow democracy techniques, recognizing that there is also a time for advocacy.

Finally, in the appendix, we offer a set of "slow democracy rules": tips and reminders to help foster slow democracy.

This is not a "how-to" or facilitator's handbook, although if you plan to embark on creating more deliberative processes in your town, we highly recommend that you get one (and we provide a list of resources at the back of the book as a place to start). There's no one single formula for slow democracy. Instead, slow democracy, like slow food, is going to look different in different places. Rural and urban, east and west, north and south: each has its own traditions and its own logic, and a genuine democratic process will reflect that.

To that end, we tell the stories of communities that are doing exciting work. Each is specific to the place from which it springs; it is the product of that particular community and the strategies it has chosen. But these stories also have a power beyond themselves, the capacity to spark ideas in those sitting far away in different circumstances. As you turn these pages, we hope you start to envision how you might bring some of their insights and strategies to work in your own community.

PART I

slow democracy:
why do we need it?

one

"TOWN HALLS" FROM HELL, AND OTHER STORIES

Chanting "Hear our voice!" and "You work for us!" the overflow crowd at the August 2009 "town hall meeting" on health care in Tampa was fighting mad. In fact, the meeting did result in violence, with at least one person treated for injuries and a freelance journalist suffering damaged glasses and equipment. Eventually, U.S. Representative Kathy Castor, one of the conveners of the event, was escorted out of the hall by police, unable to complete her remarks to the disruptive, angry crowd.

"Town hall meetings" with congressional representatives in Michigan and Denver also ended in shouting matches and name-calling. And at a similar event in Missouri, six people were arrested, some on assault charges.[1]

The media made a lot of these incidents—after all, they made for very exciting television, and for some Americans the near riots may have been lively entertainment. Some may have felt that they showed the beauty of democracy: whether you're an elite representative or a common citizen, everyone gets to have a say. But if you had an interest in civil discourse, or in actually reaching some agreement on health care reform issues, you were more inclined to avert your eyes in dismay.

Noted one press account, "Amid boos, hisses, and the occasional screaming outburst, [many attendees said] the town hall meeting did little to change their minds or clarify the basic tenets of the health care reform bills."[2] "They think they're exercising their right to free speech," said one disappointed citizen who had driven twenty-five miles to attend the Tampa event, "but they're only exercising their right to disrupt civil discourse." Even some of the members of the yelling crowd later admitted that their efforts accomplished little. Noted one protester, "Somewhere in all the screaming, no one got heard."[3]

What went wrong in the health care "town halls"? Some would fault organizers for inadequate planning; in Tampa, for instance, a hall that was designed to hold 250 drew closer to 1,500. Others would argue that Democrats were simply outmaneuvered in a game of political showmanship: the conservative spin machine had whipped up a series of orchestrated publicity stunts at the local level (rather than being real grassroots events, skeptics called them "Astroturf").

Either way, whoever concocted the idea of naming the health care gatherings "town hall meetings" must have thought it was a stroke of genius. For most Americans, the traditional image of the New England town meeting brings to mind free speech, citizenship, and the Norman Rockwell painting of the earnest "common man" addressing a respectful group of his peers. The implication is that a "town hall" meeting is self-governance, and if it doesn't go well, we have no one to blame but ourselves.

The term "town hall meeting" evokes enough sentiment that every election year, a group of candidates somewhere will hold "town hall" debates. "Town halls" sound appealing because they promise to be more informal (candidates will eschew podiums and instead sit on stools; they might even roll up their sleeves). They might be more interactive (questions are posed by actual citizens) and maybe more intimate (candidates might tell a personal story or two). In short, the term "town hall meeting" connotes something that is more *real* than politics-as-usual.

But the parallels between these so-called "town halls" and a traditional New England town meeting end there, for one key reason: power. Make no mistake about it. Citizens who participate in a real New England town meeting are themselves the legislative branch of their town government on issues of governance and finance. Here, voters are meeting face-to-face to approve or reject budgets, make amendments, and otherwise take direct action in their government. Citizens are not sounding off or offering advice to government leaders; *they are*, in fact, the government. The issues on which a real town meeting can take binding action are strictly local—generally pertaining to the town's institutions, such as its roads and schools—but the money is real, and the citizens' direct access to democracy is absolute.

Certainly traditional town meetings have their flaws, as we'll see later. But at least you are unlikely to hear chants of "You work for us!" and "Hear our voice!" Because at a real town meeting, government is a "we," not a "they."

Why We Need Slow Democracy

We all know that Americans are deeply disillusioned with our federal government. Most citizens seem to think that government is either incompetent or corrupt, or both. The Pew Research Center gave its 2010 poll of public perceptions of government a telling title: "Distrust, Discontent, Anger and Partisan Rancor."

Sometimes the situation verges on the humorous. In 2011, the *Washington Post* compiled a ranking of approval ratings for various unpopular figures, ideas, and institutions. It found that, with a 9% approval rating, Congress was only slightly more appealing to Americans than Fidel Castro (at 5%). Congress lagged behind the idea of America becoming a communist country (11%), BP during the oil spill (16%), banks (23%), and Nixon during Watergate (24%). The IRS, by contrast, with an approval rating of 40%, was practically the public's darling.[4]

But most of the time Americans are not amused—in fact, citizens today have less investment in and more suspicion of government than at any other time in the nation's history. A look at the numbers makes the case starkly:

- 89% of Americans do not trust the government to do the right thing.[5]
- Only 17% of Americans believe that Congress does an excellent or good job.[6]
- 30% of Americans believe that the federal government poses a danger to their personal liberty.[7]
- 74% of Americans rate the federal government's implementation of its programs as just "fair" or "poor."[8]

Americans are particularly angry at their national elected officials:

- 56% of Americans are frustrated with the federal government and 21% are angry; only 19% are content.[9]
- 81% of Americans believe that elected officials are more personally ambitious than publicly motivated, agreeing with the statement that they "care only about their own political careers."[10]
- 83% say that elected officials are not careful with government spending.[11]

And, as the Occupy Wall Street protests show, Americans are deeply unhappy with the relationship between government and corporations and other special interests:

- Most Americans think that government attention is misplaced, with 50% saying that Wall Street receives too much and 66% saying that the middle class receives too little.[12]
- 90% of Americans believe that corporations have too much influence on government.[13]
- 82% believe that elected officials are prey to the influence of special interests.[14]

One American poll respondent offered a widely shared assessment: "Probably the government in Washington could be trusted at one time but now it seems like it's all a game of who wins rather than what's best for the people." Another agreed: "I don't want to blanket the whole government that way, but it's getting scary. . . . Everything is for the wealthy. This used to be a lovely country, but everything is sliding."[15]

There are many reasons for this decline in confidence, some beginning with the political parties themselves. Up until the mid-twentieth century, political parties organized on the local level, with get-out-the-vote and other community campaigns. Now, rather than building relationships, most of their resources are directed at broad-based media.[16] The trend is clear, and it's getting worse. Since the Supreme Court's 2010 Citizens United decision, special interests and partisan groups have had the capability to unleash a tsunami of anonymous negative political advertising, which we can only assume will add to citizens' disenchantment.

The pervasiveness of negative public sentiment suggests a fundamental shift in the way that individuals relate to their government. And a look at the parallels between fast food and this "fast democracy" shows that many of the same dynamics are at work.

Fast Food and Fast Democracy

The dissatisfaction that pervades our politics is not about democracy itself. Instead, it is about a system that looks representative and gives lip service to democratic values but is fundamentally only a masquerade of what government by the people could look like. Over and over, this system has shown itself to be inept at creating solutions that work to solve complex problems. Rather than taking into account local situations, decisions are made in monoculture.

In his book *In Defense of Food*, Michael Pollan makes a distinction between real "food" and prepackaged "edible foodlike substances." Food is broccoli, carrots, foraged mushrooms, farm-raised chicken, milk. These are direct or near-direct gifts from the vegetable and animal kingdoms, dense in nutrients, complete in their own skins.

Foodlike substances, by contrast, magically appear on the shelves of stores with "sell by" dates well into the next year. They are wrapped in plastic and boxed in cardboard, saturated with GMO corn and laced with MSG: neon crackers, white-encrusted toaster pastries, rings of cereal in rainbow colors.

We are experiencing a similar disconnect in much of our self-government. We've become so accustomed to hype that we're confusing real democracy with an unfulfilling stand-in: the "town hall" fiascos, shouting matches between pundits, and highly choreographed debates. All of these point to the growing disconnect between Americans and our democratic power. Our connection to decision making is so attenuated that attempts to get involved often end in bitter frustration, and incendiary outbursts only increase our distaste for what we've come to think of as the democratic process. It's the democratic equivalent of junk food: junk democracy.

Not all of these so-called town hall meetings end in fisticuffs, of course. Many legislators have found that they can hold informational question-and-answer sessions with constituents that are both pleasant and productive. But even the more cordial of these gatherings are merely informational, with no assurance that public comments will be taken into account. They are not a place for making change.

What we have now is the McDonald's of democracy. It isn't necessarily a rapid process, any more than our processed foods—with slaughterhouses, processing plants, intercontinental transportation routes, and months in the freezer—are actually quick. But it's fast in the sense that fast food is fast: it's a centralized process based on the premise of efficiency, delivering a simple, easy-to-use product, but one that leaves citizens unnourished and unsatisfied. Like industrial agriculture, this "fast democracy" has encroached on our communities in a silent and invisible way. And Americans, with a deep stake in the quality of these decisions, know we are losing out.

With our current system, there is an ever-increasing distance between the community that is being governed and the people who are making the decisions. Rural towns, for example, control their zoning and how much they spend on local roads, and many still have important, albeit waning, impact on school decisions, but almost all other decisions are made outside their boundaries. Farmers cannot sell milk and meat to a neighbor without being subject to federal regulations created with industrial agriculture in mind. Unlike the days in which community members gathered together to raise a new school building, they now must adhere to strict state-mandated square footage requirements that may not even be relevant to their situation. In many states, national lobbies have pushed through laws that bring certain types of decision making to the state level, which means, for example, that municipalities cannot enact tighter laws governing environmental emissions and mining.

Decision making has been commodified and turned wholesale. Instead of decisions being made by a community with reference to its specific situation, standards are set by far-away legislators. In fact, increasingly these regulations are made by unelected bureaucrats who implement them through rule changes rather than through deliberation in the public sphere.

In many cases the standards set at a state level make sense, and communities might have adopted them anyway, but the issue of who makes the final call is of vital importance. It's not that all decisions should be made locally, all the time. Some standards must be set at the national level, especially when it comes to ensuring basic rights; we think of civil rights and environmental protection as key examples. But it is also true that many decisions that rightfully belong at the local level have been shifted to centralized arenas. In the ongoing American balancing act between our national government and our citizenry, the pendulum has swung too far from the local. In order for our democracy to work, the field of decision making needs to be matched to the decision being made.

It's also true that political participation has been reduced to walking into the voting booth and pulling a lever or ticking a box. Pundits measure citizen involvement by the percentage of people who register to vote and the percentage of those eligible voters who turn out; they engage in a constant conversation about individuals who think that their vote does not matter and how to change their minds.

Think of the countless get-out-the-vote efforts. Potential voters can now register at motor vehicle departments while they are getting their licenses;

new initiatives encourage military and overseas voting; and such institutions as Harvard's Kennedy School and the Pew Research Center have spent large amounts of money trying to figure out how to improve voter participation. The filmmaker Michael Moore even traveled to college campuses during his Slacker Uprising tour in 2004, trying to register young Americans. The right to vote—which so many people have fought so hard for over our country's history—is now something that we can barely give away.

Perhaps this is because Americans have a very limited sphere of influence on the issues that affect us. We can blog, we can give money, we can put bumper stickers on our cars—but mostly we are reduced to passively taking in what the political system serves up, watching political ads on television, and casting that single ballot. While we may be voters, many of us feel less like citizens than like consumers.

New York's Community Gardens

The struggle over New York's community gardens provides a good look at a "fast democracy" case study—one in which city officials decided to sell off green space, despite other options and to the detriment of local neighborhoods who fought to keep it.

For decades, city residents have been creating community gardens on vacant lots. Most of the gardens are on lots that the city acquired after apartment buildings were torn down. In tough neighborhoods in Harlem, the Bronx, and the Lower East Side, where no private developer wanted to build, the lots languished with neglect. Residents began to go in and clean up, carting away junked appliances and picking out broken glass.[17] "We personally threw out the drug dealers, cleared the land, and planted the flowers," said a Lower East Side resident.[18] Now, around eight hundred community gardens have sprung up on these unused plots, totaling about two hundred acres—more space than can be found in the renowned Brooklyn Botanic Garden.[19]

The gardens became informal community centers in struggling neighborhoods, populated mostly by citizens of color. In a garden on 122nd Street, for example, Harlem resident Cynthia Nibbleck-Worley and her ninety-one-year-old neighbor planted lilies and fruit trees. Volunteers gathered and built a vegetable garden, a shed, and a compost pile. They eventually established a partnership with the local school, which used the garden to teach children about growing food.[20]

For many years, the city was supportive: it called the gardeners "urban pioneers" and praised their work.[21] But in the late 1990s, the real-estate market began to heat up and developers approached mayor Rudolph Giuliani about selling the lots. The mayor decided to auction off plots of public land, some for public housing and some for luxury units. And even though the city owned 14,000 vacant lots, and the community gardens occupied only about 10% of that number, the administration targeted many of the gardens.[22]

The decision sparked a community outcry. The New York City Environmental Justice Alliance filed suit to stop the sale of the gardens. Gardeners and activists demonstrated at city hall, chanting "No Gardens, No Peas!"[23] and the Giuliani administration found itself fending off activists dressed as ladybugs and painted daisies.[24]

The director of the city's land use planning division ignored the community functions of the gardens and their history as celebrated public spaces. "Those people chose to take public land without permission," he said. The city refused to reconsider. Bulldozers razed at least nine of the gardens, taking out fences, specimen roses, tulip beds, and vegetable plots.[25]

The dramatic climax came in May 1999, when the Giuliani administration scheduled an auction in which it planned to offer 112 gardens to developers. One day before the auction was to take place, the entertainer Bette Midler swept in to the rescue. She organized a deal with the Trust for Public Land to buy the offered lots for $4.3 million, thus saving them from destruction.

The last-minute purchase saved those gardens, while leaving hundreds of other, lower-profile gardens vulnerable. It was a privatized answer to a privatization problem. It did not solve the environmental justice issues that the fast democracy process exposed. "Almost all the gardens that were to be auctioned were in neighborhoods of color," the director of the New York City Environmental Justice Alliance pointed out. "For us, it was never a question of only saving a few gardens. The issue is the city's lack of policy on open space equity."[26]

The story of the community gardens shows the ways in which fast democracy and its decision making cut against the interests of local neighborhoods—in the process undermining the garden communities, social justice, and food security. "What's bizarre," pointed out the president of the New York City Community Garden Coalition, "is that we've been living by the rhetoric of all the social scientists in the world: 'Go clean up your neighborhood, go clean up your block, make your community livable.' Gardens are the embodiment of that."[27]

Privatization and Centralization: Two Enemies of Local Decision Making

Privatization of power and public resources was the paradigm behind the sale of the New York community gardens, and one of the strongest forces that separates citizens from decision making. Centralization of power is another.

While they are often seen as opposite ends of the political spectrum, privatization and centralization paradoxically have a similar effect on real democratic engagement: decision making on local issues is outsourced and exported away from the people who are directly affected by those issues.

Privatization is the driving force of capitalism, the push to allow the free market to determine the distribution of resources in our society. In the last century, it has meant larger and larger conglomerates taking charge of services that were once provided locally or in common: water, transportation, prisons, and more. Depending on one's politics, privatization is the great engine of economic progress or an aggressive power to be contained or combated. In either case, it is formidable. As economic theorist Manuel Couret Branco argues, our economic system appears almost as a force of nature, important to watch but impossible to control:

> Nowadays, within mainstream economics discourse, economic phenomena seem to be brooding over our heads like the great mysteries of nature. Economic bulletins strangely resemble weather forecasts, commodity prices float as temperatures, and unemployment suffers from seasonality. Within this framework people are put in the position of a powerless spectator attending the dazzling show nature is performing.[28]

With this mind-set, citizens begin to feel that privatization is as inevitable as tropical storms or melting polar ice caps. Experts are supposed to interpret and predict the economy, but recession and Wall Street upheaval have made it clear that they're as adrift as we are.

Centralization is usually seen as an opposing force: the socialism to privatization's capitalism, the big government to privatization's big business. It is the consolidation of government power and services in "central" locations, so that resources are not dispersed among a host of tiny entities but rather concentrated in a single place. It, too, has been a major feature of public life over the last hundred years, as states and the federal government have taken over a large portion of the decisions that were once made locally. Pollution regulations are now determined in legislatures and the courts; school curricula are set in state departments of education and coordinated in supervisory offices; highway routes are drawn by traffic engineers in a state building somewhere.

Such centralization has often happened with the best of intentions and the desire to do things right—and we may in fact applaud the resulting regulations. But one important and largely invisible side effect has been that citizens have less and less opportunity to make decisions on issues that concern them. However different the types of power they consolidate, centralization and privatization pose a similar threat to democracy. In each case, they transfer decision-making capacity toward a larger entity—and thus away from local denizens. Both are driven by the idea of efficiency, and it is this value—more than any other single one—that has encroached on our communities in a silent and invisible way. Even if no one set out to take power from local communities, it has happened as a by-product of the promise of better efficiency.

In theory, centralization and privatization each offer the promise of improved efficiency: less overhead, better management, and increased expertise at a fraction of the local costs. On some levels these efficiencies have been realized. Fast food is famously cheaper than farm food, with Happy Meals costing under five dollars; a similar meal at a local restaurant with local ingredients would run three times as much. Even from a local food perspective, some efficiencies make sense: having local farmers, rather than each citizen growing his or her own food, frees up all of the non-farmers in the community to do what they do best. Similarly, centralization and privatization *can* improve efficiency for certain government services, and sometimes they are the right choice.

The problem comes when we allow efficiency to trump other values. Increased economic efficiency is not always worth the social and community costs. Fast food's cheaper price has a short-term appeal to the pocketbook, but it comes with little nutritional value and a huge set of social costs, from obesity to deforestation. One of the effects of organizing our society around the ideal of efficiency is that other values become obscured. In economic parlance, those values are "externalities," shunted to the margins of the discussion. But they are intensely important, and often the dearest values that a community holds. These are "prices" that we will have to pay eventually, but that are not immediately factored into the equation.

Our governments and community services—for instance, public lands or public education—were created not based on theories of self-seeking, privatized self-interest, but for the public good. William Mathis, managing director of the National Education Policy Center at the University of Colorado, examined state constitutions to see on what grounds they promoted education:

> In the 50 state constitutions, there's a remarkable absence of clauses centered on "education for economic competition." Instead, I found phrases like "Intelligence and virtue being the safeguards of liberty and the bulwark of a free and good government . . ." (Arkansas), "Knowledge and learning, generally diffused throughout a community, being essential to the preservation of a good government; . . ." (Indiana), and ". . . the encouragement of virtue and prevention of vice . . ." (Vermont).[29]

As Mathis argues, basing education on economic theory completely misreads the purpose of education in a democratic society.

We should think carefully about the ways in which we let efficiency dominate our public life. "As I see it," wrote Nobel Prize–winning economist Paul Krugman, "the economics profession went astray because economists, as a group, mistook beauty, clad in impressive-looking mathematics, for truth."[30] It is not the beauty of efficiency that we want from our food, but true nourishment. By the same standard, our public decisions—and the way we make them—must nourish our communities. All efficiencies must serve that larger goal.

School and Community: A Case in Point

Schools are a particularly ripe field for discussions of democracy because at the core of all political discussions are the things we hold in common. Without these things, we would have no need to make decisions together. In agrarian societies, for example, townspeople shared a "commons" for grazing sheep and other animals. Though many argue that our modern, mobile society is far less place-based, we still share many sets of commons. Some are concrete: the earth, the air, water. Others, like politics and culture, are more metaphorical. And one of our most beloved "commons" is our children.

As sociologists have shown for decades, schools are central to their communities. They are key building blocks in city neighborhoods and *the* central institutions in rural communities.[31] One study from 1990 identified the three factors that rural schools provide as community builders: centripetalism (bringing community residents together), inclusiveness (creating associational life and welcoming all members), and social distinction (distinguishing their own town from others).[32]

Furthermore, as observers from Alexis de Tocqueville through the present have pointed out, schools are training grounds of democracy. The famous educational philosopher John Dewey shaped his entire theory of education around its role in a democratic society. Education, he wrote, is a far more powerful tool than law:

> I believe that the community's duty to education is, therefore, its paramount moral duty. By law and punishment, by social agitation and discussion, society can regulate and form itself in a more or less haphazard and chance way. But through education society can formulate its own purposes, can organize its own means and resources, and thus shape itself with definiteness and economy in the direction in which it wishes to move.[33]

In both its form and content, education shapes the way that children ask questions, process information, and respond to public issues.

In fact, schools are important democratic training grounds not just for children but, historically, for the adults who run the schools. Local school governance has the natural capacity to be inclusive, with the professional expertise of superintendents and principals ideally funneled through the local wisdom of citizen school boards—and always with the checks and balances of parents and community budget votes. It is deliberative, as board members work late into the night, hashing out the merits of smaller class size versus cost containment.[34] And it is the source of real power, as the board works out a budget that is then voted on by the town. Many board members, having learned their skills running the school, then go on to run for higher office.

So what happens when this key central institution is taken out of the community? There has been fiery public discussion about the pros and cons of school consolidation, and we won't explore the question of whether it makes financial or educational sense; there is a huge body of research on this already. Instead we want to look at school closure from a more sociological perspective. What democratic and community functions does the school serve, not so much for the students but for the community at large? And what happens when those functions are placed at a distance? The story of Hacker Valley, West Virginia, shows how governmental "efficiency," without regard to other values, can unintentionally destroy communities.

Hacker Valley, West Virginia

April in West Virginia smells like wild leeks: pungent and oniony. In the woods, their slim green leaves look like lilies of the valley, but pull the white bulb from the ground or tear off a piece of leaf and their aroma gives them away. Appalachian people have savored that smell for generations, gathering and eating the plants as a spring tonic. And, for almost as long, they have held community feasts to celebrate both the wild leeks —known locally as ramps—and the coming of spring.

The hills rise steeply all around Hacker Valley, home to one of the finest ramp dinners in West Virginia, held in the gym of the handsome new Hacker Valley elementary school. Laid out on long tables under the basketball nets are baskets of dinner rolls, traditional fried potatoes, and, of course ramps, sizzled in butter and served by the heaping spoonful. Dinner is served family-style, and neighbors talk to neighbors. Most of the village's five hundred residents don't have a lot of money—the average household income was under $24,000 as of the 2010 census—but many are happy to come out and support the school.

Hacker Valley nearly didn't have this school. Twelve years ago, the school was a makeshift conglomerate of ten trailers that the state was pushing hard to close, but the citizens were determined to keep their children, and they won their case through a combination of intelligence, perseverance, and luck. In 2009, Governor Joe Manchin cut a red ribbon and welcomed the children into their new building. Now the school is a focal point for the town: a place to vote, a room for public meetings, and a hall big enough for the ramp dinner.

"If This Is Democracy, Then I Missed the Bus"

The new Hacker Valley school is the product of a long process that started out with high hopes for rural communities. In the 1970s, a group of parents from rural Lincoln County filed suit against the state, arguing that the existing system was unfair to children from poor rural communities; their schools were impoverished and facilities in terrible shape. In the early 1980s, a West Virginia court agreed, declaring the state's school financing system unconstitutional and ordering that a new system be put in place. When the legislature created the School Building Authority (SBA) to distribute funds for construction and maintenance, many West Virginians welcomed the news. The SBA outlined a statewide planning process that seemed like an inclusive and democratic approach: a committee from each county would develop a comprehensive plan for school facilities.[35]

In Hacker Valley, school board members and parents were delighted. It was high time to invest in the school; volunteers had fixed a leaky roof and drilled a new well, but the trailers were in bad shape, and on frosty mornings students scraped ice from the inside of the single-pane windows. The town was proud of its students—they had the highest test scores and lowest dropout rates in the county—but they needed a new building. The governor's process seemed like it would be a fair and democratic way to fund it.[36]

But Hacker Valley residents knew that something was wrong the minute they walked into the facilities planning meeting for their own Webster County. The chairs weren't arranged for a committee meeting around a table or open space; instead, they were all lined up facing the head of the room, as if for a public lecture, with the state-named consultants sitting up front. As they looked around, they realized that the committee composition didn't reflect the people of the county: of the twenty-nine members, more than half were employees of the board of education and only nine were parents. There were no students at all.[37]

The superintendent introduced the two consultants who had been named by the SBA to oversee the process: Roy Blizzard and J. Dan Snead, who had come up from near Charleston, the state capital, and were architects who designed schools. Parents reflected afterward that the consultants immediately steered the discussion toward support for a new consolidated middle school. The situation was not lost on the Webster County residents. "It seemed like a conflict of interest for an architect who builds middle schools to be giving opinions on whether or not we need a new middle school," said one of the parents.[38]

Parents from Hacker Valley and other towns on the northern end of the county were especially worried about long bus rides. Their high school students already rode an hour and a half one way to a consolidated high school; they did not want their younger children to be stuck on the bus too. As one committee member said, "West Virginia is number one in the nation in the cost per student for transportation. That tells me we are spending too much money out of the schools and learning. In this day of modern technology, there is no reason why children should have these long bus rides. The money spent on busing should be spent on buildings and learning."[39]

In a series of meetings, these same concerns came up over and over. No one from the community spoke out in favor of closing existing schools and building a consolidated one.

But the School Building Authority had already identified minimum enrollment numbers that threatened to make community concerns obsolete. In order to be eligible for state funding, an elementary school would have to have at least three hundred students, a number that was supposed to create an economy of scale but was wildly unrealistic for the small towns where 70% of West Virginia's children live. That size requirement meant consolidation and thus busing, since few Appalachian communities had that many children.

Parents felt that the consultants pushed consolidation. The architect Roy Blizzard, who ran the meetings, treated the SBA's required minimum school size as sacrosanct. His plan was to send preschoolers through fifth graders on a bus ride over two mountains to Webster Springs—a forty-five-minute ride from their existing schools. When parents and citizens looked for alternative options, they felt dismissed. As one mother on the committee described it, "Any idea we came up with Dr. Blizzard would just shoot down and say, 'That's not input, I want input.' We would give some other options. 'That's not input, I want input.' The only thing he would consider input would be something that is in accordance with SBA guidelines on economies of scale. Anything else he would not consider to be input."[40]

The mother described how the parents persisted. "We were at every meeting. He finally did admit at one meeting that we could put in a request to get a hardship waiver because of our mountainous terrain. He said the SBA probably wouldn't approve it, but we could put it in."[41]

Ultimately, the committee took an informal vote against the middle school, but it didn't matter: Blizzard explained that he would make the final decisions. Committee members realized that they had been part of a charade. The public process looked like democracy, but rather than a collective inquiry into options, outside forces had pushed them toward a preordained conclusion.

Blizzard's bluntness may have been exceptional, but similar processes were going on all over the state. The facilities planning committees, named by superintendents, were dominated by school officials; parent appointees were few and far between. Citizens who supported local schools were frozen out of the process. Committee members were told not to share information with the public. Consultants handed out stacks of charts and graphs on demographics and funding formulas but did not mention the extensive research on school size and student performance. Of the seven criteria identified by the legislature for determining school size, only one had become the benchmark: economies of scale. The six others—student health and safety, reasonable travel time, multi-county and regional planning, curriculum improvement, innovative programs, and adequate space for projected enrollments—simply faded into the background.[42]

The process left a deep imprint of cynicism and disgust, as evidenced in the voices and actions of committee members. "The consultants had a plan and the community was just window dressing," said one.[43] Another described how "the committee, the board, parents and the county had been only spectators, powerless to act on our own behalf."[44] In Preston County, fully two-thirds of the committee members simply stopped participating. "We were told what the State Board of Education would approve," a parent said. "It was like a used car lot with only one car."[45] As a former school board member described the frustrating process, "You just don't question, because the SBA has these guidelines and this authority to tell you what you can and what you can't do. So why bother us people in the community? . . . If that's democracy, then I missed the bus."[46]

Rural School Consolidation: The Impact

Hundreds of communities lost their schools as part of the West Virginia consolidation movement. In the years since 1990, the state has closed one out of every five schools, with a total of over three hundred forced to shut their doors. The state's transportation budget shot upward, with a volley of buses crisscrossing the counties.

An overreliance on centralized administrators led to committees making decisions on the basis of information that was imperfect, if not downright misleading. In Preston County, for example, the central county office had provided data that indicated a particular school was overflowing with too many students. But the parent and teacher committee members, who were in the school every day, knew that the true picture was quite different. As one said,

> All of that information [about facilities] was taken from the county office. . . . If a classroom that had been designed for a full class of 25 was being used for five special ed students, it was considered being fully used. If it was used two days a week for music class, it was considered fully occupied.[47]

Local people knew the real picture; it was they who could have suggested workable solutions. Perhaps existing part-time music and part-time art programs could be combined into one room, freeing up an additional classroom. Perhaps the small group of special education students could be moved to a private section of the school library. This kind of creative decision making can make the difference between keeping kids in the community and building a new school—a difference with vast community and financial impact.

With consolidation, many children rode up to two hours each way. In the town of Snowshoe, one county south of Hacker Valley, kindergartner Tommy Evans caught the bus at 6:30 a.m. and didn't come home until 4:40 p.m.; his bus ride took a total of two hours and forty minutes a day. To pass the time, he and the other kids counted the bolts along the bus roof. "Everyone on the bus can tell you there are 46 bolts," said an older rider.[48]

Political momentum shifted only when the *Charleston Gazette* published a series on the effects of consolidation and highlighted its human face. The SBA dropped its requirement for "economies of scale" and began funding local schools again. The new Hacker Valley school is a result of that new policy.

But the devastating effects of the badly bungled process have lasted long after the committees were disbanded. Since the state closed small schools and eliminated local school boards, parents and community members have found it harder and harder to be a part of their new schools' decision making. The effort to be involved is greater: the drives to meetings are longer and the faces at the other end are unfamiliar. And the rewards are less certain. Because the consolidated boards cover such an expanded territory, there are relatively fewer members with a direct investment in their children.[49]

In addition, towns that have lost their schools have lost their major public building. As a former school board member observed, "To urban administrators, moving a school 10 or 15 miles down the road may seem a minor adjustment on the state map, but local schools are the only town hall, gym, polling place, theater, dance hall and recreation center."[50] The loss of these functions weakens the community relationships that make local democracy so effective. "When a school is in the community, then there's a community of people there," observed parent Linda Martin, who coordinated the statewide effort against consolidation. "Once the school is removed, then we're just people who live here and there along the road."[51]

West Virginia is not an isolated case. While that state's experience with consolidation has since created a movement back toward local schools, many other states continue to promote consolidation as enrollments shrink and budgets tighten.

Lessons from the Schools

The story of West Virginia is not unique, nor is rural school consolidation the only example of misplaced priorities. In the name of such goals as "efficiency," "uniformity," and "professionalization," we have seen a nationwide trend of volunteer school boards replaced by central district offices, neighborhood planning decisions made by regional bodies, and town decisions overridden by state or federal mandates.

The case of West Virginia highlights two of the biggest problems with the current balance of power between local democracy and state and national forces. First, the process simply doesn't work very well. Over and over, our current centralized decision-making process has shown itself to be inept at creating solutions that work to solve local problems. State administrators develop "best practices" and theoretical frameworks that may be eminently useful in some situations but don't apply to others, such as when policies that work well in urban areas are applied, one-size-fits-all, to rural areas.

Second, this kind of process undercuts the institutions that foster real local decision making. School consolidation discussions generally revolve around questions of administrative efficiency and academic offerings, but especially in rural areas, the loss of local schools also has a deep impact on local democracy—a consequence that is almost never mentioned. In Vermont, for example, pro consolidation legislation will fund merger studies if they consider four criteria: real dollar efficiencies, operational efficiencies, curriculum opportunities, and student performance. And even though sociologist after sociologist has pointed out the relationship between schools, community, and democracy, somehow that connection has not registered with public policy makers: neither community nor democratic engagement is even on the list of criteria. In most policy discussions, there are—as there should be—advocates for frugality, advocates for children, and advocates for teachers. But rarely does anyone ask, "What's best for our democracy?"

two

THE RISE OF EXPERTS AND THE DECLINE OF LOCAL DECISION MAKING

Alexis de Tocqueville was astounded. Traveling through the United States in 1831, the slim, dark-haired young Frenchman studied the structures and habits of democracy and was amazed by the frequency and enthusiasm with which Americans engaged in politics. In France, he had found that residents were frequently happy to live private lives without public engagement; by contrast, the United States appeared as a scene of incessant civic action:

> The political activity that pervades the United States must be seen in order to be understood. No sooner do you set foot upon American ground than you are stunned by a kind of tumult; a confused clamor is heard on every side, and a thousand simultaneous voices demand the satisfaction of their social wants. Everything is in motion around you; here the people of one quarter of a town are met to decide upon the building of a church; there the election of a representative is going on; a little farther, the delegates of a district are hastening to the town in order to consult upon some local improvements; in another place, the laborers of a village quit their plows to deliberate upon the project of a road or a public school.[1]

Deciding, electing, consulting, deliberating: these were the habits paramount in the American character, according to Tocqueville. He was partly amused and partly appalled at this quality in the people. They had mastered none of the light and amusing conversational art so practiced by Europeans, instead treating every verbal interaction with a dogged and political intensity, as though it were a debate. "An American cannot converse," he wrote, "but he can discuss. . . . He speaks to you as if he was addressing a meeting." This habit was so ingrained, continued Tocqueville, that "if [an American] should chance to become warm in the discussion, he will say 'Gentlemen' to the person with whom he is conversing."[2]

It was hardly surprising. Americans in the 1830s had full authority over local matters like the ones Tocqueville mentioned: churches, local elections, improvements, roads, schools. There were few federal requirements—most of them pertained to elections—and no rules established by state agencies. In some cases for better and in some cases for worse, many responsibilities that are now taken over by state and national government, from raising militia to caring for the poor, were once held on the town level.

Historian Mary Ryan describes the story of democracy in this era as eminently local, calling it "meeting-place democracy." The key event of citizenship, she argues, was not dropping a ballot in a box or wrestling with printed statements of politics but, in the words of the era, "speechifying and resolutions at political meetings."[3] In the towns, public meetings were called when necessary; in the cities, they came nearly nightly—there were so many of them, in fact, that newspapers dedicated a separate column to their listings. These meetings offered citizens plenty of opportunity for political practice: "speechifying," listening, cheering, and deliberating.

For those of us used to observing twenty-first-century public process at a numbing distance, it is hard to imagine the excitement and engagement of nineteenth-century public meetings. They were not just a civic experience but a form of contact sport: a combination of politics, theatrics, and community fair, complete with noble rhetoric and occasionally rotten tomatoes.

The Great Democratic Republican County Meeting of 1835 epitomized the drama of local politics. The meeting took place in New York City's Tammany Hall, which was well on its way to dominating Democratic party politics even before the days of Boss Tweed. It was held to nominate the slate of officers for the city, and everyone knew it would be a showdown between the "Tammany Men," the party regulars who supported banks, and the group known as the "Equal Rights Democracy," who wanted to wrest control of the party.

As the meeting began, a local newspaper reported, "there [was] a dense throng collecting in front of the hall, and the leading passage and great stair way to the large room [were] crowded to a perfect jam, as if human beings were wedged together and bound fast."[4] Thousands of men stamped their feet outside the doors of the great hall. But when the doors opened at 7 o'clock, they showed that the party regulars were already onstage and trying to nominate the chair before the Equal Rights crowd could get settled.

Men rushed into the room, shouting, while the politicians onstage hurried to push their nomination through. In the crowd, competing banners were unfurled, greeted by roars of approval, and it became clear that the Equal Rights people had the majority. Onstage, the Tammany candidate was being physically pushed into the chair by his supporters, while shouting, "Let me get out gentlemen, we are in the minority here!" The chair was knocked over and the Equal Rights champion forced his way into the seat.

Realizing that they would lose, the Tammany men raced away down the back stairs and turned off the gas for the gaslights—leaving a huge crowd of pushing, shouting, excited men in total darkness. Then, one by one, tiny lights appeared in the great hall: the flickering first of matches, and then of candles, held above the crowd by the arms of "human chandeliers," until the hall was illuminated by hundreds of these lights. The place rang out with triumphant cries of "Huzzah! Huzzah!" while the Equal Rights slate was nominated and voted in—and promptly nicknamed "Locofoco," after the brand of matches that were used.

The Transformation of Political Culture

Clearly, nineteenth-century democracy was not always a model of civic dialogue; the Locofoco meeting makes our contemporary "town halls" look like model governance. What is striking is how frequently and fully citizens expected to be involved in the process. Perhaps the most important of the resolutions that the Locofocos passed that evening was a resounding statement of public support for public meetings: "The people have the right and duty at all times . . . to assemble together to consult for the common good."[5] Unlike the health care "town halls," these were not performances for the television cameras; they were an expression of the political culture of America at that time.

It is also striking to see how "local" these meetings were. Public meetings in the nineteenth century were far more personal and accessible than most cities' politics are today. Even New York City, the largest metropolis, had only 200,000 residents in 1830, with Baltimore and Philadelphia next largest at around 80,000 each. In such communities, there was still a very strong connection between individual citizens and the issues that affected them.

Tocqueville was not at all sure that the decisions themselves were wisely made, and after hearing about the process it is hard not to agree. "It is incontestable that the people frequently conduct public business very badly," he wrote. [6] But he was also insistent that, whatever the quality of the decisions, the process of local deliberation created a culture of liberty:

> Municipal institutions constitute the strength of free nations. . . . A nation may establish a system of free government, but without the spirit of municipal institutions it cannot have the spirit of liberty. [7]

Seen from the perspective of our society today, this is a sobering insight. On the one hand, American democracy has expanded its franchise impressively since Tocqueville's day. At that time the right to vote had just been freed of the last of the property requirements, allowing all white men to vote regardless of whether they owned land—but it still excluded women, blacks, and many others.

At the same time, democratic activity has now shrunk until it is unrecognizable. Instead of debating public matters on a weekly or monthly basis, American democracy now often consists of sitting on one's couch and watching attack ads, and perhaps going to the voting booth once a year.

These are fundamental shifts in the way that Americans approach self-governnance, parallel to the transformation of the American diet. "Don't eat anything your great-great-grandmother wouldn't recognize as food," advises Michael Pollan[8]. Our ancestors would certainly be surprised by—and might not recognize—what passes for democracy today. While some of the changes have been positive, others are problematic. From a slow democracy perspective, the draining of power from the local level is especially troubling.

Not only has there been an absolute shift in the power of local communities, but many Americans today are skeptical of the ability of communities to govern themselves. Local people—rural ones—are seen as rubes, hicks, and bumpkins, and in some cases right-wing extremists; those from urban communities don't fare much better. While today's movement toward "local," including the locavore and Transition Town movements, could largely be considered left-wing, the left has played a driving role in efforts to centralize control and shift the locus of decision-making power away from the local level. What has happened?

Many historical factors have shaped this transformed notion of democracy. A look at the historical rise of two intertwined phenomena—efficiency and expertise—helps us understand what has happened to local decision making and points to how we might reclaim the best of both worlds.

Efficiency as a Driving Value

The American love affair with efficiency began with a mustachioed man with a stopwatch. Frederick Winslow Taylor was a turn-of-the-century factory manager and then consultant who applied "scientific principles" to the world of work. Instead of accepting the way that tasks had always been done, he broke each job down into its component parts and studied them to maximize efficiency. At Bethlehem Iron Company in Pennsylvania, he observed as workers shoveled iron ingots off railroad cars and onto the production floor. He noted that the average output was 12.5 tons per day. Using a stopwatch, he did a time and motion study, noting exactly how long it took the most efficient workers to move the iron, which movements were "false" or "unnecessary," and how much rest was necessary for maximum productivity. He determined that workers should be able to move 47 tons of iron per day, and he offered more money for those who could do it. As a result, Bethlehem Iron increased its productivity dramatically.

Taylor's system was particularly suited to the large factories of the turn of the century, which employed hundreds of workers, and the massive unemployment that had men lining up for those jobs. Workers were expendable in his system, and he had little patience for them, calling them "stupid," "phlegmatic," and "mentally sluggish":

> This work is so crude and elementary in its nature that . . . it would be possible to train an intelligent gorilla to be a more efficient pig-iron handler than any man can be. . . . It is impossible for the man who is best suited to this type of work to understand the principles of this science, or even to work in accordance with these principles, without the aid of a man better educated than he is.[9]

Taylor relied on a clear division of labor between brains and brawn. Once Bethlehem Iron managers had organized each task for maximum efficiency, workers could shovel pig iron at far greater rates. Taylor also believed in a "one best way," determined by the science of efficiency. His "scientific management," or "Taylorism," as it came to be called, was widely influential; Henry Ford famously adopted Taylor's principles on his assembly lines.

But beyond that, Taylor is considered one of the fathers of public administration, because of the way he influenced a whole generation of public policy thinkers. "Science" and efficiency became ways to organize not only businesses, but governments and social systems as well.

The Rise of Experts

Taylor's ideas of efficiency supported the growing influence of experts on public policy. Before the turn of the twentieth century, "experts" as we know them did not exist. There were religious hierarchies to which people looked for guidance, and there were certainly public leaders, often men of power and influence, but there were few specialized areas of knowledge. It was only with the appearance of professional organizations like the American Economics Association in the late nineteenth century that the idea of expertise emerged. These organizations provided a cadre of specialized thinkers—trained economists and political scientists—who were poised to help direct government efforts.

The "professionals" found ready material in the difficult human landscape of the time. Industrialization and urbanization—the same factors that had led to the growth of large-scale factories—also led to terrible social problems. The progressives looked at the growing cities, with their terrible poverty and their millions of struggling immigrants, and objected to the entrenched power dynamics that served the corrupt party bosses who ruled the city. Instead, they envisioned a future in which public decisions would be made by experts along the best scientific and rational principles: where sewer lines, for example, would be placed on the basis of need, rather than patronage. Their vision was not necessarily capitalist, as Taylor's was; rather, it was based on the need to reform a social system that clearly was not working.

The influx of experts into policy making brought a number of legacies. Experts began to take on a new authority in public life, one that threatened to erode existing democratic practices. Sometimes this was intentional: many experts believed that they were far better suited than citizens to tackle social problems. As the American Political Science Association's Committee of Seven famously announced in 1914, ordinary Americans "should learn humility in the face of expertise."[10]

Often, though, the erosion of democratic decision making was not intentional but rather a by-product of the growth of specialized knowledge. Agricultural extension services, for example, were established by congressional action in 1914 in order to inform farmers about new technologies and practices and help with their application. Urban planning, education administration, public health, and many other areas saw similar growth. And as these forms of specialized knowledge grew, so did the administrative bodies of state and federal governments. "Public administration" had barely been heard of when Woodrow Wilson introduced the term in the 1880s; today it spans an entire field and is frequently offered as an advanced degree.

At the same time, a rise in competing forms of entertainment—for example, vaudeville and movies—meant that town and city meetings no longer formed a pillar of social life. Suburbanization, the rise of the automobile, women working outside the home—all these changes in lifestyle also affected the appeal of local politics. Twentieth-century Americans found that many of the qualities that had once attracted their great-grandparents to town and city meetings were now gone.

And with the advent of television, everything happening on the national or international level—Sputnik, the Cold War, the interstate system—was brought into the home and made a real, daily presence in the lives of many Americans.[11] Every evening at 6 o'clock, television announcers provided viewers with messages about what was important. How could a city council meeting hold up against the atom bomb? So, trumped by state and federal powers, other forms of entertainment, and global events, local democracy came to seem increasingly irrelevant by the 1960s.

This legacy defines our democratic landscape today. The federal government increased dramatically in the 1930s with the New Deal; the numbers of state and local government employees mushroomed from the 1960s to the 1990s. There are currently over two million workers in the federal government, roughly five million at the state level, and fourteen million at the local level, including school employees.[12] Decisions that were once made democratically—in town and city councils, town meetings, and other local institutions—are now made by unelected officials working in public agencies. And these agencies, instead of the democratic process, form the locus of power.

To some extent this arrangement is necessary, because of the complexity of the world that we live in. But it has had a negative effect on "the spirit of municipal institutions" that Tocqueville found so necessary for freedom. Public administration has effectively drained decision making away from local democratic rule. Most local democracy is now limited to issues such as firefighting, sewers, water, and to a decreasing extent schools; even in these areas, hundreds of state and federal regulations set forth limiting parameters.

Devaluation of Local Knowledge

The shift away from local knowledge has been most profound on the political left, and two events during the twentieth century were particularly influential in defining it.

The Scopes Trial fed into a growing sense of small towns as backward and benighted, essentially setting the terms for the rest of the twentieth century. John Scopes was a high school science teacher in the small town of Dayton, Tennessee. In 1925, the Tennessee legislature passed the Butler Act, which outlawed the teaching of Darwin's theory of evolution. Scopes was charged with violating the act and prosecuted.

Also known as the Monkey Trial, the Scopes Trial became a national event, dramatizing what many saw as a battle for the American psyche—one between faith and science. Clarence Darrow, a leading ACLU attorney and criminal defense lawyer, was brought in to defend Scopes, and the grand old Christian statesman William Jennings Bryan swept in as the prosecutor. Two hundred journalists descended on the town, and the proceedings were broadcast by radio. The trial unfolded over eleven hot days in May, and it took the jury all of nine minutes to find Scopes guilty.[13]

The irony was that the premise of the Scopes Trial was a complete fabrication: in fact, it was residents of Dayton—that small town—who had cooked up the whole trial plan as a way to challenge the Butler Act. John Scopes couldn't remember whether he had taught evolution or not. While the trial featured a prosecution of the atheists, it showed that in the larger society religion itself was on trial. The very fact of the Butler Act—and that its passage was deemed necessary—showed how much fundamentalism was loosening its grip on the American mind-set.

Already, across the nation, there was a growing rejection of small towns and localism. Sinclair Lewis's *Main Street*, published five years before the trial, had depicted the people of small towns as small-minded and petty. Now the trial, with its national publicity, crystallized that view. The atheist journalist H. L. Mencken skewered the people of Tennessee as "hillbillies," "yaps," and "primates" who could not think for themselves. Creationism, he wrote, was the "degraded nonsense [that] was being rammed and hammered into yokel skulls" by country preachers.[14] Such depictions had a profound cultural impact, as local decision making became identified with politically and religiously conservative forces.

Thirty years later, the Civil Rights movement became a second key moment in shaping how left-leaning Americans thought about local decision making. The 1954 Supreme Court case of *Brown v. Board of Education* was the first powerful assertion of federal authority against local practices of segregation. In it, the court declared the racial segregation of schools to be unconstitutional, thus overthrowing school segregation laws in more than a dozen states and local practices in many others.

Similar uses of federal power followed on the heels of *Brown v. Board*, each attacking state and local segregation practices. In September 1957, nine black students were chosen to integrate Little Rock's Central High School in response to the Brown decision. Arkansas governor Orval Faubus, a committed segregationist, called out three hundred of the state's National Guard to prevent the students from entering; their commander turned the children away. In response, President Eisenhower federalized the National Guard and ordered the soldiers to aid, rather than block, the integration. Even more dramatically, he deployed federal troops to assist them. The resulting scene, with 101st Airborne soldiers escorting black students into the school, was a vivid picture of how the federal government was overcoming local segregationist practice.

In 1962, African-American James Meredith won a lawsuit that allowed him entry to the previously all-white University of Mississippi. The state's governor, Ross Barnett, refused Meredith's enrollment, saying, "No school will be integrated in Mississippi while I am your governor," and protesters rioted. The U.S. Fifth Circuit Court of Appeals objected, holding Barnett in contempt of court, while President Kennedy sent in federal troops to stop the rioting and allow Meredith to attend.

A similar showdown between state and national powers followed a year later in 1963. Alabama governor George Wallace had promised "segregation now, segregation tomorrow, segregation forever" in his reelection bid. When two black students tried to register for classes at the University of Alabama, he made his famous "Stand in the Schoolhouse Door," physically blocking the door of the school auditorium, flanked by Alabama National Guardsmen. Reached by telephone, President Kennedy federalized the National Guard. It was only after the general then asked Wallace to move aside—"Sir, it is my sad duty to ask you to step aside under the orders of the President of the United States"—that he finally moved and the students were able to register.

And in 1964, Congress passed the Civil Rights Act, which prohibited racial discrimination in schools, public facilities, and voting rights.

In each case, local power enforced segregation and discrimination, while federal power secured civil rights and inched African-Americans toward equal opportunity. For people who cared about racial equality and free speech, it seemed that the federal government was the only way to ensure that African-American children would be treated fairly.

National vs. State vs. Local Issues: Finding the Right Sphere

An important lesson emerges from the Scopes Trial and Civil Rights movement: some decisions need to be made by the state and the federal levels. Local communities can be dominated by one ideology or race or religion, and the majority can use the democratic process to run roughshod over the rights of the minority. Tocqueville identified this habit as the tyranny of the majority, and he warned against it as a threat to democracy.

Basic human rights cannot be decided at the local level; these are the responsibility of the larger society. The Civil Rights movement was successful only because of national intervention. Southern state and town power structures, dominated by whites, consistently overran the rights of African-Americans, and it took the Supreme Court, the National Guard, and congressional legislation to override these power structures. In this case, national power—rather than local—was the instrument of democracy. Still, it took local courage and action to begin this movement, and it continues to take profound local courage and commitment to protect and further its progress.

Likewise, fundamental ecological truths cannot be tailored to fit local needs. Nature does not understand or respect political boundaries. The effects of coal burned in the Midwest can be measured on the mountaintops of New England; oil spilled in the Gulf of Mexico affects birds migrating around the world. National, and in some cases global, agreements will be necessary to ensure that nature has a voice. But people at the local level can ensure that rational ecological policies are implemented in creative, spirited ways that make the most sense for their region.

There is certainly a role for national democracy, and safeguarding individuals' civil rights and the environment is part of it. Part of the challenge facing our democratic system is figuring out which issues are appropriately national, which are best dealt with on the state level, and which are fundamentally local issues.

Our current almost-exclusive emphasis on national politics is neither inevitable nor desirable. The American founders devised a compromise—a blend of local, state, and national government levels, with a series of intermingled checks and balances to ensure that no single body wound up with too much power. However, this balance has changed dramatically over time. The time has come to reexamine which issues belong at which level—and to bring local wisdom back into the equation.

At the Bottom

Some of the most devastating effects of expert-driven, top-down decision making have played out in poor and nonwhite communities. The history of urban renewal is a powerful example—perhaps even the classic example of how well-intended government policy has gone wrong. Good-hearted experts can sometimes unthinkingly steamroll the needs of a community—especially if that community is disempowered. That is precisely what happened in one Philadelphia neighborhood when the midcentury push for housing projects ignored local wisdom, at tragic costs.

Mill Creek lies west of Philadelphia's city center, about four miles from Independence Hall and the Liberty Bell, in a neighborhood known as "the Bottom." The name refers to the topography of the area—it's a low-lying floodplain—and also, at least to some, to the social status of the people who live there.[15]

In the years after World War II, Mill Creek had been one of many low- to middle-income urban neighborhoods. Its residents were a racial mix of white and African-American, and residents lived on both sides of the poverty line; many of them were working class, while others struggled with poverty. Always troubled by structural problems because of its sodden floodplain location, the area was dominated by narrow brick row houses in various stages of repair: some, especially west of 48th Street, were well kept, with ceramic tiles and potted plants, while others were run through with faulty plumbing, flooded basements, and rats and cockroaches scurrying in the walls at night.[16]

Homeowners were caught in the contradictions of the new Federal Housing Administration, whose policies made mortgages available to middle-class families in the suburbs, but not to the residents of Mill Creek. The neighborhood had the lowest rating—red—for property values, and insurance companies and mortgage lenders were not required to do business there.[17] Still, a strong community spirit meant that the Bottom was considered one of the best of the city's poorer neighborhoods.[18]

A Model Plan

Public housing, in the form of modern, well-constructed living quarters, seemed like the answer to Mill Creek's problems. The new federal Public Housing Administration, the great hope of the postwar era, wielded enormous influence, backing two out of every three low-income housing projects in the country, and it had a stringent list of requirements, including direct sunlight for each apartment in a new project.[19] City planners, advocates for the poor, and even many residents saw neighborhoods like Mill Creek as being in dire need of a safe, sanitary new infrastructure. The buzz term of the day was "urban renewal."

Philadelphia's planners were known to be particularly thoughtful in their approach to public housing. Housing advocate Catherine Bauer, who blasted New York and Chicago development, singled out Philadelphia for its "thoughtful planning and responsible civic leadership."[20] Philadelphia planners rejected the kind of "supertenement" building projects that were being built in other cities. Their metaphor for urban renewal was not surgery—cutting the slums out entirely—but "penicillin": smaller projects on a human scale that would create "spores" of healthy communities that would then spread outward.[21] And the architects they employed were known for fidelity to the "neighborhood ideal." Their designs sought to sustain family life with a strong network of schools, community buildings, playgrounds, shops, and churches.

Against this backdrop, Mill Creek was targeted for renewal and its existing housing demolished. By 1955, the housing project that replaced it, the brand-new Mill Creek Apartments, was the picture of hope. Designed as public housing for struggling working-class families, it was a symbol of government commitment to the less fortunate.

Of the eighteen Philadelphia projects designed in the postwar period, the Mill Creek project was one of the finest: a smaller project carefully crafted by Louis Kahn, a thoughtful, liberal architect with deep social and political convictions. Kahn believed that residents should affect the planning process and was an early advocate of community input. In fact, he was coauthor of a citizens' primer titled *"Why City Planning Is Your Responsibility."*[22] His goal was not simply to plop a spectacular building in Mill Creek. Rather, he sought to create affordable housing in a space that would generate community and build on the natural features already present.

The project was centered on a lovely circular lawn surrounded by trees. A triangle of apartment towers rose around the green knoll, each seventeen stories tall, their surface defined by cement columns contrasting with yellow brick sandstone. They were a triumph of modernist architecture, and the hand of their famous designer was evident in their double columns of balconies facing the rising and setting sun. Below the buildings, children played in a spray pool and tumbled on a play sculpture, while mothers watched them and pushed baby carriages in the grassy courtyard. Each of the apartment towers was organized around a garden, and beyond them was a school, church, and community center.

Kahn linked the different parts of the project with a green necklace of natural walkways for pedestrians. That feature was part of a compromise. The architect had an instinctive dislike for high-rises, finding them unconducive to community life, but accepted them as a necessary evil that would give him the biggest possible courtyard and uphold his primary goal: shared outdoor space for the area's residents. He fought hard for the balconies, one for each apartment, as a way to provide outside space even in a high-rise. He wanted children to be able to play outside while their mothers did housework, and if he must build towers, he wanted them to look, as he said, like the Hanging Gardens of Babylon.[23]

From Heaven to Hell

The first wrinkle in the process had come in the clearing of the land. The city called it "slum removal"; residents called it "Negro removal," since it sacrificed black residents to the cause of the housing project.[24] In order to build, the city claimed the property by eminent domain. Bulldozers took out eighty-four houses, two churches, and eleven businesses, forcing over a hundred families and nearly four hundred people from the neighborhood.[25]

Personal dislocations aside, at first the housing projects were a great success. In Mill Creek and other projects across the city, many of the residents were thrilled to be accepted into public housing. Some had come from apartments without running water, toilets, or refrigeration, and the projects felt like heaven: an "undreamed of luxury."[26] They loved the balconies and the fresh paint, the sunlit rooms and the hot and cold tap water. One woman described the move as "going from a dark room into sunlight. . . . My whole outlook on life changed."[27] Over ten thousand families put their names on the waiting list for Philadelphia's projects.[28]

But the Mill Creek project lacked the community underpinnings that it needed in order to be successful. Few residents would have designed the high-rise towers, even at the price of losing their green space. The Federal Public Housing Authority knew from both tenants and managers that "the vast majority of families want enclosed, individual back yards . . . for children, for laundry, and some would like a garden."[29]

Prospective tenants had consistently demonstrated an overwhelming preference for row houses, with 91% of residents describing "complete satisfaction" with that arrangement. (Similarly, in New York, out of a thousand tenants surveyed, only 1% said they would choose to live in a three-story or higher building.[30]) Still, the towers went up.

The towers created a strange new kind of community, one very different from that shared by residents of adjoining row houses. Mill Creek had been known for its vital social life, but the tensions of the apartment buildings began to rip away at that strength. As one observer pointed out, "Nowhere is it quite so difficult to create a community as in a block of flats. With neighbors above, below, and to both sides, the natural tendency is to erect barriers against friendship."[31]

The management by the Philadelphia Housing Authority (PHA) was as hierarchical and top-down as the buildings themselves. Rather than giving tenants the freedom normally accorded in apartment houses, or organizing them to come up with their own rules and systems of self-enforcement, the PHA produced a draglet of rules and then encouraged residents to spy on each other.

It was against the rules to keep a pet, host an overnight guest, repair a leaky faucet, or make a little extra money by hairstyling for friends at the kitchen table.[32] Managers had passkeys and let themselves into the apartments for surprise inspections; any family judged "poor housekeepers" risked eviction.[33] Families' incomes were closely monitored, and any additional cash meant an increase in the rent.

It is telling that Kahn's biggest value—the leafy green spaces—did not function as he had envisioned. At first, residents enjoyed them and children from the projects and neighboring areas used them as play spaces. But the PHA did not employ landscapers, and as managers become lax, the green spaces became more and more bedraggled. Children were sent down to play unsupervised, since mothers could not watch them while doing housework.[34] Garbage piled up in the courtyards, making them hard to enjoy, especially on warm summer days.[35] Finally, tired of maintaining the grassy areas, project managers paved them over with concrete.[36]

The rules, the tensions between managers and tenants, and the increasingly bedraggled buildings ate away at residents' sense of ownership. The lack of money allocated by the city for upkeep contributed further to the problem. In only five years, the high-rise elevators and stairways had become likely places to be robbed or sexually assaulted.[37] The project's lack of solid community foundation was starkly symbolized by its ecological foundation. Under the streets, Mill Creek continued to belch and burp uneasily in its sewer pipe. Because of the underlying floodplain, the playgrounds and streets and open spaces continued to sink. The foundations of the project—literal as well as democratic—were fundamentally unstable.

Within a decade, the Mill Creek Apartments had disintegrated, plagued by all the now-familiar demons of housing projects: joblessness, drugs, violence, fragmented community. In 2000, the neighborhood was the site of the worst crime that Philadelphia had ever seen, when ten people were shot in a crack house. In 2002, the apartment towers were torn down.

By that time the apartments had become a symbol of one of the keystones of urban planning—housing projects—gone wrong. They were also a symbol of fast democracy: decisions made by experts for other people, living somewhere else. Their replacement, the Lucien Blackwell homes, are much more what the community residents wanted: low-rise buildings, each housing a small number of families.

The Mill Creek Apartments should have been a triumph of city planning. Funded by the federal government and directed by the Philadelphia Housing Authority, they drew on the resources of powerful institutions on both the national and city levels. But the decision-making process did not include those it would affect: the residents.[38] They could have told Kahn that their old neighborhood, however difficult, had its own community fabric, based on the row houses and the neighborliness of the street. The massive projects could only have been imagined by someone who would not live in them. And so a series of decisions made by experts and centralized institutions, though they seemed logical and efficient at the time, ultimately proved to have profoundly destructive effects, both financially and socially.

A Different Approach: Residents as Experts

It doesn't have to be this way. New models are transforming the relationship between experts and residents in all kinds of fields, including housing.

In the mid-1990s, the Phillips neighborhood of south Minneapolis had many similarities to the Bottom. The area was close to downtown—only ten blocks away—but had been cut off when freeways were built in the 1960s. Buildings emptied out. Businesses struggled, then closed down and left. The only trades that flourished were drugs and prostitution; one block had five crack houses. At the main intersection of Franklin and Portland Streets sat three deserted gas stations and one empty lot.[39]

As in the Bottom, residents struggled. Most were very low-income: the average family of three earned under $20,000 at the 2010 census. Seventy percent were people of color. Many were recent immigrants or refugees.[40]

But here, two groups joined forces to develop affordable housing: Aeon, a low-income housing developer, and Hope Community, an organization dedicated to community building in the area. As a partnership, they drew on years of community conversations. "Over 10 years, we have talked to about 1,500 people from the neighborhood in small groups," said Hope's executive director. "They told us they wanted a grocery store. Sixty percent of them do not have cars, yet the nearest grocery store was at least a couple of miles away."[41]

In designing their Franklin-Portland Gateway housing project, the groups used a process known as a "charrette." This is an increasingly popular design approach that brings all the stakeholders to the table early in the design process: funders, architects, tradespeople, engineers, community members, and residents. They work together in an intensive series of discussions to state concerns and develop proposals.

The charrette gave residents a chance to shape their housing, and a wide variety of them participated. In the discussions, they talked extensively about the size of the buildings, the amount and kind of green space, and the relationship between the apartments and the street—the very concerns that the Mill Creek residents would have liked to weigh in on.[42]

The resulting projects offer affordable housing with a mix of other amenities, including a grocery store, a restaurant, a children's play area, and the Hope Communities office—all within a block of a neighborhood park. And they are green, with solar hot water and rain gardens.[43]

Both the Mill Creek Apartments and the Franklin-Portland Gateway project incorporated community gardens, and their fates are instructive. Louis Kahn built gardens into his plan for the apartments. But the authoritarian management of the Philadelphia Housing Authority withered the community life of these gardens. Families were fined if they did not keep their gardens neat. Managers worried about gardeners losing the tools, so they locked them in a shed; in at least one PHA project, they allowed residents to sign the tools out only between noon and 1 p.m.—when men were working and most mothers were feeding their children lunch—effectively killing the gardens.[44]

The Franklin-Portland Gateway garden has twenty-three plots and a communal area for growing larger crops like melons and squash. Tools and compost are freely available. The project also boasts a lively gardening program that offers classes on basic gardening skills, composting, and even growing food in a bucket. And, in conjunction with the Land Stewardship Project, Hope Community shows movies about food and food politics on Tuesday evenings.[45]

A New Role for Experts in Local Decision Making

As the charrette process in the Franklin-Portland Gateway housing project shows, there is no necessary opposition between expert knowledge and local decision making. Experts have a key role to play in decision-making processes. Their highly specific knowledge allows them to highlight areas for improvement and suggest solutions that have been tried in other places. They are in a superb position to be partners in local decisions.

But instead of using outside experts to *inform* local decisions, government has too often used them to *make* local decisions. Sometimes, as in West Virginia's school consolidation, a public planning process looks like it fosters citizen engagement, but with predetermined outcomes. This is not slow democracy; it is *faux* democracy. In West Virginia, as in the Bottom, the influence of Frederick Taylor was evident: there was little respect for the kind of on-the-ground knowledge that local citizens can offer.

And despite Louis Kahn's best intentions, the Mill Creek Apartments also served their population poorly. Without direct input from the residents, Kahn did not know what they needed. And the autocratic managers did not let residents take advantage of the architectural aspects they *did* want, like the community gardens.

Even measured by the standard of efficiency, these kinds of noninclusive, speeded-up processes are often too fast for their own good. An "efficiency at all costs" mentality can lead, quickly and efficiently, to disastrous decision making. The long-term costs can be massive—economically, socially, and environmentally. And fixing things takes *more* time than doing things right in the first place.

The good news is that fast democracy is not an irreversible trend. Even in difficult circumstances, where citizens are being railroaded by the forces of centralization and privatization, they generate their own processes to protect their community. Hacker Valley builds its own school. The Mill Creek Apartments are torn down and a community garden is springing up just down the street. All across the country, local people are rallying around the need for slower, more local democracy, instituting policies that affirm their autonomy and protect their community.

three

COMMUNITIES TAKING ACTION
IN A BIG WORLD

Roz Frontiera laughs into the telephone from her family room in Gloucester, Massachusetts. She is a warm woman in her late forties with wide eyes and soft brown hair. "I grew up knee-deep in fish," she says in her telltale North Shore accent. "I was born into a long line of fishing families." She has traveled the world, lived in Italy, and worked for Microsoft on the West Coast, but Gloucester is home. She speaks with ownership about the city's artistic and historical legacies. "This is where I live. I want to make it a better place, to preempt our culture and heritage from being completely stripped."[1]

Frontiera is talking about water. You wouldn't think that water would be a problem in Gloucester, which is technically an island. As the country's oldest seaport, the city is surrounded by water: water slaps up against the fishing trawlers at the pier, crashes on the rocks under the gleaming white lighthouse, and rises in the salt marsh at high tide. This is the place where the perfect storm landed with such ferocity in the 1990s.[2] And that water has helped define the built environment. The city's historic houses face the harbor, their widows' walks a testament to the dangers of deep-sea fishing. The Fishermen's Memorial statue looks out to the sea beyond, a larger-than-life fisherman at the helm, straining to bring his boat in safely through the waves.

Public Water, Private Ownership

While the city has plenty of seawater, drinking water is another issue. The private company that until recently had managed the city's water had allowed it to become undrinkable. Gloucester's water started fresh and clean, streaming from two tree-lined reservoirs above the city. But from there it entered an infrastructure of broken and outmoded equipment, flowing through iron pipes nearly a century old, which oozed with bacteria; rushing through the corroded remnants of gates that used to keep debris from clogging the city's system; and swirling into the city's water treatment plant, where the chains and scrapers that were supposed to scrape the sludge from the sedimentation tank were broken and missing.[3]

Frontiera remembers an incident over a decade ago, before she was aware of the city's water issues, when the water main burst open in front of her mother's house. "It was disgusting," she recalls, describing a dark gunky mixture oozing from the pipe. "Here was a big twenty-inch pipe with only a tiny flow of water. The rest of it was crap." That trickle flowing through the slime was the water that spurted out of the faucet and into her glass.

Like many other cities, Gloucester owned its water system, but it contracted out the management to a private company: United Water. United is an American subsidiary of Suez Environnement, a French company that is as multinational as Gloucester is local. Named for its role in building the Suez Canal, it is one of the world's oldest corporations, dating back two hundred years. Now headquartered in glassy offices near the Champs-Élysées in Paris, Suez is one of the two massive corporations that dominate the water industry. The company has either bought or contracted to manage the water system for nearly 91 million people in seventy countries from Algiers to Bangalore.[4] Cities like Gloucester typically retain ownership of the infrastructure of pipes and plants, while hiring United to do necessary maintenance and upkeep. And the problems arise when the corporation cuts corners in order to send profits back to its headquarters in Paris.

Most Gloucester residents only became aware of how bad their water had become in 2009, when United's contract was ending. The company had let the infrastructure deteriorate to the point that the water was undrinkable: for the final twenty days of the contract, the water quality was so bad that the city had to issue a boil order. Frontiera was incredulous. If what she had seen out of that pipe was supposedly potable water, what did it look like now? Gloucester was especially interested in clean water because the city had suffered from multiple health plagues. Residents were concerned by the numbers of children with disabilities and with unacceptable levels of lead in their blood. And Gloucester had suffered more than its share of cancer cases: on Frontiera's sister's street, there have been 27 deaths from cancer alone. While nobody knows, some residents suspect the drinking water.

The boil order was the talk of the city, and Frontiera and her neighbors were infuriated when they discovered that the very company that had let the water quality run down was hoping to buy the water system. "United Water came into the mayor's office, plopped their card down, and said, 'We want to buy your water,'" says Frontiera. Residents were horrified to learn that the mayor could legally have sold the water system right out from under the people of Gloucester. "She had every right to sell it," says Frontiera. There would have been no vote, no dialogue, no way for the citizens to stop the sale. Was this possible in a democracy? Who decides something as important as water security?

In fact, the mayor did not sell the system to United. Instead, she turned to a different private water company, Veolia Water, awarding them the contract to manage the water. Veolia's parent company, Veolia Environnement, is the counterpart to United's parent company, Suez Environnement. Also a French company, it is the other major water power in the world. Together the two companies are dividing up the world's water.

Doing Their Research: Other Communities

Gloucester's contracts with United Water and Veolia are part of a silent shift taking place in who controls the world's water. Early in the twentieth century, most towns and cities had public control of their water. But for the last several decades, many American communities have been contracting out management of their systems, or even selling them outright. Private companies control water systems in forty countries, including China, Ghana, Indonesia, and England. Now, a full 270 million people around the globe get their water from large-scale private companies. With Gloucester's system run by either United or Veolia, decisions about the city's water were no longer being made by people who would drink that water; instead they became economic equations processed out of state and sometimes halfway across the world, as part of a massive logarithm aimed at maximizing profit.

With Veolia in charge, the boil order was lifted: the company improved the pipes enough for that. But Frontiera and her neighbors—who were now fully outraged—could see what was coming as they identified a predictable pattern of what happens to communities that sell their water supply. In country after country, state after state, and town after town, they found that privatization of water systems has led to lower-quality water, rate increases, and profits that flow back to the corporation rather than being invested at the local level.

Frontiera and her co-organizers made contact with one community that had already fought this fight: the town of Felton, California, on the other side of the continent. Felton, a mountain town surrounded by redwood forests and hiking trails, is home to four thousand residents. A popular historic train steams out from the town through old logging territory and down the San Lorenzo Valley gorge to the boardwalk in Santa Cruz, just a few miles south.

In 2001, California American Water (Cal-Am) bought the town's water system and promptly tried to raise rates by nearly 80%. Like United Water in Gloucester, Cal-Am was at the time an American subsidiary of a multinational corporation—in this case, the German RWE.

What followed was an eye-opening education in fast democracy. The residents of Felton protested the raise in rates, but in order to appeal they had to hire a $500-per-hour lawyer to appear before the California Public Utilities Commission (PUC). And despite their efforts, the PUC still allowed a 44% increase—in part because the commission guarantees private companies a 10% return on their investment. The stakes were stacked against the town.

"No small community could afford to travel up to San Francisco to be heard in front of the PUC," says water district employee Betsy Herbert. Even if you could, she said, "your chances still aren't very good. And you compare that to your ability to go to a local board meeting with five people who are locally elected. If you don't like what they are doing, you can unseat them."[5] The contrast between dealing with a local democratic body and a far-off corporation spoke for itself.

Residents decided to buy their water system back. A group called Felton Friends of Locally Owned Water (FLOW) mobilized the community. And in 2005, voters in Felton overwhelmingly approved a bond measure to buy their water system back, by a margin of 3 to 1—only to have Cal-Am refuse to sell. Finally, the town threatened to take the water by eminent domain, at which point Cal-Am settled.

Today, Felton is part of the San Lorenzo Valley Water District, with better service, lower rates, and a transparent system in which citizens participate. The district just put in a huge new solar installation that will provide 20% of the electricity the system uses. There have been other benefits too. Two hundred and fifty acres of watershed went along with the Cal-Am system: "This is forested land with beautiful streams," says Herbert. "When Cal-Am owned it, the company logged the land, sent the profits to the shareholders, and barely invested anything in the system; now, however, it is permanently protected."[6]

Felton started out as a typical water story, but it turned into one with an unusually happy ending. Massive rate increases are common when private companies take over a system. The advocacy group Food and Water Watch compared rates before and after the ten largest sales of municipal water systems; they found that the average yearly bill had tripled, and that households were paying more than $300 over what they would have had with municipal ownership.[7] At the same time, water quality and service often deteriorate. In 2010, for example, Illinois American Water, the state's largest water company, outraged consumers when it requested a 30% increase in rates; it received a hike of 17% to 26%.[8] Atlanta took its water system back from United Water after four years of that company's management because of water main breaks, boil orders, and brown water.[9] In Hoboken, New Jersey, United Water's management of the city's water system has also been characterized by boil orders and tea-colored water, as well as ruptured pipelines as often as three times per week.[10] Because of instances like these, many U.S. municipalities are now taking back their water systems.[11]

Who Decides?

Alarmed by what they learned about privatization, Frontiera and other Gloucester residents began organizing, trying to persuade residents that the city itself could do a better job managing its water than any profit-making entity. Their mission statement reads like a manifesto of slow democracy: "to accurately inform the public, to share in the civil discourse, and to participate in the decision making process." They called their group "Who Decides" because that was the fundamental question at stake: was it going to be the citizens of Gloucester or the Veolia corporation who made decisions for the town?

Members came from all walks of life and included a carpenter, a lawyer, a videographer, a retired police officer, a curriculum coordinator, and a Brazilian journalist. They met every Monday night in an old church and modeled their group along democratic lines, connecting their work with the Bill of Rights and insisting on making decisions by consensus. "I have an appreciation for these processes," Frontiera says, reflecting on their meetings. "What we put into it is what we get out of it."

It was not easy. "Democracy is exhausting," says Frontiera. They reached out to raise awareness in the community in every way that they could: printing leaflets, standing outside supermarkets, showing documentaries about water politics, e-mailing to targeted distribution lists, making videos, using Facebook, and creating a website to keep people updated. There were community meetings, forums, heated debates about which disinfectants to use in the pipes. There were also questions about how to pay for improvements. Gloucester is one of the poorer communities on the North Shore, and it didn't have money to build new schools, let alone take control of its water system. But the citizens were clear about their priorities; as one city councilwoman said, "We all agreed, we don't want the water to be sold."[12]

Fed by the community mobilization, the Gloucester city council took up a resolution requiring local control of their water as a democratic right. On an October evening in 2010, residents crowded into the historic city hall. Under the high tin ceilings and the hand-carved wooden balcony, they listened as the resolution was passed:

> The People of the City of Gloucester declare that access to clean and affordable water is essential for life, liberty, and the pursuit of happiness—both for the health of the people and for the ecological systems which support human and natural communities—and therefore, that it is a right belonging to the people of the City of Gloucester.

It was a statement not only about rights, but about the relationship between privatization and democracy:

> We believe that our rights are threatened when public water systems which guarantee that access are controlled by a corporate few, rather than by our community. We believe that privatization of that infrastructure constitutes a usurpation of our democratic right to make decisions about that infrastructure, and therefore, that we are duty bound under the Massachusetts Constitution to prohibit such action.[13]

Without a single dissenting vote, the city council passed the resolution and gave Who Decides a standing ovation. Frontiera described it as a "goose bumps" moment: "It was a moment of sweet respect where it all just stopped for a minute. Everyone felt that this was history in the making. It really made you understand the importance of what we were doing and the awesome responsibility of the effect."[14]

And that effect has been noticed. While Gloucester's efforts were as local as they could be, the implications were global. "This is the ordinance heard round the world," says Frontiera. International water companies are paying attention, she says. "Everybody at the statehouse knows us. Everybody in the water industry knows us." The work has linked Who Decides with other citizens working in other local communities to protect their water supply. Frontiera has connections from New Hampshire to Italy. She links that local-global dynamic to Gloucester's very specific past as a seaport, noting, "Even though it's an island, we also have that global sense. That really helped me understand why we have to reach out."

Who Decides was able to draw on its very local base and use existing government structures—with a lot of community organizing—to create a far more democratic process. Now, with the ordinance, any decisions about the water supply must be made in a way that is empowered and inclusive. It has been a long, hard road, and it is far from over: they need stronger laws on the state level to guarantee their continued control. Privatization is one threat; centralization is another. Having escaped the sale of the water system, Who Decides must now ensure that the federal government does not decide to regionalize the water system and take control, especially with a public-private partnership.

Frontiera is clear on the power of Who Decides' battle to bring decision making home. The hard work has been worth it, both in terms of water cost and quality and—beyond that—in the way it has brought people together. The work has developed her own skills in ways that she couldn't have imagined: "I'm not a speaker; I'm not a writer—but here I am developing my voice."

And Frontiera sees that possibility amplified on the community level. "Each person is a leader in their own right," she says. "You feel so alive. The synergy between us is like magic. The mission is greater than us, greater than one individual, greater than one group. The work is for the next generation or the generation after. . . . There's an ebb and a flow and a weave. It's the best of how a community can be."[15]

Acting Locally

Many Americans hold out some hope for our political system—on a local level. There is a big difference between how Americans feel about our federal and state governments and how they feel about local government. While many view the federal system with deep cynicism, citizens are more positive about the government systems that are closer to us:

- Nearly 60% (58) believe that the federal government is meddling too much in state and local business.[16]
- 53% of Americans view state governments positively, compared to 38% for the federal government.[17]
- Perceptions of local government are even more positive, with 63% of citizens looking on it favorably.[18]
- Unlike the view of the federal government, perceptions of state and local governments are not significantly different between Democrats and Republicans.[19]

So instead of beating their heads against the iron wall of national politics, citizens are finding possibility in local action—taking their own states, towns, and communities back into their own hands. Citizens are working hard to regain control of decisions that affect them, and increasingly they are using local arenas to do it.

The examples that follow embody different definitions of local—from tiny towns to whole counties—but they each show the power of communities defining their own values. In each case, people are working to bring back power that has been usurped by—or that we have given to—state and federal governments, or indirectly to private corporations. Here, citizens are rediscovering one of the most elemental of American values: an impassioned interest in governing themselves.

Maine Food Sovereignty Laws

The Blue Hill peninsula rises across the bay from Mount Desert Island and Acadia National Park. It is known for its small towns, artists, boatbuilding, and summer folk. One of its summertime attractions is the colorful Blue Hill farmers' market, where vendors sell blueberries, zucchini, pies, raw honey, and flowers, as well as local meats.

In the spring of 2011, it also became known for its fierce stand on food rights. That's when four towns on Maine's Down East coast passed ordinances declaring food sovereignty.

The impetus for the ordinances came from local farmers raising free-range chickens. Under the existing regulations, they were not allowed to sell chicken parts unless they took the birds to a licensed facility, of which there were only a handful in the state of Maine, and processed the birds with an inspector present. This requirement made a great deal of sense for large industrial farms that keep animals in barns rather than on pasture and that process tens of thousands of birds; for these operations, diseases and cross-contamination are daily issues. However, it was unrealistic for small farmers, who would have to enclose the chickens in crates, drive for hours, and pay for the facility—all of which would drive up the price of a drumstick beyond what anyone could afford. These farmers could ensure food safety at their own farms with a simple set of regulations: having their water tested, ensuring proper chilling of carcasses, and making sure their facilities were inspected, without the need for an inspector to be actually present at the time of slaughter.

So these farmers worked with the state legislature and passed a bill creating an exemption for small-scale chicken farms. But when the Maine Department of Agriculture developed a set of standards for these farmers, they were completely unrealistic, calling for indoor facilities with running water and septic systems, costing up to $40,000. This was an impossible sum for small farmers, especially considering the fact that they were not going to be using these facilities weekly or even monthly. As Maine farmer Bob St. Peter said, "The requirements didn't make economic or logistical sense for small farms."[20]

When the issue went back before the legislature, the Agriculture Committee told the farmers that Maine would lose USDA funding if the state adopted rules that were not in keeping with federal regulations. The final bill prohibited farmers from selling chickens that were processed outside.[21] It was another discouraging example of how government regulations, however well intentioned, have worked against small farms.

That is when the towns got involved. Maine is a "home rule" state, which means that any law that is not prohibited on the state level can be passed on a local level. Having been blocked by the state system, the farmers took their concerns to their neighbors. As St. Peter described it, "We talked with local farmers and producers, the local Republican Party and the local Democratic

Party, the Chamber of Commerce and the local Grange. . . . Part of that process was reminding people that our communities, as far as agriculture goes, used to look a lot different. What we were asking of the state was to return to how agriculture had existed in our communities for hundreds of years, since Europeans settled here."[22]

The farmers were not asking to relax safety and hygiene standards; an outbreak of salmonella in local foods would endanger their entire livelihood. But they were asking for ways to ensure that those standards were appropriate for small farms and familiar relationships between farmers and customers. At town meetings in April 2011, Blue Hill and three other towns passed food sovereignty ordinances that explicitly allowed small farmers and their consumers to work out their own arrangements. In Blue Hill, the ordinance read like this:

> We the People of the Town of Blue Hill, Hancock County, Maine have the right to produce, process, sell, purchase and consume local foods thus promoting self-reliance, the preservation of family farms, and local food traditions. We recognize that family farms, sustainable agricultural practices, and food processing by individuals, families and non-corporate entities offers stability to our rural way of life by enhancing the economic, environmental and social wealth of our community. As such, our right to a local food system requires us to assert our inherent right to self-government. We recognize the authority to protect that right as belonging to the Town of Blue Hill.
>
> We have faith in our citizens' ability to educate themselves and make informed decisions. We hold that federal and state regulations impede local food production and constitute a usurpation of our citizens' right to foods of their choice. We support food that fundamentally respects human dignity and health, nourishes individuals and the community, and sustains producers, processors and the environment. We are therefore duty bound under the Constitution of the State of Maine to protect and promote unimpeded access to local foods.[23]

In Blue Hill, most of the discussion at the town meeting centered not on the content of the ordinance itself but on what would happen if the state or federal government decided to challenge it. And in fact, in November 2011, the state of Maine filed a lawsuit against a Blue Hill farmer for selling raw milk. As of publication, this suit was still pending.

Similar food-sovereignty resolutions have passed or are being considered in towns in Vermont, Wyoming, Arizona, Massachusetts, and California. The momentum behind local food sovereignty is growing. And as Dan Brown, a Blue Hill farmer, says, "One of these times, they're going to come after one of us, and it's going to be that Rosa Parks moment. I'm hoping the public will realize what's going on. . . . They've got to get involved. We've got to fix what's wrong with the food system."[24]

Boulder: Municipal Utilities, Local Power

Boulder, Colorado, has a long history of action on green energy and climate change. While the U.S. government ignored the parameters and goals set by the Kyoto Protocol to combat climate change, Boulder made a commitment to them. The city imposed a carbon tax, created goals to lower emissions to 1990 levels, and funded practical, hands-on energy conservation programs. But in 2009, Boulder realized that conservation alone wasn't going to be enough; if it was going to cut emissions as much as it wanted, citizens would have to rethink the sources of their energy.

The city has been served by Xcel Energy, an electric and natural gas company that actually has one of the better environmental records as far as electric utilities go. But Xcel still has a strong reliance on coal, and there seemed to be no alternative. As environmentalists have pointed out, the company's entire business model depends on it. "The whole system seems to be rigged against maximizing non-coal-based electricity," said Boulder mayor Susan Osbourne. "We were just being hog-tied." So after negotiations with the company failed, the city decided to propose ballot measure 2C, which would allow the city to create its own municipal electric utility. With it, the city could control its own energy future, choosing power sources based on local production of renewable resources.[25]

Since 2000, a dozen other local governments have taken utilities into their own hands in a similar way. Winter Park, Florida, voted overwhelmingly to establish its own utility in 2005, based on the reliability of service. Jefferson County, Washington, also established its own utility.[26]

In November 2011, Boulder voters approved measure 2C, and the companion measure that raises a tax for planning for the utility. The vote was close, passing by 51% for the utility and just over 50% for the tax.[27] The city is not sure whether it will actually go ahead with the utility, which will be expensive; several cities that have tried to municipalize their electricity have foundered on the costs. The city will do it only if it can provide electricity at rates equal to or lower than the ones that Xcel charges. It may instead lobby the state legislature to legalize community choice aggregation (CCA), an approach that has been used in Massachusetts, Ohio, California, New Jersey, and Rhode Island. CCA would allow the city to choose the sources of its electricity without having to become a municipal utility and invest in infrastructure.[28]

For Boulder residents, the debate is about the ability to define their own energy future, making sure that it is compatible with the city's values. "It's essential that all of the parts of the community stay involved at a high level," said one of the municipalization advocates. "Our goal is to bring our community together, not split it apart."[29] Or as Jonathan Koehn, Boulder's regional sustainability coordinator, says, "We didn't go into this with the aim to own power poles and wires. The goal is to have control over the decisions being made."[30]

Mendocino County: Moratorium on GE Crops

Mendocino County, California, was the first North American county to outlaw the use of genetically engineered (GE) crops within its boundaries. Mendocino stretches north of San Francisco, a beautiful and rugged agricultural county that includes Big Sur along the coastline and dozens of small towns and unorganized townships inland. It has long been a center of local and organic activism. The county seat is the small town of Ukiah, which boasts the country's first organic brewpub, owned by Els Cooperrider and her husband.

Cooperrider is a short woman in her sixties with a broad smile and wavy white hair. A former research scientist and now grandmother, she once played country rock in honky-tonk bars. She is famous in Mendocino County and in anti-GMO (genetically modified organism) circles but thinks of her actions as a natural outgrowth of awareness. "People call me an activist," she says. "I bristle when I hear that word because I am just an ordinary person who cares about what is going on around her."[31]

In the early 2000s, alarmed by the growth in GE seeds and the federal government's refusal to monitor it, people in Mendocino County were talking about the need to label GMOs. With her background as a scientist, Cooperrider was convinced that a more fundamental change was needed: "I said, you know, we can go one step better. Why don't we in Mendocino County say, 'You can't grow them here'?"[32]

So with the brewpub as a hub, she and fellow citizens formed a citizen's initiative called GMO-Free Mendocino. They started a series of community conversations about GE foods. And in 2004 they put on the ballot Measure H, which prohibited GE produce and livestock within the county. As Cooperrider said, "The biggest challenge was educating the people of the county about GE. Most people didn't have a clue. It was a matter of educating, *not* convincing them that GMOs were bad. People would have to conclude for themselves when they had the facts."[33]

The citizens were opposed by CropLife America, a big Washington lobby representing Monsanto, DuPont, Dow, and other huge industry names. CropLife came into the county calling Measure H "the H-bomb."[34] Advocates for Measure H soon saw how powerful and necessary the democratic process would be to their efforts. Environmental activist Britt Bailey spoke at many events:

> I quickly realized my first words needed to focus on voting and registration. "Are you registered to vote?" I would ask. An unnerving though common answer was "why should I register to vote—my view is never represented."
>
> For many of the people who had become involved [with] the "Measure H" campaign, it was the first time in years they had voted much less been caught up in politics. Many had left behind the idea that they would see the benefits of their voting efforts.[35]

In March 2004, supporters gathered at the Ukiah Brewing Company as the votes were counted. They drank organic beer and seasoned their organic burgers with organic ketchup as the votes came in. By the end of the night, the measure had passed, with an impressive 57% of the county voting in its favor. And Mendocino became the first county in North America to outlaw the use of GE crops.

The vote of this one California community had national ramifications, provoking both action and reaction.

Industry advocates responded by trying to shift power from local communities to the state level, where they were more likely to prevail. They launched campaigns to pass preemptive seed laws in California and twenty-one other states, laws that would ban local communities from taking action like Mendocino's and ensure that only the state would have authority over seed laws. While six of these bills failed, sixteen of them passed.[36] Sponsors of these bills insisted that local people were not smart or informed enough to be appropriate caretakers of this kind of legislation, and that it should be left to national experts and state agencies. As a Georgia representative said, "We wanted to keep authority pertaining to seeds within the Department of Agriculture. The Department has the knowledge; the brain trust if you will, to better control the types of foods we grow. We do not want a small voting segment of the population which has limited knowledge to wipe out a sector of our crops."[37]

Since Mendocino, three other California counties have banned GMOs. At the same time, Fresno and other Central Valley counties—where industrial agriculture dominates the economy, producing half of the country's fruits and vegetables—have passed pro-GMO resolutions, actually banning the banning of these seeds.[38] Still, local actions are far more likely to prevent GMOs. Eighty-three Vermont towns have passed resolutions against them.

Rural Pennsylvania:
Industrial Hog Farms, Sludge Dumping, and Local Sovereignty

Some communities have decided to actively challenge the existing hierarchical relationships between nation, state, and local laws. Rural Pennsylvania, with its largely Republican and conservative population, seems like an unlikely place for such a challenge to rise up. But it was here, in 1995, that a baby-faced blond lawyer named Thomas Linzey, fresh out of law school, cofounded the Community Environmental Legal Defense Fund (CELDF).[39] His initial goal was to provide free services to local governments and grassroots environmental organizations. But after three years of appealing permits, only to have companies come back with a different permit or new legislation from friendly lawmakers, Linzey was looking for a different approach.

His quest coincided with two big environmental developments in Pennsylvania, brought on by the passage of a waste-disposal law called the Nutrient Management Act. In theory, the law was supposed to regulate waste from factory farms. With backing from agribusiness, however, it took away the rights of local communities to impose their own requirements on manure dumping, leaving them with only the weak state standards to rely on. In this, the act was a classic example of a preemption law: a law that sets standards on a state level while denying the ability of local authorities to make more stringent rules. With its passage, over a hundred towns had their regulations effectively repealed.[40]

As a result, industrial hog farms started flooding into rural Pennsylvania. These huge operations, known as CAFOs (concentrated animal feedlot operations), kept tens of thousands of animals crowded in pens and stored entire ponds' worth of liquid manure in "lagoons" that frequently leaked into the watersheds.[41] They moved in right next to the small family farms that had populated the rural Pennsylvania townships for generations. Franklin Township alone found itself with nearly a dozen CAFOs—for a population of 1,400 people.[42] Citizens were horrified by the pollution, the stench of ammonia, the antibiotics being washed into the soil, the plummeting property values, and the incredible amount of water extracted from the aquifer (30,000 gallons per operation on average).[43] So they began calling Tom Linzey. "[We] started getting calls from municipal governments in Pennsylvania, as many as sixty to seventy a week," he recalls. "Of 1,400 rural governments in the state we were interacting with perhaps ten percent of them."[44]

The same law that allowed CAFOs over the objections of local towns also loosened the regulation of other kinds of dumping. Waste-management corporations, seeking a cheap way to get rid of municipal sludge, began sending trucks full of it directly from the treatment plants to the region's defunct coal pits; they also gave it away to farmers as free fertilizer for their fields. Pennsylvania became a magnet for waste from New York and New Jersey. As one resident said, "We've become the toilet bowl of the East Coast."[45] The sludge contained heavy metals—including lead and mercury—as well as chemicals that do not break down in the treatment process. In 2009, when the EPA randomly tested sludge samples—those that had been treated and were ready for spreading on fields—they found twenty-eight metals, eleven flame retardants, seventy-two pharmaceuticals, and twenty-five steroids or hormones.[46]

The sludge, it turned out, was lethal. In 1995, two teenage boys rode their ATVs in a field that had been spread with the "fertilizer" shortly before. One of them died from the fumes.[47] Another boy died after being exposed to the sludge while hunting.[48] It was then that Pennsylvanians realized what a toxic brew was coming into their midst, and how powerless they were to stop it. And they too began calling Tom Linzey.

"These are small neighborhood groups," said Linzey. "Often you have no more than ten people around a kitchen table. Usually they do not consider themselves a real group, but they are. . . . They represent real democracy. People coming together at a kitchen table to look over a problem represent real democracy."[49]

From his experience with permitting, Linzey knew that regulation was not the answer. "When these municipal officials started asking for help," he said, "[our answer] was not to tell them that their only option was to regulate odor, regulate water pollution, or regulate things, because when you regulate something, you automatically allow it in. . . . What we were looking for was a much more long-term type of solution."[50]

So he devised a different approach: he would focus on local sovereignty. Using century-old anti-corporate farming laws from the Midwest as a model, Linzey helped towns draft local ordinances to ban activities they did not want. Southampton Township, Pennsylvania, provided the model: its Family Farm Protection Ordinance explicitly prohibits corporations from owning land or engaging in farming, while allowing and encouraging the operation of family farms. As Linzey explains, "The Southhampton Ordinance focuses on the core of the problem."[51]

The ordinance was quickly adopted by other towns—by late 2004, nearly eighty Pennsylvania towns had passed similar ordinances—and Linzey adapted the model for towns fighting sludge dumping. When towns like Tamaqua, Pennsylvania, were unable to stop the dumping of chemical coal residues by working through regulatory agencies, they chose local sovereignty ordinances. They knew that this approach defied the state preemption laws, and they knew that they might get sued. But it was worth it. The Tamaqua mayor, who cast the tie-breaking vote in the town's passage of the ordinance, said, "If I am going to be sued, so be it. You want to take my row home, my little car, good luck, you can have them. We are going to protect our community."[52]

The town sovereignty approach is a movement to shift the locus of government power. As Linzey's CELDF says, "Communities we work with are realizing that these seemingly 'single' issue threats share something in common—that the community doesn't have the legal authority to say 'No' to [that issue]."[53] So instead of accepting the dominance of national and state laws over local power, these ordinances explicitly assert the right of towns to govern themselves.

Such tactics have been used for an increasing range of issues, as other communities have passed local ordinances calling for limits on corporate power. Barnstead, New Hampshire, banned corporate water mining, after watching bottled water company USA Springs take hundreds of thousands of gallons per day, lowering the water table in neighboring towns.[54] Pittsburgh and a number of other towns have used local ordinances as a way to ban fracking, a controversial natural gas extraction method, within their borders. In all, over 125 local sovereignty ordinances have been passed.

Some towns have been sued. When Pennsylvania's East Brunswick Township adopted an ordinance prohibiting sludge dumping, the state's attorney general filed suit against the town. His brief asked the court to overturn the law, stating, "There is no inalienable right to local self-government."[55] And when challenged, these ordinances tend to be struck down in court. In the case of New Brunswick, the attorney general and the town eventually settled in an agreement that allowed the town to regulate, but not ban, the sludge.

Yet most of the ordinances have gone unchallenged. It is easier for corporations simply to go elsewhere, to the next likely spot, than to bother with the legal hassle of suing a town.

In addition to defending the rights of communities, local sovereignty ordinances have become a valuable organizing and informational strategy, sparking discussion and awareness of the ways in which state and federal laws empower corporations while tying the hands of local communities. And they are indicative of an increasing community-based movement to take on local decision making.

Reclaiming Local Decision Making

All over America, communities are struggling with the balance of power. Each of the cases we've discussed has its own story; some issues should clearly be decided locally, and others may need guidance from the state or federal levels. What is abundantly clear, however, is that citizens are ready— past ready—to reopen the question of "who decides." The pendulum has swung too far toward centralization and privatization, and Americans want more opportunities to make decisions locally.

As these diverse stories show, claiming local power is not just about making a law. It often requires a change in the structures of government itself, one that shifts power from the state or federal to the local level. In Boulder, this meant allowing the municipality to run a utility; in Maine, it meant overruling state laws that counter a town's values.

Corporations try to push decision making to state and national levels because laws made at those levels inherently favor them. A former lobbyist for the tobacco industry made an excellent case for this point in an interview with the *Journal of the American Medical Association*. He knew the power of "local" precisely because he had butted up against it. He fought communities' rights to make their own ordinances, pushing for federal and state preemption laws, and his explanation is a testament to the power of local action:

> We could never win at the local level. The reason is, all the health advocates, the ones unfortunately I used to call health Nazis, they're all local activists who run the little political organizations.
>
> They may live next door to the mayor, or the city councilman, and they say Who's this big-time lobbyist coming here to tell us what to do? When they've got their friends and neighbors out there in the audience who want this bill, we get killed.
>
> So the Tobacco Institute and the tobacco companies' first priority has always been to preempt the field, preferably to put it all on the federal level, but if they can't do that, at least on the state level, because the health advocates can't compete with me on a state level. They never could. On the local level, I couldn't compete with them.[56]

This reasoning says it all: the relationships on the community level are far more genuine and immune to political maneuvering than those on a bigger political stage. As a farmer and state representative who worked against Iowa's seed preemption bill explained, "It is a lot easier for the agribusiness industry to buy a legislator than it is to fight each individual local community concerned about genetically modified organisms."[57] Or, as Anuradha Mittal, the former codirector of Food First, said, "Although corporations are able to buy influence in Washington, they can't fool the American public."[58]

Measure H in Mendocino County is a striking example of this principle. Corporations tried to undermine the measure by forcing the action onto the state stage. Their sponsorship of the GMO preemption laws, in which the state refused to let communities set their own standards, is a telling reminder that the higher the rung on the legislative ladder, the more the power structure favors big business over individual or community concerns.

When local communities make their own policies, one of the most powerful legacies is not just the political effects of the action, but the sense of democratic possibility that it engenders. Britt Bailey, who was involved in the Mendocino anti-GMO campaign, described the scene at the Ukiah Brewing Company the night that Measure H was approved:

> For me the greatest outcome from the victorious news embracing the crowd was witnessed in the eyes of everyone I saw. The eyes of the public were lit with the passion and enthusiasm that comes from being involved in the democratic process. People were ecstatic to find that their involvement in an internationally powerful and controversial issue effected change. And, folks were truly joyous to know that Mendocino County agriculture would be secured against the spread of GMOs. As I scanned the faces in celebration, I caught the eyes of one of the county's supervisors present. I said, "it is like we the people retrieved our souls." Before he offered a hug, he nodded in agreement.[59]

The campaign was powerful on levels that Bailey had not anticipated. It was certainly about protecting Mendocino from GMO seeds, but it was also about something more personal and transformative: a sense of engagement, empowerment, and self-determination.

From Local Action to Slow Democracy

Local, community-based empowerment is a key element of slow democracy. But while local power is absolutely necessary for slow democracy, it is not sufficient. Slow democracy is not just about local, as slow food is not just about local. You don't support the industrial farm, even if it is within fifty miles. Slow is about sustainability, about respect, about relationships, about transforming the way we do things.

So slow democracy does not simply equal local advocacy. Although there is a role for advocacy (see chapter 12), advocacy alone—however local—is not sufficient for slow democracy. There are a couple of reasons why.

For one thing, advocacy depends on the traditional political model, in which an issue is divided along lines determined by interest groups. Sometimes those groups are political parties, sometimes industry groups, sometimes environmental or social justice organizations; sometimes we like those groups and sometimes we don't. But they are the ones who determine the menu of choices, and it is a very short menu, with usually two or sometimes three items. People choose their side and vote for it. There is a debate, with winners and losers, instead of public deliberation, out of which something creative might emerge: a synthesis and reshuffling of the original terms.

Second, advocacy takes an extraordinary amount of energy and is not sustainable for most people, most of the time. Some of us might have energy for advocacy some of the time, but most people don't—which is why so many Americans are turned off by the way we currently practice democracy. It takes a huge investment of time and energy. As Frontiera said, "Democracy is exhausting." In order to be heard, you have to research and organize and educate and network and convince—and even then you might simply be blown off. While there can be a righteous thrill in preparing for battle on the side of right, most people are not willing to do it most of the time. And that means that real power is distributed among the fraction of the people who are invested in an issue.

So if we want slow democracy to be sustainable and creative, it has to be more than the same old political system transposed to a community level. We will need a transformative shift from local action to slow democracy. And as we will see, the circumstances and the timing couldn't be better.

PART II

---

slow democracy:
why now?

four

THE TIME IS RIGHT

Today's technologies—improving daily—are expanding our organizing capabilities exponentially. They allow us to transfer information in volumes, over distances, and at speeds we could only dream of a few years ago. Today, citizens are using these tools to self-organize. We're better informed and more quickly engaged than at any point in history.

The new tools, from old-fashioned conference calls and e-mails to wikis, texts, tweets, and whatever they've invented since we wrote this, are not only inexpensive, ubiquitous, and effective. They're also changing the way we think.

In *Next Generation Democracy*, Jared Duval argues that the generation born between 1979 and 1997, often called the Millennials, has already changed expectations for public engagement.[1] As online natives, Millennials will use electronic media as a powerful tool to ensure that government decision making is open and inclusive. To illuminate the source of this revolutionary change in thinking, Duval offers a brief history lesson—that is, if you count 1970 as history.

In the 1960s and '70s, the relatively new world of computer science freely shared its progress and discoveries for peer review, especially in academia. This tradition stood in stark contrast to the culture of the corporate world, where trade secrets were kept tightly under wraps. However, as the potential for profit became clear, some artificial intelligence researchers began to withhold their findings. MIT researcher Richard Stallman was appalled by that development and eventually decided to dedicate himself to creating a free computer operating system.

As Stallman saw it, software was information and should not be proprietary or "non-free." (The concern about "free" software here was about not money but intellectual development; as Stallman put it, "Think free speech, not free beer.") He championed the idea of the general public license (GPL), which is so different from a copyright that it is nicknamed the "copyleft." Work licensed this way guarantees that anyone can have free access to use or copy the source code, to improve it, and to share the improvements. No more hierarchies, no more secrecy. The concept of "open source" was introduced to the world.

Stallman's commitment to free information inspired a brilliant young computer student halfway across the world in Finland, named Linus Torvalds. Although Stallman and Torvalds did not meet to collaborate, their ideas did, and from their work emerged the Linux operating system. Rather than being created by a small, secretive group of handpicked experts, the computer operating system that runs some 90% of today's supercomputers emerged collaboratively, through the free and open exchange of information.

Perhaps the most important element of this computer innovation was not that it changed technology, but that it changed the way we interact. In an essay called "The Cathedral and the Bazaar," computer historian Eric Raymond noted that before Linux was developed, software developers assumed that anything as complicated as a large operating system needed to be created in a tightly supervised process, the way great cathedrals were constructed; after Linux, people realized that transparent, participatory processes, more like a "great babbling bazaar," were in fact more successful.[2] That babbling bazaar is now known as the open-source revolution.

Emergence of the Mind and the Spirit

Like the open-source revolution that has surrounded and shaped their experiences, Duval makes the case that Millennials value shared power and collaborative decision making.[3] As it becomes clear that this mind-set is both dynamic and effective, the technology that has shaped Millennials is having a cross-generational effect across society. We are seeing a shift toward flatter hierarchies and public demand for transparency and shared information.

For instance, community organizers have always focused on connections—finding the church groups, workers' networks, and neighborhood clubs that might collaborate toward a particular end. While today's wiki-style organizers do the same thing, for them, each connection is also an end in itself. Network expert June Holley calls them "network weavers"—people who are increasingly seeing the value of simply fostering connections and watching where people will take them, confident that great new ideas will emerge and grow.[4]

"Emergence" is the term used by systems thinkers to describe the exciting phenomenon of many local collaborations producing global patterns. When we work together, our efforts are not simply the total of your work plus mine, but also the synergy created by the interaction. In the same way that schools of fish or flocks of birds move in sync, these emerging meta-level patterns are naturally self-organized and not under any central control.[5]

Researchers at Stanford call this emergent, bottom-up style of collaboration and decision making "working wikily," after the wiki websites (such as Wikipedia) where anyone can contribute or edit information.[6] And increasingly, businesses, nonprofits, and (slowly but surely) government entities are switching to more decentralized, self-organized strategies that reward innovation and information sharing. Groups that continue to hold onto all the power at the "command-and-control" center are being left behind. These new technologies and the thinking they inspire are uniquely suited to today's needs for bottom-up, creative, slow democracy.

The United States saw an example of emergence in its largest scale, and hence most unwieldy embodiment, in the fall 2011 Occupy Wall Street protests. Early reactions to the protesters were scornful—just a bunch of ratty kids who didn't know what they wanted. And even traditional organizers' first reaction was to worry that Occupy Wall Street was doing it upside down (*first* you define your demands, *then* you protest). But it soon became clear that an entirely different process was at work. The people occupying Wall Street—and soon dozens of cities and college campuses on six continents—were all part of the same emerging wave. As media theorist Douglas Rushkoff explained for CNN during the third week of the protest, "[Occupy Wall Street] is less about victory than sustainability. It is not about one-pointedness, but inclusion and groping toward consensus. It is not like a book; it is like the Internet."[7]

Emergence is not left-wing or right-wing. Arguably, the Tea Party started out the same way as Occupy Wall Street. It's also not guaranteed to create the change the activists originally envision. Occupy Wall Street protesters found that consensus is slow and group energy is difficult to maintain, and some Tea Party observers might comment that high energy early in a process can't ensure that a group's vision won't be co-opted later. But both are strong evidence of a new, emergent change paradigm.

The Transition Town concept, a movement to formulate creative community responses to global warming and shrinking energy supplies, has also taken off in ways its originators never imagined. In his book *The Transition Companion*, Rob Hopkins answers the question, "What if the best responses to peak oil and climate change don't come from government, but from you and me and the people around us?"[8] In chapter 1 (revealingly titled "The Emergence of an Idea"), Hopkins describes the origins of the Transition concept, when, as a college instructor in Ireland, he and his students learned about the peak-oil phenomenon and were inspired to create a plan to wean their town off oil.

Hopkins notes that when they unveiled their plan at a small conference in 2005, they didn't think it was anything special, but those who read their ideas thought otherwise. The first five hundred printed copies of the plan sold out immediately, and a digital copy was downloaded thousands of times. He recalls, "Other people started getting involved and bringing pieces from systems thinking, psychology, business development and the power of the internet to spread ideas. The right people seemed to turn up at the right time."

In just a few years, Transition initiatives had been picked up in hundreds of communities from Ireland and the United Kingdom to the United States, Canada, Australia, New Zealand, and Europe, each with its own personality and local adaptations. Hopkins notes that Transition continues to surprise him, and that such surprises are delightful and amazing as long as he remembers the idea of "letting it go where it wants to go." He notes, "Transition can be very challenging for control freaks . . . it develops its own momentum and, because it builds on what those involved feel passionately about, it tends to head off in many unexpected, but usually delightful, directions."

Slow, Radical Change

Whether emergent ideas are moving at a global scale or simply from neighbor to neighbor through a community, our expectations are changing. Rather than waiting for experts' answers or leaders' instructions, we are becoming accustomed to the idea that each of us can make a difference, and more and more of us are ready to add our ideas to the mix. At the local level, slow democracy offers processes for change that make it easy to join in.

The connections we foster today will help make our communities powerful yet responsive, resilient yet flexible. Not only will we use these connections to address today's problems, but they can be useful in ways we cannot even imagine, in addressing issues we have yet to identify. Rather than defining a particular outcome ahead of time, this new breed of slow democracy leaders and activists is working to create conditions that foster connections and the emergence of new solutions—solutions they themselves may not even have imagined.

There is almost never only one right way to solve a problem. Indeed, often even the perception that there is a "problem" needs to be reexamined. Veteran facilitators Marvin Weisbord and Sandra Janoff describe the learning curve of history this way: In 1900, experts solved problems. In 1960, "everybody" solved problems. By 1965, experts had progressed to improving whole systems. The next step, Weisbord and Janoff hopefully predict, will be "everybody" improving whole systems.[9]

That time has come. If we work at the community level to catalyze the types of connections we want to see, we "network weavers" are, in our own small way, actually guiding emergence.

Some who look at the world more spiritually have seen this day coming all along. In The Tao of Democracy, Tom Atlee urges us to use "co-intelligence" to create wise self-governance systems that allow the best solutions to emerge. His discussion of co-intelligence—a wisdom that goes beyond logical "command and control" to embrace collaborative, collective, even universal intelligence—offers hope that slow, emergent democracy will ultimately be not more work, but less. Its minimalist systems will naturally self-regulate, not using any more force, funding, or energy than is needed to get the job done. Lao-Tzu's famous quotation takes on fresh meaning in this light: "The masterful leader governs so well that the people are hardly aware she exists. When she has completed her work, people say 'That happened naturally' or 'we did it ourselves.'"[10]

Allowing citizens not merely a choice between two "solutions" but the ability to frame the issues and craft collaborative action is a superb match of today's skills and mind-set and today's complex problems.

Citizen-Powered Governance: It's Happening Now

The goal of slow democracy is to strengthen communities through citizen-powered decision making. And the good news is that the timing is perfect. "Despite their disgust with politics, or perhaps because of it, citizens have become a stronger, more vocal force in public decision-making than at any time in the last 100 years," notes Matt Leighninger, director of the Deliberative Democracy Consortium.[11]

Most of these initiatives are launched not out of an idealistic notion of community building or democratic reform, but out of necessity. Citizens are desperate for better outcomes, while declining budgets and a changing political landscape mean that local leaders are opening up to citizen-based solutions. City managers are increasingly seeing the value of creating buy-in through participatory budgeting processes. New models in natural resource planning depend on the creative ideas of community members to make real changes toward sustainability. And small but encouraging numbers of neighborhood councils and committees are emerging in communities across the country, not only to react to local topics, but with actual control of a share of public resources.

Not surprisingly, polls show tremendous support for laws and policies that strengthen public participation.[12] As we will see in the following chapters, communities across the United States are reawakening to the advantages of deliberative decision making, with "hundreds and perhaps thousands of these efforts launched in the last twenty years," notes Leighninger, adding:

> The vast majority have been local efforts initiated by local leaders. They include mayors, city council members, city managers, employees of community foundations, human relations commissioners, nonprofit directors, planners, leaders of interfaith groups, policy practitioners, community organizers, school superintendents and school board members, school communication officers, police chiefs, librarians, youth program directors, members of the League of Women Voters, neighborhood association presidents, real estate agents, employees of university Cooperative Extension services, active recent retirees, and policy advocates.[13]

While some are "bottom-up" grassroots advocates, others are local elected officials reaching from the "top down" to engage citizens, and all are calling for collaboration. To see what the process looks like in action, let's take a detailed look at one of the longest-running and best-integrated examples today: a little coastal city that will give us an up-close look at the inclusive, deliberative, empowered techniques that make up slow democracy.

Portsmouth, New Hampshire: A Case Study in Slow Democracy

At the mouth of the Piscataqua River, where the waterway serves as the state borderline with Maine, sits the historic city of Portsmouth, New Hampshire. Sun sparkles on the water, and gulls wheel and cry over the naval shipyard. While tourists browse the city's craft shops and explore the exquisitely restored historic buildings (by some reckonings, Portsmouth is the third oldest city in the United States), students from the nearby University of New Hampshire join the locals downtown in the city's busy stores, restaurants, and watering holes. Portsmouth was once a bustling port and shipbuilding center. Now, this little city of twenty thousand people has the history, scenery, and culture to ensure that it's listed in various magazines as one of America's "prettiest," "most walkable," "most distinctive," or simply "best" places to visit or live.

But Portsmouth has also seen plenty of problems. From changing economic realities to divisive education issues to growth and development conflicts, the city has experienced the same polarizing politics that trouble most American cities. The difference in Portsmouth isn't the city's lack of problems. It's how it deals with them.

A New Way to Hear Each Other

In 2001, Portsmouth was stuck. The Pease Air Force Base, a major local employer, had closed down ten years before. The move had dislocated some four thousand military personnel and civil servants, along with their families. An estimated 2,400 jobs related to the base were also lost. With this major population shift, as well as the ebb and flow of the city's population over time, two Portsmouth elementary schools were now operating under capacity. At the same time, however, a third elementary school in a wealthier neighborhood was bursting at the seams. Here, students were being taught in the corridors. Closets were being used for office space. Modular classrooms were installed as a stop-gap measure, but in reality there was no end in sight to the overcrowding.

From the outside, the answer looked obvious: redistribute the kids. But anyone familiar with local politics and the culture of neighborhoods won't be surprised to learn that redistricting proposals went nowhere fast.

Changing cultural configurations and patterns of interaction is always a challenge. And although Portsmouth looks homogeneous to the visitor (people of color make up just under 10% of the population), it is not immune to the many other forms of prejudice that plague most American cities. In the early public discussions regarding redistricting, residents resorted to painful insinuations about class and culture. Recalls Portsmouth lawyer Jim Noucas, "People stood up at public hearings and denigrated the elementary school that was literally 'on the other side of the tracks.'"[14]

Attempts to redistrict became heated and bitter. Portsmouth city manager John Bohenko observes, "Changing the way schools work, especially elementary schools, is . . . probably one of the most intense things a city can go through."[15] Noucas puts it more bluntly: "Tackling the issue was political suicide."[16]

The issue was so divisive that despite the crowding, leaders did not dare to open the conversation for a decade. Finally, supported by a superintendent who valued shared decision making, the school board appointed a redistricting committee consisting of representatives from the school board, city council, and a neighborhood association, as well as parents from each of the three elementary schools. The committee enlisted the help of an existing school-community partnership group, along with the University of New Hampshire's Public Conversations Project.

The redistricting committee settled on an approach called "study circles,"[17] one of the best-known community dialogue and deliberation processes being applied by cities, towns, and associations across the United States. Every study circles process is adapted to the particular needs of the community, but all study circles processes involve actively recruiting a diverse group of citizens to share information, build understanding, explore solutions, and connect with policy change or action.

Members of the redistricting committee were able to recruit a diverse group of 105 Portsmouth residents to participate. This large group was divided into eight teams to take part in small-group discussions that were held over the course of four weeks. Each group included representatives from all three of the city's elementary schools. Local residents were trained as facilitators and moderated each group, to ensure that everyone had a chance to speak and the conversations stayed on course. Each group developed its own ground rules to make sure that all participants were comfortable with the process.

The groups rotated their meetings among the three schools, beginning each session by meeting the principal and touring the facility. Many participants had never visited any school but their own, so the visits offered new information in a hands-on, "see for yourself" setting.

Given the past divisiveness of the issue, participants were not yet ready for deliberative decision making. Small, trust-building conversations were needed to bridge the deep community divides. As is traditional with the study circles approach, the small groups began with dialogue, sharing personal stories and finding some common ground as parents and neighbors.

After establishing that base, the groups took a deep collective breath and contemplated the question of what issues and criteria the redistricting committee should consider in balancing the enrollments of the three elementary schools. Unlike traditional public processes, this question did not jump immediately to proposed solutions. Instead, they presented the question as an open-ended query that focused on values and had no wrong answers. The question framed the issue in a welcoming way and invited all participants to tell their story.

Having considered their responses to that question, the groups went on to work together on an honest appraisal of recommendations. Each group created its own report, and a steering committee also wrote a summary report highlighting the common themes among them.

After their sessions, each team presented a report to the school board. And it was a testimony to the power of the process that rather than sending a representative from each group, about three-quarters of the 105 study circles participants chose to attend the meeting to stand behind their findings.

The final report, *Rethinking instead of Redistricting*, showed the significant overlap and agreement in the eight teams' findings. Its ten recommendations included specific space and facilities suggestions. In addition, participants were clear that they did not want any fifth graders involuntarily moved during the first year of redistricting, and the groups also agreed that socioeconomic balance among the schools was a priority.

It was not only citizens who found the process valuable; leaders appreciated it as well. A diverse, representative public process such as this one, and the recommendations it generates, offer several things to leaders:

- They get a valuable reading of citizens' perspectives and the political pulse of the community. For instance, Portsmouth residents' strong consensus about fifth graders' vulnerability during redistricting might only have been guessed at without the face-to-face conversations.
- Leaders benefit from in-depth, customized research. Dozens of taxpayers trooping through all three school facilities made numerous observations that informed their recommendation to abandon the formula for calculating school capacity—on-the-ground insights that even an expensive consultant might have missed.
- As an important factor in financial decisions, leaders discover the courage (some would say political cover) to make difficult program

cuts or spending increases, knowing that the moves are backed up by an engaged, informed public.

In Portsmouth's case, this new courage meant that after ten years of avoidance and frustration, the school board drafted a long-awaited redistricting plan that called for $2 million in facility improvements. With the help of 105 knowledgeable "ambassadors"—participants in the citizen deliberation—the resulting plan ended up receiving broad support from the community, and the spending was approved.

And most importantly, because the plan was so well informed by the citizens it would affect, it made sense on the ground. Only sixty-five students ended up needing to switch schools.

Noucas, who was involved in the process, is convinced that the deliberations helped open minds. For instance, every community seems to have a citizen (some have many) who takes on a consistent public role, using every issue to tout his or her pet issue—fiscal prudence, environmental responsibility, or whatever matters to him or her most. In Portsmouth's case, one resident—let's call him Bill—always made a point at every public hearing to speak out against spending. So imagine the effect when, after participating in the study circles, Bill attended the public hearing and testified in favor of the school bond issue. "[He said] he had to agree, after talking with people and seeing the inside of the schools, that the City had to spend this money," says Noucas. "My chin dropped to my chest."[18]

In another example, Noucas recalls,

> The night of the very first study circle meeting, one participant declared to me that he was there to re-open [a specific school] as the solution to the overcrowding problem. On the last night, he made it a point to tell me that, after the study circles, he realized that his solution was not the best one for the community.[19]

In the end, over eight hundred person-hours of dialogue had its effect on the community, dispelling myths and weaving trust and understanding among Portsmouth residents. Simply put, says Noucas, residents "came to realize that . . . the parents from the other schools loved and cared about their children and their education just as much as they did."[20]

Listening to Children

It is only appropriate that this major shift in community dynamics was launched in an education setting, because Portsmouth had first discovered the effectiveness of dialogue and deliberation techniques by listening to children.

A year before the school redistricting issue arose, parents had been concerned about violence at Portsmouth Middle School. Based on a report in the local newspaper about a street fight, as well as frightening national statistics about drugs, alcohol, and physical violence in schools, concerned parents won a $5,000 grant in 1999 to address violence problems at the middle school. Parents joined with the school principal and chose the study circles approach to explore the issues. Their first act was to invite the sixth-grade student council to cosponsor the study.

Many residents were skeptical. With the deluge of national research on this topic, what expertise could twelve-year-old students offer? But the plans for dialogue went forward, and ultimately some two hundred sixth graders combined with seventy-five parents, community members, teachers, and officials to make up sixteen study circles. Over the course of five weeks, each group met once a week for forty-five-minute sessions.

Knowing that getting kids and adults to talk together might be difficult at first, organizers began discussions with a question everyone could relate to: What was your very first day of school like? Following the study circles model, participants started out by getting to know each other and telling about their personal experiences.

"Whether you're 12 or 60, everyone has a first day of school that is usually a little scary but exciting too," notes Noucas. "Kids were amazed to hear that a city councilor was nervous and scared their first day of school."[21] The opening dialogue quickly warmed up the group by helping their commonalities come to the surface. Only after a sense of trust had emerged did they move on to addressing questions about problems within the school.

At the end of the five weeks, each study circle drafted findings and conclusions, which were summarized in a report and presented to a first-ever joint meeting of the city council and school board. The results took them by surprise.

Violence, it turned out, was not the problem—not the dominant problem, nor even a major problem for Portsmouth middle schoolers. Nor, as it turned out, were drugs and alcohol a major factor in their daily lives. The problem was bullying. The sixth graders spoke eloquently about where and how bullying was occurring and were able to make specific recommendations to lessen its occurrence.

A telling incident occurred at the midway point in the five-week conversations. On April 20, 1999, horrifying news flashed across the nation: in Columbine, Colorado, two high school seniors had gone on a shooting rampage, killing twelve students and a teacher and injuring at least twenty others before turning the guns on themselves.

Americans hardly knew how to react. What had caused the teens to explode? Drug abuse? Bullying? Mental illness? Educators and political leaders shook their heads in horror and scrambled to make sense of the violence. Parents everywhere hugged their children closer. Meanwhile, the media was torn between offering analysis of possible causes and airing lurid details of the gruesome scene.

In New Hampshire, the only commercial television station in the state caught wind that Portsmouth Middle School was hosting an event dealing with violence. According to Jim Noucas, immediately after the Columbine shooting:

> They arrived at the school unannounced with cameras rolling. Live, they wanted to know about the violent incident that occurred at [Portsmouth Middle School] and created this study circle activity. As soon as they were told that there had been no violence and that community members were meeting with students to talk about what safe and respectful schools should be, they turned off their cameras and left. It never made the news.[22]

Hundreds of students and parents in thoughtful, preventive dialogue do not, apparently, make for exciting television. They did, however, make for important changes within the school community. Administrators implemented the specific recommendations emerging from the study circles, including increased adult supervision in the hallways, bathrooms, and school buses. After these changes, the school appears to have experienced a decline in bullying.[23] Perhaps as importantly, the community strengthened important relationships: students felt validated and empowered by being listened to by grown-ups; adults recognized profound value in the students' thoughtful input; and parents and community members who had never been past the school lobby gained a deepened understanding of their school.

While community leaders across America shook their heads in bafflement about the issues that may have caused the Columbine shootings, Portsmouth was doing the slow, heartfelt work needed to ensure that such horror might never strike home there.

Portsmouth Listens

Portsmouth didn't set out to "build community" or "improve democracy." Like the vast majority of communities that embrace deliberative dialogue, they were just trying to solve problems that they couldn't solve any other way.

But somehow, along the way, inclusive community conversations were becoming woven into Portsmouth's fabric. In the decade that followed, when the city found itself struggling with difficult problems, leaders and community members repeatedly turned to dialogue and deliberation.

- **Race relations.** In spring 2002, when the police department faced allegations of racial profiling, the city's response was not denial, finger-pointing, or writing a report and putting it on a shelf; it was to convene study circles on racism and race relations.[24] Cosponsored by Portsmouth's police department, the local chapter of the National Association for the Advancement of Colored People (NAACP), and the school district, the study circles involved high school students and improved interactions between the police and the community. As an example, the deputy chief of police noted that the study circles eased communication, so that representatives from the NAACP could simply contact him or other officers directly instead of using formal protocols.
- **Master plan update.** With the Portsmouth master plan update in fall 2002, the city was ready to take participation to a new level. Citizens formed "Portsmouth Listens," a new, all-volunteer group that, in collaboration with the city administration, proposed a study circles process for the planning board's update. Attorney Jim Noucas, who had been involved in previous study circles, helped lead the new group, with John Tabor, the publisher of the local newspaper, the *Portsmouth Herald*, as cochair. The *Herald* was a key partner in getting the word out to gain diverse public participation, but it was not the only communication tool; at one point, seventy-five volunteers fanned out across the city with five thousand flyers. Ultimately, over

four hundred citizens were involved in the master plan study circles, which took place in several stages over two years. And citizens saw their work incorporated into policy. The Portsmouth Listens vision statement was adopted as the vision statement of the city master plan, and every one of the study groups found its major recommendations within the master plan.[25]

- **Middle school renovation.** In 2007, Portsmouth was again faced with a difficult issue: whether to renovate or relocate the middle school. Either the seventy-five-year-old historic downtown school needed an overhaul, or a new building would be constructed next to a nearby tidal estuary. A joint city council/school board committee hired consultants and engineers, but after six months, it was deadlocked. A public hearing seemed to show that residents were also evenly divided—and increasingly agitated. Finally, the superintendent asked Portsmouth Listens to convene study circles.

  Fourteen groups of about ten residents each, plus two high school groups, made site visits, combed reports, and deliberated on the options. Significantly, participants were also mindful of the work of the Portsmouth master plan study circles, where both historic pres- ervation and land conservation had surfaced as priorities. Ultimately, the majority of the groups wound up in favor of renovation. While many observers had predicted that the school board was leaning strongly toward relocation, within forty-eight hours after the study circles made their report the board came out unanimously in favor of renovating the school.

- **Environmental sustainability.** In addition to influencing the school renovation decision, the participatory master plan update inspired the city to make environmental sustainability a high priority. The com- munity sponsored a study circle on the "Natural Step" sustainability model, which was eventually adopted by the city. And in 2009, to open a five-year sustainability plan process, citizens participated in a one- day community conversation and responded to an online survey.

  Since then, thanks to this community support for sustainability initiatives, the new library became the first municipal building in New Hampshire to be awarded the prestigious LEED (Leadership in Energy and Environmental Design) certification, with special recognition for energy conservation, sustainable construction materials, and recycling. The city has achieved substantial energy savings in the new parking garage, and new designs are under way for the water treatment plant, fire station, and middle school. A sustainability fair hosted by Portsmouth's mayor, city council, schools, and Portsmouth Listens has evolved into an annual information exchange including sustainability tours of local homes and businesses, speaker forums, arts, and education. And a new citizens group called Sustainable Portsmouth now leads the implementation of the sustainability plan.

- **City budgeting.** After several years of economic recession, in 2011 Portsmouth leaders realized that they could no longer get by with small cuts here and there. As in many other municipalities, in that year the city council would be forced to make fundamental alterations in public services. Portsmouth Listens proposed a study circles element to the city budgeting process. While city councilors were initially resistant to the idea and made it clear that this was not an empowered citizen budgeting process, Portsmouth Listens moved ahead. After participants took a "Budget 101" class, council members and representatives from all four of the city's departments met in small groups with over sixty citizens. Leaders noted that the process helped highlight areas where the city needed to offer more education about proposed changes. The tax rate came down, and the budget passed.

Portsmouth Listens has found success with the study circles, but the group has also branched out to other public engagement processes, including the "World Café" technique[26] and a variety of Internet communication tools. Portsmouth Listens also regularly hosts candidate forums. Preceded and substantially informed by candidate questionnaires developed by a citizen panel and published in the local paper, the candidate forums feature direct dialogue with the candidates.

In short, the city has come a long way. One city councilor described the impact of a Portsmouth study circle this way:

It showed the face of contemporary local citizenry—it's not the small group of perpetually angry guys who show up at public comment— but thoughtful, well-spoken people who are willing to discuss values and principles in addition to taxes and land use, and are willing to get involved if they see the path to do so. . . . There can be no going back to the old ways of doing things for anyone who was there.[27]

The Results of Listening

Portsmouth hasn't solved all of its problems, and its leaders know they never will; every city faces a continual parade of issues. What has changed is the way the city approaches problems. Public deliberation in Portsmouth has become, in the parlance of academics who study such things, "embedded."[28]

In most communities (and almost always at the state and national level), the story of public decision making involves professional politicians and interest groups applying adversarial organizing techniques, money, and accumulated power to make policies. In contrast, embedded deliberation means that public institutions are skilled at bringing citizens together, engaging them in useful research and discussions, and then taking action based on people's contributions. In some cases, the citizens themselves have the power not only to advise but to decide and take action.

Many communities seek citizens' opinions through an occasional survey or small-group process, but these one-off exercises have limited long-term effect. Embedded public reflection changes the community dynamic. While still relatively rare, communities that have embedded deliberation into their decision making are inspiring others to follow suit. As in Portsmouth, leaders can improve policies and public service delivery because they have consistently better information. Citizens, through practice, become better at making public judgments and informing decisions for the common good.

According to scholars, "Unless competent institutions are ready to *listen* and *act* on the public's suggestions, deliberations are likely to have only a modest impact."[29] For Portsmouth leaders, listening has become a way of life.

Making the change has not been easy, nor has it been unfailingly successful. For instance, the 2011 budgeting study circle was not embraced by the city council, for fear that it would not represent the full community. Portsmouth Listens went through with the process anyway, but some council members were strongly critical. According to city councilor Chris Dwyer, citizens could not understand the complexities of the budget in such a limited time frame, which meant they could not participate in the sophisticated discussions. "It wasn't a good match of process with content," notes Dwyer.[30]

However, Dwyer feels that the use of the study circles process with the city's master plan update was citizen participation "at its very best," and she notes that the city would definitely use it for the next city planning process.

Dwyer, who has served on the city council since 2006, notes that the study circles and other processes have changed expectations about civility and civic engagement in Portsmouth. For instance, in a recent election two candidates got into a political dogfight trying to ensure that their opponent did not gain a particular group's endorsement. Dwyer notes that although such negative skirmishes are commonplace in American politics, things are different now in Portsmouth: many residents commented that they were disturbed by the dirty dealings.

"It was wrong, and the people involved agreed it was wrong, and we're going to try to figure out how not to have that going forward," says Dwyer. "Maybe it's naïve, but it's a wonderful kind of naïve. We don't want to be like that. We've raised the bar."

Portsmouth has become more gentrified in the past decade, but Dwyer often hears from elderly residents who remember a more rough and tumble "old Portsmouth." "They tell me they never thought it was possible to come from this kind of town—the kind of town they could be *proud* to be from," she says. "It's attractive, it's active, it's proud of its downtown center. The work with study circles is a big part of that."

John Bohenko, who has served as Portsmouth's city manager since before the city's first study circle, agrees that the changes in Portsmouth have rippled through the community. For instance, he points to study circles as an inspiration for the "contact design" work his office engages in, where the city invites citizens' opinions on public works projects such as repairs to streets, a water or sewer system, or—in this coastal town—sea walls.

"The old days of designing the project and just focusing on the engineering and getting it done on time, without public input—those days are gone," he says. "Especially in Portsmouth. . . . Now, before you design the project, you go out into the neighborhoods and lay out plans and invite the neighbohood in. We tell them right up front that not everything is feasible, but we want their ideas, and we'll see what we can do to make it happen."[31]

When talking with other officials about the advantages of including citizens in project design, Bohenko tells them, "you avoid having people come in and want changes afterward—changes that could cost more money in the long run, not to mention the aggravation."

"There's nothing worse than finishing a project that you've spent resources on, and the staff has worked hard [on], and [finding] that people don't like it," says Bohenko. "And there's nothing *better* than finishing a project that you've spent resources and staff time on, and people are happy."

In 2011, Portsmouth was a runner-up for the prestigious international Reinhard Mohn Prize for groundbreaking projects in vitalizing democracy through participation. Meanwhile, other communities in New Hampshire have taken up the torch: the city of Keene used study circles in its master plan review, and nearby Dover has launched the dialogue initiative "Dover Listens."

Portsmouth, the new poster child for dialogue and deliberation, has been featured in scholarly research and numerous articles about community engagement. It now has something to add to its travel-guide claims of being among America's "prettiest" places to live: Portsmouth is arguably among the most participatory.

Perhaps Portsmouth's biggest prize is in opening new pathways for individuals to find their voice. Noucas points out that small-group processes can serve as a valuable training ground. It's not unusual for local candidates to mention in campaign literature their participation in study circles. In fact, it is common for citizens in Portsmouth to start out in a study circle and then find the courage and inspiration to serve on a local board or even run for office.

"Part of that is developing your own confidence—that what you have to say is not stupid," says Noucas. "But hopefully in the process, you learn not only to have your say. You also learn how to listen."

An Explosion of Deliberative Civic Engagement

Portsmouth is special in the breadth and depth of its deliberative processes, but it is far from alone in its citizen participation efforts. In many public arenas across the United States, on issues ranging from schools to public lands, planning to budgeting, public safety to the treatment of criminals through such programs as community diversion, leaders are in desperate need of the energy and expertise that strong community engagement will offer. And citizens are diving in to help.

The United States is hardly the epicenter of the deliberative civic engagement explosion. Indeed, there is no center—"emergence" has been at work here, with parallel initiatives popping up all over the globe. Participatory budgeting had its start in Porto Alegre, Brazil, in 1989 (two decades before it picked up steam in the United States), citizen-based planning has taken off in India, and citizen participation efforts are on the rise in South Africa and across the Global South. Australia is a leader in deliberative democracy experimentation; public deliberation initiatives are in play across Europe and Canada; and eastern European countries are using citizen-driven initiatives to implement post-Soviet environmental reforms. Deliberative democratic techniques are even being implemented in places that aren't considered to be democratic; for instance, the Zeguo Township in Wenling City, China, has employed the Deliberative Polling technique several times to gauge citizen opinion on public infrastructure choices.[32]

As interest in deliberative civic engagement has been expanding, it is no coincidence that academic research and professional development have kept pace. While fifteen years ago the topic might only have been broached during a hallway conversation at an environmental or social services conference, or addressed at one lone workshop at a political science symposium, now the field (yes, it's become a field) has come into its own.

The growth of professional and academic interest in the field—whether it's called "deliberative democracy," "deliberative governance," "dialogue and deliberation," or some other buzz term—has inspired a host of academic alliances and professional consortia.[33] And scholars and practitioners are coming from all angles to get involved in this phenomenon. A look at the various social media links on the National Coalition for Dialogue and Deliberation website shows participants from political science, public administration, policy making, law, business, natural resource and urban planning, sociology, psychology, spiritual studies, communication, education, and information technology, just to name a few.

The dialogue and deliberation approach used in Portsmouth, Everyday Democracy's study circles, is in wide use, but it is far from being the only tool. Scholars and practitioners have worked diligently to define and develop the field and have created tools for a variety of applications. Some are dialogue methods for preventing and transforming conflict, such as those used by the Public Conversations Project,[34] and for deepening mutual understanding, such as the World Café.[35] Some, like the National Issues Forum process, help citizens weigh the trade-offs of public issues.[36] Others, such as Future Search[37] and the National Charrette Institute's Dynamic Planning process,[38] are designed to help a body of stakeholders plan their collective future. Local online issue forums are hosted by e-democracy.org. Another cluster of organizations and techniques convenes representative samples of citizens in order to gather their considered ideas to advise policy makers; America Speaks (21st Century Town Meeting),[39] Citizen Juries,[40] and Deliberative Polling[41] are examples. And this is only the beginning of the list. One comprehensive source called *The Change Handbook* offers details on sixty different methods "for engaging whole systems."[42]

The academics and practitioners who work in this whatchamacallit field come from a variety of organizations—governments, universities, foundations, nonprofits, and for-profit businesses.[43] The body of work is extensive and evolving rapidly. And it is being applied at many levels—within businesses as well as nonprofit organizations, at the town, county, and state levels, and even on national-level issues.

Funnily enough, the name of the field is a problem. Most of the time, the leaders and community members who are working together at the local level don't call it anything at all—they just *do* it. Scholars and professionals need something a bit more official, but their jargon is hard to get excited about. Our unscientific scan of the literature suggests that if you select a word from each of the two columns in the chart on the following page, and it's not too redundant, you'll probably come up with a label that someone uses.

These terms can mean any number of things to any number of people. However, for the purposes of slow democracy, one element deserves special attention: deliberation. When it meets the rigorous standards being defined by scholars and professionals in the field, effective deliberation raises the bar and adds a level of richness to our decision-making process not seen in many public venues.

As deliberative processes have been increasingly successful and widely applied, "deliberation" has come to be defined and studied more carefully. As the field has developed, it has become clear that despite its variety, the characteristics of this work have amazing overlap and profound internal consistency. And they are in keeping with the principles of slow democracy, which include three elements of local democratic decision making: *inclusion*—making sure

FIRST WORD (choose one):	SECOND WORD (choose one):
Public	Engagement
Democratic	Governance
Citizen	Participation
Participatory	Democracy
Civic	Involvement
Citizen-Centered	Work

there is broad, diverse citizen participation; *deliberation*—ensuring citizens are engaged in defining problems and solutions, based on good information and trust; and *power*—defining a clear connection between a community's participation, its decisions, and the actions that follow.

Before we explore each of these elements, though, it makes sense to understand why dialogue and deliberation techniques offer such a revolutionary approach to political problem solving. What are the forces that push us toward the same old "fast democracy" style? Why are political stereotypes so hard to break through? What can we do about them? For that, we turn to another emerging field: cultural cognition.

five

CULTURAL COGNITION AND SLOW DEMOCRACY

Politics, communication, and psychology have combined in a new field of inquiry that has emerged in the last decade: cultural cognition.[1] Cultural cognition leads to some powerful insights about how political discourse becomes polarized—and how these same polarizing mechanisms might be applied instead to help us understand each other.

The Cultural Cognition Project, based at Yale Law School, involves scholars from a number of universities in the fields of political science, social psychology, anthropology, and communications. Funded by the National Science Foundation, these researchers use a comprehensive mix of surveys and experiments to understand how our cultural values—mine, yours, your neighbors'—shape our policy beliefs. While their work is rigorously academic, it isn't merely an academic exercise. The researchers hope to improve democratic procedures by ensuring they include a diversity of cultural outlooks, so that we can create sound public policies and resolve differences.

Cultural cognition researchers have identified key values that influence us—values that relate to individualism and community, and to equality and authority. We will explore the specifics of these values more in a moment; for now let's just say that these values are vastly more effective at predicting our stand on issues than the usual liberal-conservative dichotomy. In addition, these cultural values play a huge role in our daily lives—in the way we hear the news, in the way we take in new information, and in the way we form opinions.

"Just the Facts"?

All of us would like to think that we respond to facts. Whether the issue is economic, environmental, or social, we'd like to think our opinions are based on objective data. If only others could see the charts we've seen, hear the expert speakers we've heard, watch the YouTube video we've watched, surely they would change their minds. But if you're waiting for the truth to prevail, think again. Neuroscience is revealing disconcerting news about the way we absorb information.

In a well-known 2006 study, researchers wired up some voters to explore what exactly happens inside our brains when we receive new information, especially when the new information doesn't fit our worldview.[7] A group of self-described Republicans and Democrats were subjected to unflattering information about their own party's candidates. According to their MRIs, when subjects were confronted with information that contradicted their biases, their brains actually underprocessed the information. The prefrontal cortex, responsible for conscious reasoning, hardly even fired.

Instead, the emotional circuits of their brains lit up, including those associated with regulating feelings and resolving conflicts. Effectively, participants' brains used emotion to ignore information that they didn't like to hear but could not discount intellectually. And once they had used emotion to reinforce their preexisting beliefs, the reward centers of their brains lit up—essentially patting them on the back for ignoring information that contradicted their beliefs. Every time our brains go through this emotional rationalization, researchers believe that the process subconsciously reinforces our preexisting beliefs, associating the act of revisionist reasoning with positive emotion or reward.

Comedian Stephen Colbert, in his conservative persona, complains that "reality has a well-known liberal bias" and that he does not want to hear what the "factinistas" have to say. But neuroscience researchers tell us that it's not just conservatives who prefer Colbert's "truthiness" to objective facts. Citizens of all political persuasions have a tendency to ignore information they don't want to hear. In a cyclical, self-reinforcing, and scary way, then, we're wired *not* to take in new information that threatens our existing beliefs.

The Pathway to Political Opinion

So our brains may be partially to blame for our political polarization. After all, if I am unwilling to accept new information, I am certainly unlikely to move from my political opinion. How do we form those political opinions in the first place? The field of cultural cognition offers some answers.

It's a fact, fortunate or unfortunate, that citizens can't become experts on every economic, environmental, or other controversy that comes down the pike. There are a host of reasons why—the daunting number and complexity of the issues and the lack of time, interest, and training, to name a few. We can generate opinions when necessary; we do it every time we have a political conversation with a neighbor, respond to a poll, or vote. But unless it's an issue about which we're experts, our opinions often aren't based on a great deal of research.

As cultural cognition researchers have discovered, most of us depend to some extent on cultural cues to figure out where we stand. These cues have mapped out the roadway that most people use to arrive at their political opinions. And as we'll see, that road is rife with shortcuts.[3]

Considering the Source

The first factor affecting our opinions about the information we receive is the context in which we receive it. The cultural signals from our information source are critical, whether that source is the media or a friend or colleague.

Before any of us ever consider a scientist's data—or for that matter a candidate's platform or a neighbor's point of view—we've received dozens of coded messages about the person delivering the information. His suit and the way he stands telegraph authority; or his rolled-up sleeves and use of homey stories suggest he represents the "common man." Her accent and vocabulary speak to her origins and her links to our world—or lack of them.

Unlike receiving and retaining political information, for which policy training is helpful, picking up these social cues takes no special schooling. We all receive cultural signals loud and clear. We each have our own cultural orientation with which we interpret these signals, and it can affect how we process the information we hear. Often, we allow these signals to stand in for learning about the deeper economic, environmental, or social issues we care most about.

Selective Listening

On our pathway to political opinion, it's worth noticing not only the information sources we choose but also those we avoid. The media we select will affect the information we hear, especially in today's polarized climate, and where we choose to get our news depends on our political viewpoints. Increasingly, Americans are gravitating toward cable and online news sources we agree with, closing ourselves off to ideas that conflict with our worldview.[4] A steady diet of Fox News reinforces a very different picture of the world than does a scan of the *New York Times* or a nightly dose of *Democracy Now!*

Ironically, even the Internet, supposedly an information highway, can steer us toward familiar viewpoints, effectively isolating us from new ideas. Online organizer Eli Pariser points out that web companies' efforts to personalize service has created what he calls a "filter bubble." By tailoring search findings to individual users' interests, these "algorhithmic gatekeepers" are narrowing what comes across our screens. Rather than offering new ideas, they edit what we see to match with what we have seen in the past.[5]

Choosing Our Friends

Even more common than our selection bias in news channels or web links is our bias in choosing the people with whom we talk and exchange views. Whether we mean to or not, most of us have weekly rhythms. We talk with certain colleagues at work, and we avoid others. We run into friends at the mall or the farmers' market, at the local church or at the synagogue, on the basketball court or at the beach. Unless we are making a pointed effort to change our usual path, we naturally move within our tribe; we hear what they hear, and as a result, we tend to think what they think.

Residential patterns suggest that some Americans are choosing where to live based on factors that ultimately segregate us further, clumping us by socioeconomic factors such as age, income, and race. Gated communities and other lifestyle choices that stratify or pixilate population patterns only exacerbate our inability to see and hear a variety of viewpoints.[6]

Filtering

As we continue on our path toward a political opinion, we may find it convenient to use an "umbrella" to keep out troubling information. As the Republicans and Democrats' MRIs showed, our brains tend to deflect information we disagree with, deploying a "cognitive filter" at the first hint of information that threatens our view of the world.

Filtering out information is not only natural, it's almost primal. As researcher Dan Kahan notes, "People find it disconcerting to believe that behavior that they find noble is nevertheless detrimental to society, and behavior that they find base is beneficial to it. Because accepting such a claim could drive a wedge between them and their peers, they have a strong emotional predisposition to reject it."[7]

Last Message In, First Message Out

The more recently we've considered something, the more likely it is to pop into our minds when we're asked for an opinion. That's why politicians are advised to "stay on message" and to give the same sound bite no matter what question is asked. Combined with the repetition of the twenty-four-hour news cycle, this technique ensures that their view is front-and-center in our minds.

Shortcuts for Everybody?

Whether we're taking a stand on a local development proposal or on some other issue, there's a good chance we are using one or more of the above cultural cues to replace issue-based information. We may have subconsciously judged the various spokespeople, probably have an idea where our friends stand on the issue, and might feel prepared to vote based on these factors alone.

Here's a simple test recommended by communications scholar John Gastil to check whether you are relying on shortcuts. Think about an issue on which you have a stand (but not one on which you are an expert). Can you offer some specific, data-based arguments for your side of the issue? Now here's a harder question: Can you make a credible case for why a reasonable person on the other side believes the opposite? If you are able to explain both sides of an issue, you have probably gotten to your opinion the long way. If not, you have probably used a shortcut.

People use these shortcuts because, in general, they work. They are effective in the sense that they often lead us to opinions that we might hold if we studied the empirical data. Shortcuts don't mean we're lazy or stupid; they're valuable tools that we use to make sense of a complex world. We simply can't all be experts on everything. We've all acted on instinct or intuition, and often such judgments serve us well. Rapid cognition, or even gut instincts, may be invaluable in job interviews or blind dates.[8] But we will need to be informed by more than first impressions to make long-term policy decisions.

We now live in a world where the potential to manipulate public messages has exploded. It is increasingly dangerous to rely solely on shortcuts to solve complex problems, or to depend on them to choose leaders we hope will solve them. These cultural shortcuts are the "convenience food" of politics—a simple, ready-made way to decide on complex issues. But partisans have become infinitely more adept at "processing" and "packaging" issues and candidates for mass consumption. They are expert at marketing to appeal to targeted audiences, while not necessarily offering the actual contents we see pictured.

A Better Way

Cultural cognition research tells us that in addition to the cultural shortcuts we are prone to, there's one more factor on our path to forming an opinion. We may not come across it often, but when we do, we come away changed. That factor is deliberation. We're all familiar with politicized exchanges in which participants don't waver from their "position statements" to hear what the other side has to say. But most of us are also familiar with another refreshing phenomenon: those "aha" moments when someone's mind (occasionally our own) opens or changes. Here, the link between cultural cognition and deliberation is often at work. John Gastil notes that democratic deliberation processes "have shown the power of thoughtful, respectful, public exchange in generating consensus among citizens of diverse moral persuasions. We believe that appropriately structured deliberation achieves this result first by slowing people down."[9]

As we saw with Portsmouth's study circles, "deliberation" doesn't mean just "talk." It means an inclusive exchange, based on trust, in which participants examine the issues, evaluate a range of options, and open their minds to new perspectives. Rather than depending on cognitive shortcuts, participants in deliberation slow down and engage with real people and their real concerns, in order to find solutions they can all agree on.

Damariscotta, on coastal Route 1 in Maine, provides a classic illustration of how deliberation can help us move beyond cultural shortcuts. The town was ravaged by a Walmart battle in 2005. In the end, residents approved a size-cap ordinance to keep out big-box stores, but they were left with a bitter community divide and unsolved questions about their economic development strategy. In the wake of the struggle, residents recognized that they needed stronger tools to manage community development, based on participation from all residents. They didn't want simply to sit back and wait for the next fight to come along. But what tools would draw citizens into a community conversation *before* another crisis?

The town decided to launch an inclusive, citizen-driven visioning process. Working with the Orton Foundation's Heart and Soul Community Planning process, the town's planning committee reached out to citizens from both sides of the divide.[10] The process focused on dialogue, including one-on-one interviews, storytelling, small-group discussions, and community forums. A grassroots recruitment effort ensured that residents of all backgrounds were invited to participate. In a four-day charrette, hundreds of community members discussed creative plans for the downtown as well as busy Route 1. The variety of events ended up involving over a thousand people in reimagining the community waterfront and devising a plan to protect their historic downtown while also adapting to new growth and economic opportunities.

It hasn't been easy. The community voted down a complex development code proposal that emerged from the process. However, there were also notable successes: A local land trust purchased the property originally slated for the Walmart development, with an easement so it could be sold to a local farmer at a discount. The selectboard passed a resolution to use the community-identified values from the Heart and Soul process in their future town planning efforts, and an ongoing citizen committee will work to maintain high rates of community participation.

"It's more than one vote or one action that builds community," noted Arianna McBride, who helped with the Heart and Soul planning process. "It takes many actions, large and small over many years to ensure that communities are vibrant and enduring. It takes a local government willing to share power, and it takes energy, creativity and community values to steer the change."[11]

Damariscotta hasn't solved all of its issues. But its deliberative efforts have strengthened relationships and the community's capacity to engage citizens in making decisions for the long run.

We Are Not a Nation of Ideologues

As Damariscotta discovered, deliberative dialogue paired with perseverance can help us find common ground. Although we can always find something to disagree about, Americans generally are not as far apart as the frequent headlines about "culture wars" would suggest.

The good news about cultural cognition findings is that despite the exhortations of some politicians, the great majority of Americans are not ideologues. Indeed, political science research has been clear for decades that ideological thinking is extremely rare among Americans. The vast majority of us want the same things from our political system: security and economic health. While we may differ in our opinions on *how* to reach these goals, most of us have arrived at our policy opinions via shortcuts—quickly, and with little information. This means we are much more open to the richness of slow democracy than you might think.

As we have seen in Damariscotta, Portsmouth, and communities around the country, when issues are framed in an inclusive way, citizens welcome the opportunity to join in conversation about them. When we actually sit down in a deliberative setting, we can get beyond the initial impressions and shortcuts we rely on. In Damariscotta, structured techniques like story circles allowed residents to transcend their "positions" and understand the values and everyday struggles of their neighbors. Through a multiday visioning session, a diverse cross section of residents could take the time to examine, absorb, and question information. Then, citizens were ready to dig in and create policies that fit the specific needs of their community, working across perceived divides to generate new ideas and new solutions.

A Tale of Four Quadrants

Slow democracy is about inviting neighbors into community conversations about issues that matter. If we're serious about making change, we want as many people to join the conversation as possible, not just those who already agree with us. Cultural cognition research offers hints about how best to frame those conversations so they'll appeal to a wide range of worldviews.

In their ongoing exploration, cultural cognition researchers have used empirical testing—surveys, polls, and experiments—to evaluate the basic values that underlie our political outlooks. Researchers engaged with the First National Risk and Culture Study explored findings from in-depth interviews with a random sampling of 1,800 Americans.[12] The Second National Risk and Culture Study explored findings from experiments and surveys involving some 5,000 Americans.[13] Researchers also conducted follow-up ethnographic studies and experiments to corroborate and extend the survey findings.

Based on these studies, the researchers created a simple chart, with X and Y axes, to describe Americans' fundamental preferences about how society should be organized.[14] An understanding of these axes, and the four quadrants they create, offers us insights into political polarization and how to reduce it. As we will see, gut-level instincts about these worldview quadrants have helped advertisers and political partisans influence our thinking for years. A more nuanced understanding can help those who value democracy invite everyone into the conversation—for everyone's benefit.

Cultural Cognition in the United States: Four World Views

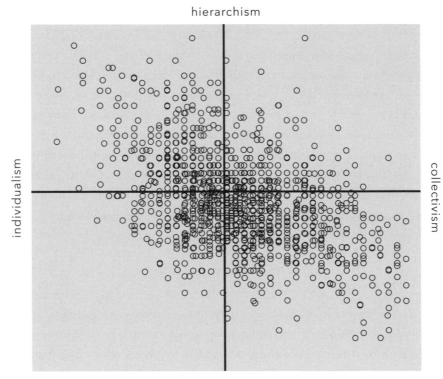

Distribution of cultural orientations in the United States. Adapted with permission from Gastil et al.[15]

As the chart above shows, worldviews can be broken down into four distinct categories. On the vertical axis, "egalitarianism" and "hierarchism" sit at opposing ends. A *hierarchical* viewpoint embraces authority as natural. To the hierarchist, social duties and rights should be allocated based on expertise, merit, or recognized spiritual leadership and well-defined factors such as gender, ethnicity, or lineage, thus reinforcing tradition. The *egalitarian* worldview is that all people should be treated equally and have equal opportunities.

On the horizontal axis, "individualism" and "collectivism" occupy the poles. Here, personal liberty faces off with a collectivist spirit. *Individualists* believe we should all be on our own, responsible for our own success without help or interference from society. *Collectivists* believe that the needs and interests of society as a whole should take precedence over those of individuals, and that society is responsible for ensuring that everyone has a chance to succeed.

Thus, citizens favor one end of each of the two axes and so wind up in one of the four quadrants. Each quadrant represents our most important cultural values—our fundamental view on what constitutes a good society.

Terms like "hierarchical individualist" can be quite a mouthful. So, with all due respect, and a wink to that favorite uncle we argue with at Thanksgiving, we offer an archetypal image for each quadrant.

In the upper left corner, a classic example of the "hierarchical individualist" is Gordon Gekko, the fictional corporate raider played by Michael Douglas in the 1987 film *Wall Street*. Gekko's most oft-quoted line is "greed . . . is good."[16]

In the upper right corner, an easily recognizable example of "hierarchical collectivism" is the Catholic church. People in this quadrant believe very strongly in the collective and their responsibility to each other, but only in the context of a deeply held respect for established hierarchy.

In the lower left corner, the "egalitarian individualist" is the true libertarian. People in this quadrant believe in free markets, personal liberty such as gay rights, and strictly limiting the role of government. Two-time presidential candidate Ron Paul is among America's best-known self-described libertarians (although he differs with this worldview on some key issues).

In the lower right corner, the "egalitarian collectivists" concerned with social justice and equality might include American labor organizer Mother Jones, or if you prefer, Mohandas Gandhi, who led India's nonviolent resistance to British colonial rule.

Obviously, these are archetypes, and some of them are extreme. Any of the viewpoints can be caricatured or taken to an illogical extreme. That's why it is important to note that survey results placed most respondents closer to the center of the axes than at the poles.

Still, the four quadrants are more nuanced than the usual liberal-conservative depiction. They also turn out to be a far more accurate and consistent predictor of our policy views than left-right ideologies, political parties, or demographic factors such as our region, sex, race, or ethnicity. This simple framework allows us to compare data on how our worldviews interact with daily life and to understand our reactions to policy ideas.

How Does It Work?

When we think of the political quadrants, we may see impossibly polarized viewpoints. And in one sense, we'd be right. In the United States, surveys have shown that the most populated quadrants are the hierarchical individualists (upper left quadrant) and the egalitarian collectivists (lower right quadrant)—in other words, diametrically opposed groupings. According to Gastil, this divide "is at the heart of American politics, encompassing (among other things) the partisan divide between Democrats and Republicans, as well as the . . . split between feminism and religious conservatism."[17]

But this doesn't mean that our neighborhood political conversations are shouting matches between Gordon Gekko and Mother Jones. Usually, the signals are much more nuanced. What matters more about the quadrants is how we process information based on our cultural perceptions.

Keep in mind that human beings are enormously adept at recognizing cultural orientation. Some messages are infinitesimally subtle, such as tiny differences in body language or word choice. Some are more obvious: your new neighbor driving up in a bright yellow Humvee sends you one signal, but if he arrives in a Prius hybrid, you receive a different one. Whether he climbs out wearing an American flag lapel pin or a peace button, a baseball hat or a goatee, you'll take it all in and process it.

We take in signals from everyone—politicians, scientists, and media sources. And the closer our information sources are to our own quadrant—our cultural orientation—the more likely we are to accept their message or adopt the view they advocate, *regardless of the facts.*

Climate change is an issue that reveals these worldview distinctions. Exposed to identical data on climate change, people in differing quadrants will interpret the data differently, trusting some pieces and discounting others. Researchers have found, for instance, that those who hold egalitarian and collectivist values readily accept global warming arguments. These Mother Jones types are likely to be suspicious of profit-seeking industries such as greenhouse-gas-creating coal and oil. Meanwhile, those who value individualism and hierarchy (Gordon Gekkos) are likely to value industry and commerce; voters in these quadrants are likely to doubt claims of global warming, suspecting deep down that resulting policy would threaten free enterprise.

In fact, cultural worldviews have predicted voters' views on global warming better than any other characteristic. Notes cultural cognition researcher Dan Kahan,

> How liberal or conservative people are, for example, explains less than one-third as much of variance in such beliefs as how egalitarian

or hierarchical and how communitarian or individualistic they are. Whether one is a man or a woman—a characteristic known to influence environmental risk perception generally—explains [less] than one-tenth as much.[18]

So far, so good—if you're a political junkie, you might have guessed this much. But researchers went a step further and found decisively that voters' views on issues are strongly correlated to which policies people expect will *result* from their viewpoint.

For example, in one experiment, researchers supplied two groups with a newspaper article about global warming. In both groups, the article summarized identically a scientific study that showed rising Earth temperatures due to human activity and predicted catastrophic consequences.

One group's article concluded, however, that the scientists called for "increased anti-pollution regulations," while the other group's article concluded that scientists were in favor of "revitalization of the nation's nuclear power industry."

Guess what? Those of the hierarchical individualist persuasion (Gekkos) were *more inclined to believe data about global warming*—the earth is heating up, human activity is the cause, and the results will be disastrous if we don't take action—if they read the article with the pro-nuclear power conclusion.

The Gekkos who received the article calling for "increased regulation" were clearly triggered by the threat of more government interference, and it affected their perception of the risk of climate change. In fact, they wound up *even more skeptical* about global warming than a control group of the same worldview that received no newspaper story at all.

Researchers discovered similar results on other polarizing issues. For instance, does gun ownership lead to better self-defense or more violent crime? Such a question sets off sirens in our cultural quadrants. Hierarchists associate guns with protective authorities such as fathers and the military, and individualists link them with such virtues as self-reliance and bravery. Meanwhile, egalitarians are likely to link ownership of weapons with racism and sexism, and collectivists view gun ownership as symbolic of a lack of communal trust and caring.

This is where we stand, and this is where we are likely to remain, unmoved by new information. During the course of one cultural cognition study, news of a shooting massacre on the campus of Virginia Tech rocked the nation. Americans mourned the brutal murder of thirty-two students. Researchers took the opportunity to conduct a 1,500-person national survey. The results were predictable: collectivists and egalitarians (Mother Joneses) continued to be skeptical that stricter gun control would make it harder for potential victims of shootings to defend themselves, while hierarchists and individualists (Gekkos) remained dubious that stricter gun control laws would improve safety. Neither side had shifted from a similar survey taken three years before. In fact, such events may even serve to reinforce our preexisting opinions.

Policies must always be informed by cultural values. But we must also have the ability to stay open to new information, especially in these complex and challenging times. If we are committed to finding the best answers, based on the soundest research, we will need to come out of our corners—the sooner the better. But there is a lot working against us.

Is There a Culture War?

The hierarchical individualists (Gekkos) in the upper left quadrant and the egalitarian collectivists (Mother Joneses) in the lower right quadrant are at the heart of most American political disputes. If we got out our pens and colored in this chart, there's no question which hues we would select: red and blue.

In fact, many political professionals make their living doing exactly this: reducing issues to a simple matter of red and blue. In a cynical sense, it's less important to focus on what constituents actually value and more critical to know which words and phrases will activate their supporters.

Republican political strategist Frank Luntz demonstrated the value of keywords in a 2002 memo circulated to GOP leaders.[19] The Luntz memo admitted that anti-environment policies were unpopular with Americans: "If we suggest that the choice is between environmental protection and deregulation, the environment will win consistently," the memo noted. Thus, although the party was staunchly antiregulatory, the memo urged Republicans not to talk about "rolling back regulations"; instead, it offered a list of "words that work" when discussing the environment ("limited role for Washington," "thoroughly review" environmental regulations, eliminate "unnecessary rules"), as well as details on which terms were most appealing to their base ("freedom," "responsibility," "accountability").

Democrats, in turn, have been accused of using the same tactics. One conservative columnist complained that President Barack Obama used euphemisms to obscure an agenda that would be unpopular with voters if they understood it: "Just know that when the President invokes 'revenue enhancement' and 'shared sacrifices' and 'a balanced approach' . . . he's trying to make his single-minded obsession with tax increases more palatable to a government-weary, overtaxed electorate."[20]

With the tactical use of keywords, partisans invite us to use shortcuts to make political choices. Their bold colors and broad brushstrokes encourage us to categorize incoming information and place it neatly into one of our preconceived boxes without examination.

Evoking hot-button issues is a powerful mobilization tactic. For those who are raising money for a political cause or rallying voters toward a particular electoral outcome, it makes political sense to focus on the issues that separate us. Rather than gather women together on the vast majority of issues they have in common (children's health or breast cancer treatment, for instance), it is advantageous for partisans on both sides to choose highly charged issues—like abortion—that trigger us to deploy our "cognitive filter" and shut down our rational brains.

Once our cultural orientation alarm bells have been rung, the analytic processes associated with deliberation lose traction. As Gastil put it, "Cultural filtering corrupts information pools, limits the range of alternatives considered, and biases the weighing of pros and cons."[21] The walls that divide us into our cultural corners also serve to shut out new information.

Each of us fits into a quadrant. However, as discussed above, most Americans are not ideologues; most of us locate ourselves much closer to the center of the chart than at its extremes.[22] And many if not most of our policy positions are based more on shortcuts than on entrenched ideologies. So if we are interested in inclusion, understanding more about each of the quadrants will be helpful in inviting the occupants of each of them into our conversations. It is important to keep in mind that some quadrants are more naturally drawn to deliberation than others. The majority of deliberation practitioners, by far, describe themselves as left-leaning.[23] However, as we will see, a well-run deliberative process has intrinsic appeal for people in every quadrant. It is up to organizers to communicate this. Indeed, different values from each quadrant can weave together to strengthen the process.

Egalitarian Collectivists: Mother Jones Is Always Ready for a Meeting

It shouldn't surprise anyone that egalitarian collectivists respond well to the idea of getting everyone together to share ideas. It is often people from this quadrant who initiate dialogue and deliberation processes, and it is only natural that they would use their own language to invite people in.

"Inclusion," "equality," "consensus," "finding common ground," "coming together," "building community"—these are the terms that make the people in this quadrant sing. But if they use only these terms, they will be singing alone.

"The trouble with Socialism," Oscar Wilde reportedly said, "is that it takes too many evenings." Indeed, few but the diehards in this quadrant relish the thought of another meeting, so egalitarian collectivists will need to convince others—using terms that resonate with people from other quadrants—that their deliberative process is worth another evening.

Egalitarian Individualists: Respect Individual Opinions

A well-organized deliberative process will ensure that everyone is heard and that groups are not urged toward "groupthink" or false consensus.

"Deliberation shouldn't get equated too quickly with consensus, which is a very collectivist enterprise," noted communications scholar John Gastil. "Some of our best deliberative institutions—such as the jury—have not used the principle of consensus, but the principle of unanimity."[24]

Gastil, who has conducted groundbreaking research on the effects of jury deliberation on civic engagement, noted that in the American jury, individual dissent is respected highly. Jury members are encouraged to hang on to their opinions and change them based only on the facts, not because of pressure. While judges will encourage deadlocked juries to continue their deliberation, Gastil said, they also accept "hung juries"—testament to the fact that dissent has its place in deliberation.

In community deliberation, individual opinions and liberties play a critical role for citizens in this quadrant. Skilled facilitators who have the expertise to maintain group confidence and patience during the tension of indecision, and not reward conformity or rush groups to find agreement, will be critical to ensuring that this freedom-loving group remains at the table.

Hierarchical Individualists: Mr. Gekko Wants Expertise

Those in the hierarchical quadrants are less instinctively drawn to community decision making. Hierarchical individualists may be suspicious of an inclusive deliberative process, since they tend to believe that decision making is a job for experts and authorities.

Here, it is important to remember that well-organized deliberative processes do indeed call on experts. Far from simply responding to the impulses of the mob, thoughtful deliberation emphasizes informed engagement and ensures that public decision making and the government itself are accountable to expert analysis. It features independent research, balanced discussion guides, expert panels, and other objective information. These are the elements that will legitimate deliberative processes for people in this quadrant.

Hierarchical Collectivists: Clarity and Closure

Hierarchical collectivists feel deeply responsible to the community, and as such they might be expected to support inclusive deliberation. However, people in this quadrant also strongly support certain established hierarchies. Some hierarchical beliefs (for example, racism and sexism) can have no role in an inclusive deliberation. However, anyone hosting a public deliberation event must be conscientious about including groups that subscribe to a hierarchical collectivist worldview (for example, by being respectful of a variety of religious traditions).

Above, we offered the example of the Catholic church in this quadrant; another example comes out of a different spiritual tradition entirely. Deliberation expert Martha McCoy, executive director of Everyday Democracy, the organization that created the study circles approach, has been working recently in the Southwest on childhood nutrition and other issues with a number of communities with large Native American populations. Although every nation is different, many of these communities are centered on time-honored hierarchies and long-standing spiritual leadership traditions.

McCoy noted that working with Native American cultures "has really caused us to question some of our assumptions—maybe we're not 'everyday democracy' to them." Study circles focus on inclusive community deliberation, but in a culture that has long respected spiritual leadership and traditions over group decision making, McCoy pointed out, "the idea that people should have an equal voice isn't the most powerful driver of their work."

However, with sensitivity and open communication, these differences can be transcended. Hierarchical collectivists will appreciate that effective public deliberation results in a well-ordered set of preferences. Clarity and closure are of great value to people in this quadrant, and for them, deliberation will ideally result in some form of agreement on social, political, or economic issues.

Framing for Inclusion

The same studies that tell us what will ring those cultural alarm bells also offer insights on how to avoid them. Cultural cognition highlights the value of two tools in particular: framing and cultural vouching. Although you may not have heard of these techniques, you've undoubtedly seen them both at work.

In *Don't Think of an Elephant!* cognitive scientist George Lakoff argued that people vote according to their values and identities (somewhat akin to cultural cognition's worldviews).[25] He noted that conservatives excel at "framing" issues to their advantage, and he advised progressives to copy their framing techniques for advocacy success.

Whoever frames the issue wins the day. If you succeed in convincing the media to refer to the "inheritance tax" as a "death tax," your battle is already half-won. Likewise, Lakoff argued that conservatives succeeded at framing tax cuts with the value-laden term "tax relief"; here, the right wing embedded its worldview into the policy debate so that its point practically self-advocated every time the issue made headlines.

Both sides have long since caught on to issue framing. The abortion debate, with its "pro-choice" and "pro-life" labels (and what they suggest about "anti-choice" and "anti-life"), is a classic example. Likewise, "physician-assisted suicide" has an uncomfortable ring, so proponents on this issue coined "death with dignity."

At the national level, issue-framing techniques have reached such a level of sophistication on both sides that we have reached a sort of Cold War stand-off. With spin machines, talking points, and sound bites whirring around us constantly, the truth is hard for anyone to discern.

Slow democracy needs to be aware of framing. But rather than framing to win, slow democracy frames for inclusion. Slow democracy takes the framing knowledge that enables partisan manipulation and turns it on its head, using it instead to encourage engagement and understanding. To enable diverse and open-minded participation, slow democracy frames issues in a diverse, open-minded way, respecting the perspective and values of all four quadrants equally. Slow democracy refers to people as they prefer to be referred to. And as much as possible, slow democracy frames issues in ways that do not back people into their corners.

When framing for inclusion, organizers should view the wording and design of publicity, informational materials, events, and online interactions with each of the four quadrants in mind. Will the process value all participation, while also emphasizing the importance of sound technical expertise? Do the word choices strike a balance between individual freedom and community responsibility?

Remember that even the way we describe issues sends subtle signals that will, whether we mean to or not, tell people about our perspective. For instance, a work party to insulate the attic of the town hall might get only half as many volunteers if you bill it only as an event to "fight global warming." To ensure you include other worldviews, you could also tout the effort as promoting "energy independence." Or, perhaps for maximum inclusivity, you might just promote it as a community event about "saving money." (And no matter what, serve pizza.)

Portsmouth Listens chair Jim Noucas notes that in his work, the convening question is always what drives the discussion. He calls the question "the compass," and he notes that it must be neutral and avoid the perception of any hidden agendas. For instance, when Portsmouth began the review of its master plan, Noucas recalls, "We didn't ask: 'How can we control growth and traffic or provide more affordable housing?' Instead we asked, 'How can we make Portsmouth the best place to live and work for everyone?' Whether you were pro- or anti-growth, you were not threatened by the question."[26]

Slow democracy is most readily successful when communities are dealing with issues that have yet to be framed by some advocate. Where polarization is, as yet, refreshingly absent, we can lose the quadrants for a little while and see each other as fellow human beings. This is the time when we can most easily and pleasurably build neighbor-to-neighbor relationships.

Can You Vouch for Me?

Cultural vouching, a second key lesson from cultural cognition, can best be explained by reviewing another research experiment. In this experiment, researchers created balanced arguments for and against mandatory HPV vaccination. The issue here was whether this new vaccine, known to prevent cervical cancer, should be mandatorily administered to girls before the onset of sexual activity. At the time of the experiment, the issue had not received much media coverage, and so it was not yet polarized. However, in the first phase of the experiment, researchers found that their subjects' reactions broke down predictably along cultural quadrant lines. Issues like strengthening parental autonomy, discouraging premarital sex, and freedom from government mandates made individualists and hierarchists suspicious of the HPV vaccination program, while the idea that society should protect young people and discourage widespread infection made egalitarians and collectivists more likely to support it.

Researchers then invented four "policy experts," one for each of the four quadrants. Each of these fictional experts had his own résumé that reflected his cultural identity, and even an accompanying photo. (This is our favorite part of the experiment. What does a "hierarchical individualist" expert look like? Apparently he has white hair and wears a tie. The egalitarian individualist had mod little glasses that made him look savvy. And not surprisingly, the Mother Jones expert had a beard.) Pre-testing proved that subjects easily associated these "experts" with their intended cultural quadrant.

Researchers then asked eight hundred new subjects to review materials about the HPV issue. However, they randomly assigned the arguments to debating pairs of experts. The results will fascinate anyone who has ever tried to initiate change in his or her community, because it turns out that the perceived cultural worldview of the experts significantly affected participants' views on the issues.

It worked like this: When an expert from one of the egalitarian quadrants (for instance, the Mother Jones guy with the beard) was presented as the author of an argument supporting the mandatory vaccination, and the white-haired hierarchical expert was introduced as the author of an argument opposing the program, the polarization between egalitarian and hierarchical subjects became more pronounced. But if the authorship was reversed—that is, if the white-haired hierarchical individualist expert was presented as being in favor of the vaccine—the gap between the subjects shrank. In these "unexpected alignment" conditions, the arguments for the other side began to make more sense to people, and polarization along cultural quadrants effectively disappeared.

Thus, we introduce the concept of "cultural vouching," one of the most powerful ways to get past the automatic cognitive cuing and filters we protect ourselves with, and to encourage more open-minded listening. A person who is a "cultural voucher" is effectively a go-between—someone who can represent one worldview, but do so while "speaking the language" of another worldview.

In slow democracy, cultural vouching is neither cynical nor symbolic. It is a form of gracious invitation, and an important type of positive modeling. It offers an image of open-minded behavior that research shows is enormously compelling. It is a critical tool in helping communities sort through and apply information in an unbiased way.

Framing and Cultural Vouching at the Local Level

When we understand cultural vouching, keeping decisions local makes all the more sense. Cultural vouching comes naturally at the local level. Living in the same community makes it more likely that even people from different quadrants still have much in common. Public schools are one of the great equalizers; they bring all quadrants of a community together. Place-based efforts—town forests, community gardens, historical societies, urban parks and recreation efforts, downtown revitalization projects, local arts festivals— bring diverse people together around a common element. Once we have worked together with people who are different from us, we begin to break down stereotypes and may not be so quick to jump to conclusions the next time we hear a message from a different group. We begin the process of seeing beyond the barriers that divide us and finding ways to move forward together. At the local level, we can inhabit the commons—both literally and politically.

The following examples show that the most participatory communities already intuitively understand how framing and cultural vouching create broader, more open-minded participation.

Randolph Community Forest

Through community ownership and management, forestlands can be protected from development while providing access for recreation, hunting, and sustainable forestry. Land trusts are among the less polarizing environmental protection strategies, since they rely on free-market forces (purchasing land or development rights) rather than government regulation. But such techniques cannot be implemented if community members do not trust or understand the way they work.

So when Randolph, New Hampshire, wanted to consider a community forest project, the town purposely brought together all cultural quadrants. Organizers instinctively applied cultural vouching in an extensive public education and engagement process.

Even the informal organizing team included an unlikely duo. One member, the town's planning board chair, was a senior member of the New Hampshire state police and was well known in the hunting, fishing, and snowmobiling communities. Another member, who sat on the town's conservation commission, was employed by a local hiking organization and worked actively with environmental groups. Being able to recognize at least one like-minded representative leading the community forest project helped people from different cultural quadrants open their minds to the complexities of land protection.

Noted the state policeman, "You need three people. One on the right," referring to himself, "one on the left," referring to the environmentalist, "and one in the middle," referring to another planning commission member who, as a retiree with time to write grants and host meetings, was credited with keeping the group moving.[27]

Maintaining friendly communications was key to success; many of the complex negotiations were held around a local lunch or dinner table. Ultimately, residents succeeded in protecting over ten thousand acres of land—roughly a third of the town's total land base.

Samsø, Denmark—The Island That Listened

We can look across the Atlantic for another example of how respecting all elements of a community can create substantial positive change.

The little island of Samsø sits off the east coast of Denmark's Jutland peninsula. Approximately forty-four square miles and home to about four thousand inhabitants, Samsø is a traditional, conservative agricultural community—in most ways. It is known for its dairy, pig, and potato farms and for tourism—and for being a global leader in energy sustainability.

After winning an energy-planning contest in 1997 sponsored by the Danish government, the community reached 100% energy independence in under five years. Not only does Samsø now create enough renewable energy to export power, but it also cut its polluting sulfur dioxide emissions by 71% and its nitrous oxide emissions by 41%, and by some measures the community is carbon neutral.

The people of Samsø achieved this extraordinary success by combining residential energy efficiency with the construction of straw-fired heating plants and eleven offshore wind turbines.[28] Their success was also based on many individual lifestyle changes: solar panels glint on barn roofs, and farmers now fuel their manure-flecked tractors with rapeseed oil they have grown themselves.

As the community moved forward, Samsø was able to take advantage of progressive Danish energy policies, grants, and utility partnerships. However, engineering and money can only get a project so far. A significant part of Samsø's extraordinary success was due to community visioning, listening, and collaboration. While one island's alternative energy mix might not be applicable everywhere, the lessons from Samsø's social change work are eye-opening and largely transferable.

Søren Hermansen, a self-described "educated farmer," took the lead on the energy innovations. Now the director of Samsø Energy Academy, Hermansen often speaks publicly about Samsø's energy innovations, and he emphasizes the value of starting change at the local level.

In this traditional agricultural community, one journalist reported, residents were "not wealthy, nor were they especially well educated or idealistic. They weren't even terribly adventuresome. 'We are a conservative farming community' is how one Samsønger put it."[29]

As he launched this project, Hermansen knew that Samsø residents were far from liberal and had very little interest in environmental issues. With this in mind, he visited every local club and community meeting and began asking neighbors about their dreams for the future. Learning that they were anxious to replace jobs that had recently been lost when a local slaughterhouse closed, he spoke of the jobs and economic boon that going green would bring. Knowing that islanders valued their history, he spoke about the historic use of windmills in the area. He urged environmental leaders to keep a low profile until longtime residents had developed an interest in the project.

Clearly, Hermansen intuitively understood the value of cultural vouching. Key community groups had to be on board before most community members would accept an idea that was not, at first glance, in their "cultural quadrant." Likewise, issue framing was critical. According to Hermansen, his neighbors would not respond to "green and hippie"; he needed to prove that the project would result in "green" in residents' wallets first.

Hermansen is a passionate and well-informed energy activist. But as important, at the center of his work is a deep respect for his neighbors, his native island's culture, and its pivotal role in creating sustainable change.

Shares of the wind turbines were set aside for purchase by the general public, including local farmers, and one of the straw-fired heating plants is community owned. In the turbine siting process, public participation was not symbolic; plans were fundamentally altered, at significant expense, based on public comments. In a recent presentation to the Institute of International and European Affairs, Hermansen attributed much of Samsø's success to decentralized decision making that treats energy consumers not simply as customers, but as integral members of the process. "If they have objections," noted Hermansen, "we shouldn't just say we should overcome the objections, or we should teach them to think differently. Maybe they have another solution that's better."[30]

He went on to display a PowerPoint map showing that Samsø is at the geographic center of Denmark. Next, he showed a map of the European Union and noted that Samsø was at the exact center again. He then projected an image of the globe and joked that Samsø not only was at the center of the world but would undoubtedly be at the center of the universe once it was mapped.

The serious point, he said, was that "when it comes to decisions locally, you are in the center of your own life at all times, and the next wise decision has to be taken from where you are. . . . There are a lot of things you can do where you are."

Hermansen tells the story of when the Egyptian ambassador to Denmark visited Samsø to admire the alternative energy efforts and inquired how many people lived on the island. The small number exasperated him. "That's three city blocks in Cairo!" he exclaimed. Hermansen was unfazed. "That's maybe where you should start," he replied, "not all of Egypt, take one block at a time."[31]

"People say, 'Think globally and act locally,'" noted Hermansen. "But I say you have to think locally and act locally, and the rest will take care of itself."[32]

a recipe for
slow democracy

six

THE PROMISE OF LOCAL

Let's, for a moment, step outside the local sphere and contemplate a larger canvas. It doesn't take long to see that our nation—indeed, our world—is in rough shape, and we need answers to vast economic, environmental, and social problems. A huge array of pressing issues demand outstanding thinking, tremendous cooperation, and fast action. In short, these issues demand extraordinary citizenship. However, we also know that our current system of getting answers isn't up to the task. Most Americans are not engaged.

In previous chapters, we have offered hope that engaged, empowered deliberation opens minds and might just help us find answers. But with this much cynicism about the national political and economic process, what hope is there that anyone can make a difference? How many would even try?

One answer is to begin at a human scale: start local. While many Americans have a disdain for politics—disdain that trickles down even to the local level—our need for connection remains. Polls show that Americans have a deep need for social interaction, and a willingness—more than that, a passion—to give back.

Each of us cannot make change at the national level, but we can usually see how to do so in our neighborhoods. What if we decided to turn our attention to our local places and to make the time to be involved there? What difference might it make? We'll begin our answer with three key lessons from the environmental movement.

Lessons from Environmental Education

For decades, environmental groups have offered compelling images of habitat destruction in an effort to move us to action. Clambering playfully on its mother's neck, a baby polar bear adorns the poster in a second-grade classroom as a poignant reminder of a topic the children have been hearing about: melting polar ice caps. Meanwhile, on the adjoining science bulletin board, a colorful toucan sends a message of similar concern to the students: save the rain forests.

Although classroom materials about endangered species, polluted oceans, and toxic spills have been well intended, all of this bad news hasn't done the cause much good. In recent years, those in the field have discovered a disturbing trend. Environmental educator David Sobel calls it "ecophobia": children have been so inundated with news of ecological catastrophe that they start to fear the natural world.[1]

Smaller children should be shielded from distant environmental tragedies until they are emotionally and cognitively ready, Sobel says. Environmental educators now take into account the importance of children's developmental stages. Rather than learning about the huge, the faraway, and the systemic, children should first be allowed to focus on the small, the local, the touchable.

Ideally, a youngster in the southwestern United States will learn about desert flora and fauna. He will come to appreciate the smell of sage when it's rubbed between the fingertips, and to notice the shadow cast by a golden eagle. Meanwhile, a child in New England will explore a northern hardwood forest and all of its mysteries, with bluejay feathers, squirrels' nests, and club mosses that look like tiny trees—a perfect place for a fairy house.

"What's important," Sobel emphasizes, "is that children have a chance to bond with the natural world, to learn to love it, before being asked to heal its wounds."[2] This is *Lesson #1: You have to love a thing before you will work to save it.*

Child advocacy expert Richard Louv agrees, and adds that such elements as a lack of metropolitan park space and an increase in societal fear, as well as simple overscheduling, have further decreased the likelihood of children bonding with nature, or even venturing outdoors.[3] Skyrocketing screen time has compounded the problem. Now quoted mournfully at environmental education conferences nationwide, a fourth grader interviewed by Louv put it best: "I like to play indoors better 'cause that's where the electrical outlets are."

Louv makes a compelling case that this alienation from the natural world— he calls it "nature deficit disorder"—is directly linked to troubling trends including attention deficit disorder, obesity, and depression. The solution, says Louv, is not more complex educational programming; it is more time. Young people need the lazy afternoons, muddy adventures, and surprising explorations that add up to falling in love with the outdoors. They need the freedom to build treehouses, catch turtles, lie in a field and look at clouds, and develop a bond with the natural world around them.

"It takes time—loose, unstructured dreamtime—to experience nature in a meaningful way," Louv argues.[4] And that is *Lesson #2: Real connections take time.*

What happens if we make the time? What if we do allow ourselves to open, to feel the pull of place, to fall in love? What difference might it make?

For decades, environmental educators had assumed that offering sound information to people would change their attitudes toward nature, and that with changes in attitude would come changes in behavior. But at a worldwide conference sponsored in 1990 by the United Nations, educators Harold Hungerford and Trudi Volk presented a landmark paper arguing that environmental education had "not been successful, on a widespread basis, in convincing world citizens to act in environmentally responsible ways."[5] In fact, they argued, if the point of environmental education was to create environmental citizenship, the field had been going about it exactly backward.

Facts are important, but what really gets environmental citizens out of bed in the morning are three interconnected factors: whether they have feel empathy toward the environment; whether environmental issues resonate for them personally; and whether they feel confident that they can effect positive change.

So to Lessons #1 and 2 we add *Lesson #3: We won't get involved unless we think we can make a difference.*

In other words, we become citizens when we go out and get our hands dirty. It's those issues that we care about personally, and for which we can take action and make a difference, that will create that democratic "click." For decades, environmental education conferences featured some variation on the theme "From Awareness to Action." But all that time, the theme should have been "From Action to Awareness."

Again and again, studies show that we do make time for democracy if we can see our personal role in human-scale issues. And real life bears them out; just ask any political leader how he or she got started, and you'll almost always hear that it was through a local issue—the development proposal in his backyard that got him involved in the planning process, or the need for a school bus stop that inspired her to run for school board.

And yet, over and over, we create policies that shift power from local entities to state and federal ones. (Ironically, these so-called efficiencies often even replace local volunteers—free labor—with paid employees.) Local, empowered school boards are forfeited in favor of the superintendent's office staff, and town decision making is supplanted by federal or state mandates.

Democracy requires citizens who are willing to put time into the systems that keep us free. But like the students who are scared by images of a failing ecosystem, adults' democratic impulses have been worn down by attending pointless public hearings led by far-off bureaucracies, and filling out yet another ballot in an election in which we feel we won't make a difference.

One last example from environmental education brings the point home. In his research on nature-deficit disorder, Richard Louv spoke with an environmentalist who was active in creating a state park in California. Once the large expanse of land was preserved, Louv asked, how would children use the park?

> "Well, they'll go hiking with their parents . . . " He paused.
>
> Would a kid be able to wander freely on this land, and, say, build a tree house? My friend became pensive.
>
> "No, I don't think so—I mean, there are plenty of more constructive ways to experience nature."
>
> When asked how he first interacted with the outdoors, the environmentalist answered, sheepishly, "I built forts and treehouses."[6]

Removing opportunities to play freely, get our hands dirty, and build treehouses in the natural world causes a nature deficit. Removing opportunities for citizens to sit on empowered boards, craft creative local solutions, and experience real, hands-on decision making has a similar effect: it is causing a democracy deficit.[7]

Dismantling school boards, privatizing public water supplies, and otherwise removing local influence is in direct conflict with the human-scale needs of a democratic citizenry. As goes our local power, so goes our connection to place, to community, and to each other. As citizens, we need opportunities to get personally involved—to roll up our sleeves, dig into an issue, exercise our dreams. From there, we will move on to reflect on the larger purpose of our work. From action to awareness. And that action begins with the very local.

Head, Hands, Heart

Environmental educators know that every good lesson engages not only our heads, but also our hands and our hearts. Students might remember facts or concepts long enough to report them back on a test, but only hands-on involvement and personal connections to the subject matter will make the lessons truly their own.

But just as many young people have become disconnected from nature, so have many of us become alienated from political participation. In his book *Healing the Heart of Democracy*, Parker J. Palmer, founder of the Center for Courage and Renewal, writes of the current malaise among American citizens today as the "politics of the brokenhearted": "When *all* of our talk about politics is either technical or strategic, to say nothing of partisan and polarizing, we loosen or sever the human connection on which empathy, accountability, and democracy itself depend."[8]

Palmer likens the severance from heartfelt decision making to the shell shock of a soldier returning from battle. Violence does not happen only in war, he notes. "Violence is done whenever we violate another's integrity. Thus we do violence in politics when we demonize the opposition or ignore urgent human needs in favor of politically expedient decisions."[9]

This divisiveness, demonization, and polarization have become ingrained in our current political landscape. We perceive ourselves as right and left or red and blue, and many forces have become expert at—and make huge profits in—portraying us to ourselves that way. But this is no way to run a democracy. Neither side can win—or if one does, it is only until the next election. If we are to solve our problems, we will need to transcend these divisions.

Local may be one place where this reconnection can begin, as the lessons from environmental education suggest. If you have to love a thing in order to save it, then local is the place to start. It's where we find issues that are so central to our homes, our families, or our heritage that we feel they're worth working on. Real connection takes time, and local is where we spend our time, exploring, eating, arguing, laughing. We simply need to make the connection between living in a place and truly, democratically inhabiting it. The third lesson—we won't get involved unless we think we can make a difference—offers profound opportunities at the local level. Here, issues are personal enough to understand and the power structures are accessible enough to affect.

Building Sustainable Communities

Environmental educators and their colleagues have one more lesson to offer slow democracy: the lesson of sustainable communities.

The term "sustainability" has been used to mean many things, but perhaps the most widely used explanation, offered by the United Nations in 1987, is meeting "the needs of the present without compromising the ability of future generations to meet their own needs."[10] In the ensuing years, environmental educators and others have picked up the banner of sustainability: while environmental protection is critical, it must be considered in the context of the whole community. Indeed, it is part of a sustainable community triumvirate of needs: environmental, economic, and social.

At the local level, an understanding of the balance among these three factors is critical. As passionate as any of us may be about our own project—whether it is protecting an environmentally fragile wetland, pursuing economic development for our downtown, or advancing a critical health or education initiative—our project exists in the context of our entire local community. The more fully our project can fulfill the triumvirate of needs for local sustainability, the more sustainable—and popular—that project will be.

At the local level, the lessons of sustainability come naturally. If we are paying attention to the place where we live, we can hardly take a step outside without sensing the connections. The farm where the chickens lay my eggs has a place in nature; it is also has an economic link to the downtown grocery. The factory nearby belches chemicals into my environment; it also provides income for my neighbors. Every decision we make, whether we sit on a planning commission, a community visioning task force, or an arts committee, affects at least one side of the triangle, and through inclusive local processes we come to comprehend the need to consider its connections with the other sides. A vibrant local democracy ensures that we interact with and understand the balance that creates a sustainable community.

The Promise of Local

Here, locally, we can step away from polarizing national divisions and build sustainable communities. And perhaps, slowly, we can renew our vital connection with democracy. But what might "local" mean for slow democracy?

The slow food movement defines local as being within a hundred miles. This definition reflects the realities of food production. While ideally food is grown in the consumer's backyard, some staples—like wheat—may be grown up to 100 miles away.

The Transition Town movement offers a different perspective on local, defining it simply as the area in which we can effectively travel as gas becomes scarcer and prohibitively expensive. The Transition movement, which works to strengthen the resilience of local communities in the face of climate change and energy scarcity, argues that we need to rethink all of our systems; we need to ensure that food and work and schooling are all easily accessible without cars. Our sense of place has been dramatically expanded by the age of cheap oil, and as that age ends, Transition Town advocates point out, that reach of place will probably contract again.

"Local" by definition implies a place-based system, as in "local community." But it's also true that we live in an age where people define "community" in ways that have nothing to do with geography. Many of us value our associations based on interests, professions, or hobbies far more than the associations defined by our town borders. In fact, we may "commune" more online with people on the other side of the globe than we do face-to-face with our next-door neighbor. And that raises the question: In the age of the global village, do we even have time for the village outside our front door?

In democratic terms, the answer is yes. Geographical communities are the way we have historically defined our democratic system—we register to vote in our towns and cities and choose representatives by districts, counties, and states. And as we'll see in the stories that follow, communities—the old-fashioned kind you can find on a map—are increasingly using those democratic systems to bring power back to citizens.

Geographical communities are a necessary component of slow democracy. And that is something to celebrate, because place-based communities are a great setting to explore common values.

So "local," in slow democracy, must mean small-scale and place-based. Beyond that, it can draw on a secondary meaning of the term: the Latin *locus* means not only place but also "center or focus of great activity or concentration." For citizens, that meaning is especially important: "local" signifies a sphere in which citizens can act, can concentrate their energies, can make a difference.

"Local," then, is a necessarily flexible, relative term in slow democracy. The local level will be different for different people. While one person may find his or her sphere of action on a town planning commission, another will find that "local" means his or her county or perhaps even a small state. It is the larger perspective that matters: in slow democracy, any individual needs to be able to clearly see his or her relationship to the issue.

Local Is a School for Democracy

If we leave all the policy and decision making to the "experts," the rest of us will lack the experience we need to be part of a democratic society. Slow democracy means everyone gets involved, at least some of the time. This will lead to stronger citizens, and better decisions. Human-scale, local democracy can foster millions of informed citizens, who will work every day to shape the sustainable energy, food, economic, and education systems of our communities.

The United States and the rest of the world will be facing excruciating decisions in the coming years. Indeed, the time for many of these decisions has already come and gone—with no action taken. We desperately need leaders with clarity, wisdom, and courage—and voters to elect them. These voters need to be wise in the ways of leadership, able to recognize integrity, and able to distinguish—immediately—between deliberation and bullying, policy making and politicking.

If we have been in leadership positions ourselves, we will have a much better idea about how to do it right. When we elect leaders, we will know enough not to expect miracles; we will not anticipate that agreements will be reached overnight. But we will also expect leaders not to waste their time and our resources on political posturing when a viable compromise is at hand. We will know how to spot b.s. when we see it.

Relying on far-off elected officials to make decisions for us is an integral part of the American system. Indeed, our representative government was designed that way. But when official accountability is too far out of reach, and deftly obscured by professional spin, it is easy for citizens to lose interest in the political process. Indeed, citizens' democratic skills can slowly atrophy. We get out of the habit of coming together to make difficult decisions, and in the infrequent circumstances when we have to exercise our public judgment, we often do so poorly.

Slow democracy is not just an add-on to representative government. Ideally, the two systems will complement each other. As communities become more engaged and more skilled at decision making, larger entities such as state legislatures and government agencies can step back from their micromanagement and work instead to support and connect local efforts.

At the same time, these agencies draw their authority from the consent of the governed. Engaged and informed citizens will be that much better qualified to strengthen and support government's legitimacy.

So, slow and local democracy can set off a virtuous cycle: discussions that create connections and reveal creative new solutions; citizens who become more open-minded and ready to help implement their problem-solving initiatives; and smart, sustainable results that could, slowly but surely, change the world.

seven

INCLUSION

Readers who enjoyed the 1970s radio comedy and novel *The Hitchhiker's Guide to the Galaxy* will remember its spoof on the public planning process:

> "But Mr. Dent, the plans have been available in the local planning office for the last nine months."
>
> "Oh yes, well as soon as I heard I went straight round to see them, yesterday afternoon. You hadn't exactly gone out of your way to call attention to them, had you? I mean, like actually telling anybody or anything."
>
> "But the plans were on display . . ."
>
> "On display? I eventually had to go down to the cellar to find them."
>
> "That's the display department."
>
> "With a flashlight."
>
> "Ah, well the lights had probably gone."
>
> "So had the stairs."
>
> "But look, you found the notice didn't you?"
>
> "Yes," said Arthur, "yes I did. It was on display in the bottom of a locked filing cabinet stuck in a disused lavatory with a sign on the door saying 'Beware of the Leopard.'"[1]

Most of us have been involved in a public process at one point or another where, like the frustrated Arthur Dent, we wondered whether those who were hosting it really wanted us to be there. And, dirty dealings aside, even honest public officials admit that sometimes it would be easier if we stayed home. Why?

Most processes involving the public require that officials relinquish some element of decision-making control. Involving the public usually takes more time than making the decision by themselves. It may cost more money—in the short term, for the hall rental and coffee, and in the long term, because the public may come up with expensive ideas. And, especially if you're not very good at it, it can be confrontational and unpleasant.

However, inclusivity is critical to the success of public decision making. Without it, the effort is likely to fail on multiple fronts. Issues are not likely to be explored as thoroughly or with as broad-based perspectives, and solutions will not be as well informed by local perspectives. In addition, the process is less likely to produce the surprising, synergistic new solutions that are so often sparked when different perspectives bump into each other.

Diverse participation—inclusion across all of the socioeconomic, racial, religious, geographic, and other lines that we may draw among ourselves—takes a substantial up-front investment from organizers. But a lack of diverse participation increases the likelihood that any decisions made will be questioned or rejected by excluded groups. What at first might have looked like a time-saving corner to cut leads to a drawn-out revisitation of issues, creating ill will and headaches for all involved. Without the initial investment in gathering all viewpoints, the likelihood of the decision being upheld over time diminishes. After all, democracy's legitimacy depends on the consent of the governed.

An inclusive process will include everyone who may be affected by the issue on the table.[2] It will include those without power and those with it—whether they have power to move things in a positive direction or power to impede progress. And it will include those with important background knowledge or experience on the issue being addressed.

"The short answer to the question of *who* should be in the conversation is everyone," note leaders at the community engagement group Everyday Democracy.[3] Calling for "the marriage of community organizing and deliberative dialogue," these and other professionals advocate using many traditional grassroots organizing techniques—for instance, recruiting participation via known and trusted neighbors and reaching out through existing organizations—to get a broad turnout. Like almost all forms of democratic participation (including ballot-box voting), deliberative processes generally see more participation from people from higher socioeconomic levels. However, organized, targeted recruitment techniques can improve the balance of participation.

But here, slow democracy offers a twist on classic community organizing. The goal is not simply to make sure "your side" shows up and gets heard. By using techniques such as diverse steering committees and framing the issues to include all perspectives, slow democracy works to ensure that *all sides* are at the table. The truth is, if all of the stakeholders are heard, we all might learn something new—and the resulting project has a better chance of succeeding.

Chicago's Policing Alternative

People don't often turn to police departments for slow democracy. But the Chicago police department offers a powerful example of the value of inclusion, and of how government agencies and residents can work together to solve problems. In the early 1990s, like many major cities, Chicago was struggling with drugs, homicides, gun violence, and gangs. And the police were unpopular in poor and nonwhite neighborhoods, where many black and Latino residents experienced the department as racist.

Since it began as a pilot program in 1993, the Chicago Alternative Policing Strategy (CAPS) program has been based on a rethinking of the relationship between police and the community. The traditional model is essentially reactive: citizens call in to report a crime, and police go to the scene and arrest the offender. The CAPS model is based on a different idea, called "community policing," in which residents and officers build relationships in order to create a community where the crimes are less likely to occur in the first place.

The Chicago police decided to focus on the city's 279 police beats, which are where the interactions between community members and police take place, rather than the district or larger level. Instead of moving officers randomly between beats, they assigned them to work the same beat, on the same shift, each day, thereby allowing them to get to know the neighborhood and vice versa. And they began to hold "beat community meetings" every month to get officers and residents to identify shared priorities and shared solutions.[4]

These community meetings were very successful. In Chicago's North Side neighborhood, Gill Park had been a troubled spot for a long time, drawing drug dealers, prostitutes, gang members, and occasional drive-by shootings. The area's beat meetings were well attended, typically drawing from seventeen to forty-five residents, and residents named the park as a top concern. Many simply wanted to close it down as too dangerous. But as the police explained the concept of the "crime triangle," with its three elements of offender, victim, and location, residents realized that much of the problem was due to the park's layout, with its overgrown bushes and trees and shallow pool that concealed activities from observation.[5] By changing the layout and features of the park, they could keep a valuable resource for the neighborhood and make it much less attractive for criminal activity.

So residents, police, and the city went in and transformed the park. Police expertise and city resources, paired with the new inclusion of local residents' energy and willingness to work for the project, created widespread momentum. City agencies provided better lighting and trimmed trees; a local architect volunteered a new design; the Chicago Cubs donated $20,000 for a new baseball field; a neighborhood school planted flowers and "adopted" the park; and community members who lived in the high-rise next door agreed to monitor activity from their apartments. Officers also began patrolling the park by foot.[6] The very first summer, reported offenses on the Gill Park beat dropped by 14%.[7]

The CAPS program had similar success across the city. In the first decade, residents reported much higher community satisfaction with the police department, with increases of ten percentage points or more in the categories of responsiveness, performance, and quality of service.[8] By the end of 2000, seven years into the program, nearly four hundred thousand residents had participated in the beat meetings.[9] City crime rates have dropped dramatically since the early 1990s, though it is unclear how much credit CAPS can take for that; still, a comparison between districts suggests that the program has had a positive effect.[10] And dozens of new neighborhood watch organizations emerged from the discussions.

Getting Everyone into the Room

In Chicago, residents showed up because they wanted safer neighborhoods. But it's not always as easy to get people to show up, particularly when issues don't affect their daily life in such a profound way. That said, strategies to get everyone in the room do exist, and the Vision-to-Action Forum (VAF) is one of them. A VAF is a 1½-day participatory planning process aimed at bringing together a broad cross section of community members to assess their community's strengths and opportunities and to create an action plan to achieve their goals. Created by the League of Women Voters of the Upper Valley (Vermont and New Hampshire) and the Antioch New England Institute in order to engage citizens in planning for sustainability, the model has since been applied in communities across the United States and eastern Europe. Although a 1½-day event could be planned relatively quickly, organizers advise taking a full three months to organize in order to ensure that everyone in town has a chance to hear about the event, and using every outreach tool possible for advertisement—especially word of mouth.

In order to ensure real inclusion, it is critical to begin with a diverse steering committee, preferably with cochairs from various spheres of the town. As the VAF organizer's guide points out, "The Steering Committee should represent all parts of your community, including citizens who may not have been involved in town affairs before. If you look around the room at the first Steering Committee meeting and recognize only your friends and neighbors, you may not have looked far enough for Steering Committee members."[11]

The guide also suggests that the steering committee should mirror the diversity of the community itself. This doesn't mean planning for gender balance and racial and ethnic diversity alone, though these are crucial elements. There are many additional groups that you may want to reach out to specifically, such as:

- Longtime residents and newcomers
- Local business owners
- Retirees/senior, middle-aged adults, and youth
- Wealthy residents and economically disadvantaged residents
- Schools—staff, teachers, parents, students
- Government employees
- Various political parties
- Handicapped residents
- Funders and philanthropists
- People from different geographic regions of town
- Religious groups
- Civic groups
- Local government representatives
- Local employees
- All lifestyles, including married people, couples, and single people
- Farmers, foresters, fishers, miners
- Community leaders
- Homeless people
- Managers of publicly owned land (such as parks, forests, or preserves)
- Managers of publicly owned buildings (such as museums and historic sites)
- Active and inactive citizens

- New parents, parents with school-age children, and parents with older children
- Artists and craftspeople
- Representatives of local clubs
- Nonprofit environmental, social, economic, or cultural organizations
- Introverts (people who prefer to process information internally) and extroverts (people who prefer to process information by talking)
- Day- and night-shift workers
- Computer- and Internet-savvy residents as well as non-computer users.

Of course, no individual can speak for any given population, so achieving real inclusivity is more of an art than a science. Good organizers and facilitators continue outreach throughout the process to ensure that no groups or interests are excluded.

Another approach to inclusion is a process called "asset mapping," which encourages community organizers to make a list of all of the resources contained within the community and to use these resources as a source of strength. Instead of the traditional approach of looking at the community in terms of problems that need solving—unemployment, crime, illiteracy, and so on—asset mapping focuses on capacities, including any institutions and citizen associations, as well as any informal networks that may exist among these groups. Organizers using this technique reach out to the leaders of these groups and also to individuals, including those who are poor and traditionally marginalized. As organizers John Kretzmann and John McKnight argue, "Whether these marginalized citizens are young people or older residents, or various kinds of labeled people, the fact that they too are involved not as clients or recipients but as citizens and contributors can help to define this path as one which everyone can travel."[12]

Getting everyone in the room is especially important because so many people have been shut out for so long. The laws that upheld racial and gender discrimination have left lasting legacies in our culture, so that even now—with legal barriers gone—women and racial minorities are underrepresented in government decision making. And many of the social structures that provide civic skills and foster community engagement among people in lower socio-economic brackets have weakened. Unions and community organizations once drew working-class people into political activity, and homeownership gave them an economic investment, but as these institutions have declined, so have their accompanying triggers for democratic engagement.[13]

Slow democracy processes require full-bodied, diverse participation from everyone, not just the well heeled and empowered. And the reality of our social structures means that inclusion doesn't just happen; communities have to pay special attention to get robust, well-rounded participation.

Inclusive Planning, Creative Process

Although getting participants in the room is a big part of inclusion, it's not all there is to it. It is just as important to engage people in a way that allows them to participate as fully as possible.

In her powerful critique of deliberation, political scientist Lynn Sanders argues that the status of those deliberating—based on factors such race, power, and privilege—often affects the process and the outcome. "The goal of democratic discussion should not be teaching everyone to deliberate, but trying to figure out a way to make sure that everyone participates and is effectively represented and taken seriously in discussion," she writes. [14] In an effort to address group dynamics and dominance problems implicit in more formal deliberative processes, she proposes the idea of "giving testimony" or telling one's personal story to those assembled, which has precedents in African-American churches and political discussions. Instead of focusing on finding common ground, including the opportunity to testify invites different perspectives to emerge.

A trained facilitator, if involved from the outset, can help plan the structure of the process in a way that takes advantage of different perspectives and styles. Here, inclusion means recognizing and accommodating differences in the way people—from different racial, cultural, economic, and educational backgrounds, men and women, shy and assertive people—express themselves. It might mean using Sanders's idea of giving testimony, or perhaps a process that integrates informal small-group conversations as well as large-group discussions. In any case, an awareness of different communication modes, learning styles, and perspectives is critical.

Some of the more creative efforts at inclusion are coming from the arts. The arts aren't where people traditionally go to solve political problems, but they can be a place where people step out of formal societal roles and analytical thinking into a more accepting and empathetic mentality. This shift can make the arts a powerful means for exploring new ways of seeing the world, from the perspective of other cultural traditions and alternative worldviews that are often left out of rational, linear deliberation models. The arts can help awaken interest in residents who might not consider themselves "political," but whose engagement and perspective we sorely need. Divisive issues can often turn people away from engagement entirely. A few examples of the creative use of music, visual arts, theater, and storytelling show how the arts offer us inclusive ways to begin to understand the issues and our options for addressing them.

Deliberative Theater

Rather than pushing an advocacy agenda, "deliberative theater" is learning oriented, a creative way to help participants understand many points of view. Most of Pennsylvania sits atop the Marcellus Shale, a vast geologic formation containing natural gas. New drilling technologies, especially hydraulic fracturing or "fracking," have had a huge impact on the region. Almost overnight, fracking has created new jobs and economic development. But it has also overwhelmed government regulators, and many citizens are outraged about its effect on the water and their health.

In the midst of this community-rending controversy, director Shannon Deep decided to invite residents to the theater—deliberative theater. *Managing Marcellus* was a twenty-five-minute play that dramatized the voices of landowners, elected leaders, environmentalists, and the natural gas industry and illustrated how communication had broken down between them. A "playbill" provided information on the landowner groups, the municipal entities, and the task forces that area residents were using to cope. After the play, the audience heard from a diverse panel of local leaders on the issues and broke into small groups to evaluate the best ways to manage the complex relationships among industry, government, and community. *Managing Marcellus* was intensely engaging; after one event near Pittsburgh, three-quarters of the attendees reported that they would "probably or definitely be more engaged in their community" as a result of the theater.[15]

Storytelling for Change

Social media consultant Barbara Ganley has worked with communities on using storytelling to help build trust, help people identify what really matters to them, and help them envision solutions to current challenges.

By inviting the personal experiences and information that "non-experts" bring to community issues, storytelling promotes inclusion. And it offers an alternative to the more linear, rational deliberative techniques that can deepen feelings of power disparity for those who are less familiar with them. Telling stories is something everyone can enjoy, from small-group story circles to whole-community storytelling festivals.

Ganley relates the experience of Victor, Idaho, a town with approximately a thousand residents. Here, a painful rift was growing. On one side were Victor's longtime residents, many of them owners of agricultural land, members of the Church of Jesus Christ of Latter-Day Saints, and descended from the town's founders. On the other side was a growing population of newcomers, young entrepreneurs who enjoyed Victor for its access to outdoor recreation and who were eager to bring more amenities to town. In Victor, town officials decided to use storytelling to begin the town planning process.[16] A broad cross section of the community came to hear three longtime residents tell stories; the Boy Scouts and other local residents also collected neighbors' stories digitally. One storyteller described a time when Victor was less harried, recalling that residents used to feel a natural community connection and wave to each other when they passed. The story made people wonder, where had the waving gone? Could they bring it back? Sharing laughter and images from the town's history through storytelling led many new volunteers to sign up for the town planning initiative.

Ganley points out that, like any powerful tool, storytelling can be misused. Stories can be used manipulatively to gloss over important information, oversimplify complex situations, reduce the conversation to stagnant nostalgia, and even polarize us further. But used judiciously, in combination with other planning tools, this important technique can be used to enhance listening and open our minds to new perspectives. In Victor, rather than exchanging the usual "positional statements" about land use issues, people are starting to have real conversations. The storytelling process even led to the first "Victor Wave Day," a day for Victor residents to appreciate their community and, yes, wave to each other.

Canadian Creativity

Two examples from Canada demonstrate the power of expression. In 2004, three young Canadian artists cofounded Apathy Is Boring, a national, nonpartisan nonprofit that uses the arts and technology to improve civic engagement. In their first effort on a national election, the group used concerts, digital media, and a host of other strategies to reach over five hundred thousand young voters in under four months and awaken their interest in the democratic process. Since then, Apathy Is Boring has hosted events including concerts, fashion shows, and video competitions. They have become a model for creatively convening young people, artists, and community leaders to discuss topics that matter to them and generate excitement for action.

Meanwhile, Canada's 2011 national elections featured "vote mobs." A spin-off of flash mobs, where artists use social media to convene in a public space and treat onlookers to a surprise performance, Canada's nonpartisan vote mobs emerged from dozens of college campuses from Montreal to Saskatoon to British Columbia, even popping up from high schools and elementary schools. The cheering vote mobs encouraged surprised onlookers, as well as the many who viewed them online, to celebrate democracy and cast a vote.

A Case in Point: Austin, Texas

Austin, Texas, takes inclusion seriously. Consider, for example, that Larry Schooler has been working for over three years as the city's full-time community engagement staff person. Schooler works with departments across city government to develop diverse participation on projects ranging from land use planning to bond votes.

The many department heads with whom Schooler collaborates take their cue from the city council, whose members unfailingly inquire about the public process when evaluating any city endeavor and may derail projects that have not adequately engaged citizens. The city council, in turn, has taken its cue from citizens, who were known to push back strongly in the days when community engagement was not a priority.

"[Cities] assumed for a long time that people weren't interested, because they didn't come to meetings," says Schooler. "But it doesn't mean they don't care. Their issues will surface later, whether you ask them or not. You'll see protests, or lawsuits, or recall elections—they want to get their way."[17]

A neutral, non-policy-making body, the communications and information department where Schooler is housed is right next to the city manager's office, helping to ensure that public input gets implemented by management.

With a population of eight hundred thousand, Austin has had to get seriously creative to engage citizens in a personal way. From addressing mobility, transportation, and technology challenges to crossing language barriers, the city needs to use a variety of channels to engage Austin's diverse population. With a multitiered mandate to hear from large numbers of residents while also digging deep for thoughtful feedback, Schooler and his colleagues have devised a range of engagement tools.

- **Speak Week.** During Austin's Speak Week, the city sets up kiosks in parks and areas with a lot of foot traffic, where citizens can weigh in on issues like city planning proposals or a bond development process. Residents offer input on their overarching values (for instance, on maintaining older buildings versus building new, or on the importance of sustainability initiatives) to help guide the city in the early stages of planning. This individual-comment stage leads into later phases that are more deliberative.

- **"Meeting in a Box."** Austin's "Meeting in a Box" gives existing clubs and neighborhood groups the tools to hold their own gatherings to collect input on key city issues. The "box" is an actual box with printed materials, and it is also available as a downloadable PDF. Schooler notes that it makes sense to go where people are and "take advantage of all the social capital already in existence." Whether at the Asian American Cultural Center or the Jewish Community Center, residents feel comfortable expressing their opinions in these settings, Austin reaps the benefit of honest citizen feedback, and participants gain the benefit of more meaningful discussion with their peers on issues that may affect them.

- **CityWorks Academy.** The CityWorks Academy for adult community members trains residents in the ins and outs of Austin government and includes field trips to departments and public works sites. The program is popular—in 2011, it received some one hundred applications for thirty spots. Applicants range from young professionals to retirees, and newcomers to longtime Austin residents. Graduates go on to serve as "ambassadors" who understand the city, carry this informed perspective into their participation, and often become volunteers and leaders. Austin also uses these graduates to participate in issues-based focus groups early in many of the city's engagement processes. The Austin Corps, a similar program for high school seniors, is another popular "city government 101" leadership training.

- **Community task forces.** Austin has a number of community task forces, which convene diverse residents over a period of months or years on key issues. The Imagine Austin Citizens Advisory Task Force is helping with the comprehensive plan, while the Austin Bond Election Advisory Task Force comes together every time there is a potential bond election. Another task force looks at street closures; when streets are blocked for parades or marathons, local businesses, churches, and residences can suffer, and the task force offers citizen feedback to complement the city staff's recommendations.

- **Interactive community forums.** In Austin's innovative interactive community forums, the municipal television station broadcasts a community conversation live and enables people to participate in person, on the phone, or online, with the ability to send in questions or comments through those media and via voicemail or text messaging. Hundreds of Austinites have embraced this tool as a way to engage in live dialogue even if circumstances keep them from making the trip to city hall. Schooler explains that this combination of tools stretches the city's ability to include all Austinites while still facilitating a meaningful deliberative discussion on important issues.

- **Online tools.** The city is also using a variety of interactive online tools to engage its voters. SpeakUpAustin.org offers a space to post suggestions and comments; any Austin voter can sign up to participate, and city staff can respond. In addition, the site allows government representatives to present specific topics where voters can offer comments or rank ideas. For citizens, "it's less commitment than serving on a task force, but it's more than a one-shot deal," explains Schooler. Participants have the ability to flag and temporarily remove any postings that they deem inappropriate until the site moderator—another of Schooler's jobs—can take action, and online discussions have with few exceptions remained civil. Since users must register to use the site, the tool discourages personal attacks and encourages constructive comments. Like the CityWorks Academy, the registered participants have become a pool of informed residents that the city has drawn upon for focus group discussions.

To Schooler, it simply makes sense for Austin government to make its big city feel human-scale. He notes, "The more cities can connect with populations and see them as part of the same team, the more harmonious, long-lasting, cheaper, and more efficient the decisions will be."

Online Inclusion: Challenges and Possibilities

Austin is just one of many cities using online tools to engage citizens. Today, a wide and ever expanding array of online deliberative tools promises to improve inclusion efforts even further. Whether through formally moderated e-consultations, online forums, social networking sites, wikis, or other tools, citizens are increasingly embracing, and even demanding, online participation opportunities, and any community considering expanding their engagement would be well advised to include online techniques in the mix.[18]

While the more elaborate tools can be pricey and may require special skills or trained staff to use them, there are also many simple tools for straightforward tasks (for instance, surveying public opinion) that can be downloaded for free.

Some participants who may not shine in face-to-face settings can find online participation formats welcoming. Online participation can work especially well, for example, for those who dislike or fear crowds, and for those who prefer to take ample time to collect their thoughts before expressing them. They are also a boon to participants who cannot make a 7 p.m. meeting, but who can register their comments before work in the morning or after the kids are in bed.

As communities move to online tools for deliberation and detailed comment, one of the big questions is about whether participation should be anonymous. Online deliberation experts generally advise against anonymous participation processes. When participants' identities are known, engagement tends to be more civil, resulting in better mutual understanding and stronger community-building bonds. However, anonymity or pseudonymity can be useful in certain moderated dialogue settings, allowing participants to raise difficult issues and safely reveal "the elephant in the room." Manon Abud, a designer of online deliberations at Ascentum, Inc., notes that online processes must walk a fine line: "The key is to create this opportunity for participants to express their creativity or concerns without allowing them to disrupt the process for other participants."[19]

Electronic media have their drawbacks. Policy makers have long expressed concerns about a "digital divide" caused by such diverse factors as age, race, income, and geography. A recent survey about online government participation showed that 25% of white Internet users engage with government this way, while only 14% of African-Americans and Latinos do so. Even among those who regularly use the Internet, those who access government social media tend to be more well educated and affluent.[20]

Any political conversations or decision-making tools that rely entirely on the web will still systematically exclude some portions of society, and so they must be paired with other engagement tools. As with most public processes, one technique is not enough, but with clear guidelines and careful moderation, online resources are a valuable addition to the slow democracy toolbox.

Whether online or face-to-face, inclusion is a good start, but it's not enough. A number of other ingredients are needed to make local government work effectively. As we will explore in the next chapter, communities must address the curious and perennial challenge of trust.

eight

DIALOGUE AND BUILDING UNDERSTANDING

We promised that slow democracy featured three elements of local democratic decision making: inclusion, deliberation, and power. But, as you may have guessed from the story of Portsmouth, we need to sneak in one more element—a partner to deliberation, but one that must precede it in order for decisions to be resilient and lasting. That element is the building of community understanding.

One reason slow democracy is slow is that it requires a thoughtful engagement with citizens' concerns. Unlike executive power, where someone makes a unilateral decision, and unlike adversarial democracy, where people simply vote for their side of an issue, slow democracy requires that people understand each other. It is only then that they can talk clearly and figure out the best decision—one that will last.

One way to get to that understanding is through the techniques of dialogue. And dialogue is not about making decisions, or even about finding agreement; it is about speaking honestly, listening, and learning as a precursor to those goals.[1] For example, the study circles used in Portsmouth usually begin with participants sharing personal experiences and storytelling.

With clear ground rules agreed upon by the group, dialogue organizers emphasize the importance of active listening: not only remaining silent while others speak, but also being willing to reflect back what you hear. This is exceptionally powerful in situations when speakers and listeners disagree, since it forces the listener to understand the speaker's words well enough to summarize them without judgment.

The Occupy Wall Street movement created an inadvertent twist on active listening, when groups used the human microphone technique. Because electronic microphones were not permitted in the public spaces where they gathered, OWS protesters would repeat a speaker's comments, sentence by sentence, in unison, so that those in the back could hear. Here we saw a fascinating example of a group process literally giving voice to all opinions, whether they agreed with them or not.

The Power of Dialogue: Three Stories

To give a better understanding of what a dialogue process can look like in practice, we offer three examples of dialogue in action.

Living Room Conversations on Climate Change

A new project called Living Room Conversations asks whether it's possible to gather people with disparate political viewpoints for an evening of conversation around a political topic and have them look forward to future conversations by the end of the evening.[2]

The project is the brainchild of progressive activist Joan Blades (cofounder of MomsRising.org and MoveOn.org) and conservative leader Amanda Kathryn Roman. Their goal is to short-circuit national political polarization and reweave the fabric of communities by launching 2½-hour living room gatherings. Designed to be used by friends, neighbors, or members of community groups, Living Room Conversations calls for two cohosts: one self-identified conservative and one progressive. Each invites two additional people who share their political positions to participate. Is it possible to overcome polarization, find real connections, and have everyone leave willing to continue the conversation later? Their initial answer is yes, although getting started wasn't easy. But after a successful pilot, Living Room Conversations are being launched across the country on topics from voting practices, food and health, to money in politics.

The pilot conversations focused on "energy independence / climate change," related issues deliberately chosen to accommodate both conservative and progressive viewpoints. Living Room Conversations are set in a welcoming space and designed to encourage listening, personal connections, and understanding of diverse perspectives.[3] They do not require a trained facilitator, but ground rules suggest that rather than trying to find "agreement" (shared beliefs or opinions), the goal is to discover areas of "alignment" (shared intention)—in other words, common ground.

One of the hardest steps for cohosts is recruiting participants. Few Americans make time for democracy for democracy's sake; most people engage only if they can make an immediate impact. Some who have declined say they're fearful to discuss controversial issues, even in a small group. Finding cohosts with different political beliefs can also be a challenge. Both conservatives and progressives note that they did not have many acquaintances of different political persuasions.

Living Room Conversations demonstrates that civil conversations on difficult issues are not only possible, but something that people ultimately appreciate. Although the goal was not consensus or decision making, and there was plenty of disagreement about the causes of global warming, participants in the pilot conversations discovered they liked each other and found common ground on efficiency and increasing renewable energy sources. They noted surprise and pleasure that the conversations could, as one participant put it, "go so deep." More than half of the participants indicated they'd like to continue with similar conversations. Blades calls the project "perhaps the most radical potentially culture-changing initiative I've ever been engaged in."

The findings have strongly reinforced the value of small and "local" in encouraging dialogue; organizers say the friends, and friends-of-friends, relationships among the cohosts and the participants were part of "the glue that held the process together."

"We did what most people out there are not doing," reported a conservative participant in a California conversation. "If I had these kinds of interactions, I would interact more in my community."

"The Year of Civil Discourse" on Israel-Palestine Issues

In the Bay Area of California, four synagogues teamed up to make 2011 the Year of Civil Discourse. This comprehensive dialogue effort involved nearly a thousand people, from rabbis to congregants, in facilitated discussions, trainings in dialogue and listening skills, issues workshops, and many one-on-one conversations.

The topic of Israel and Palestine had become so heated in the Bay Area Jewish community that 47% of those surveyed before the program said they felt "unsafe" asking questions about Israel-Palestine issues in a Jewish institution. More than half of the effort's participants felt "marginalized in the Jewish community" because of their views—although, revealingly, the views of those who felt marginalized showed up at both ends of the Israel-Palestine debate. Having tried town-hall-meeting-style conversations that ended in blaming and unproductive diatribes, leaders realized they needed to begin with a more fundamental dialogue program.

"The purpose was not to have people check their opinions at the door," said Abby Michelson Porth, the Jewish Community Relations Council's associate director and organizer of the year-long event. "We wanted people to bring their passionately held views into the room, and give them the skills to have meaningful conversations about Israel."[4]

At Congregation Beth El in Berkeley, Rabbi Yoel Kahn said that the training caused participants to experience several changes. "One is being open to the possibility that the person I disagree with might have some truth to offer, that I don't have an exclusive claim on the truth. So it's a spiritual movement, to a place where one can say, 'I believe I'm right *and* I can hear what you have to offer.' Instead of saying, 'You are wrong,' say 'Tell me more.'"

Rachel Eryn Kalish, the conflict resolution consultant who led many of the groups, used a tug-of-war metaphor: the war is over, she noted, when you let go of the rope. "Letting go does not mean letting go of your values, your facts, beliefs or that there's no room for bringing those into the conversation. [But] if you scream 'You're an idiot,' and I say 'Tell me what it is that makes you feel this way,' you're going to run out of steam pretty fast, so now we can have a real conversation, finding common ground where we can, and learning from each other when we disagree."

Follow-up surveys indicate that the overwhelming majority of participants felt they had increased their ability to discuss the issues, describing the process with words like "breakthrough." Organizers are now receiving requests from around the country to copy the training model.

"When you get underneath the noise and get to core values," said Kalish, "people find that their morals and caring are far more in common."

Pro-Choice, Pro-Life, Pro-Dialogue

Few public issues in the United States are more polarizing than abortion, and after fatal shootings in two Planned Parenthood clinics in Brookline, Massachusetts, in 1994, tensions were at their peak. Perhaps one of the best-known examples of dialogue serving as a breakthrough tool was coordinated at this moment, although because of its sensitive nature, it was not made public until years later. Spurred by the shootings, the Public Conversations

Project, a group that designs and conducts dialogues about divisive public issues, convened pro-choice and pro-life leaders in what turned into a multiyear dialogue process.[5]

Six women activists, three from each viewpoint, agreed to meet confidentially, with the help of dialogue professionals who would facilitate the conversations. They hoped to find some common understanding, de-escalate the conflict, and reduce the possibility of more shootings. Participants on both sides went into the dialogue with deep trepidation. The pro-life activists met together to pray before the initial dialogue session. One pro-life participant noted that she was afraid that if the dialogue effort was discovered, it could create a scandal "if people thought I was treating abortion merely as a matter of opinion on which reasonable people could differ." Another expressed a "gut fear of sitting with people who were directly involved with taking life." Pro-choice participants were also concerned. The president and CEO of a Planned Parenthood League asked herself if she could afford the time for dialogue when recovering from the shootings was a top priority; a representative from the National Abortion Rights Action League wondered how to "justify to my board and colleagues spending time on something that arguably could be futile."

The discussions began painfully. Even initial ground rules were difficult to settle on, given profound disagreements on terminology. (One pro-choice activist refused to use the term "pro-life" because, she argued, her cause was equally pro-life. Similarly, pro-choice activists preferred the term "fetus," whereas pro-life activists preferred "unborn baby." They settled, with difficulty, on "human fetus.") But with tremendous effort, participants agreed on a process, which included a promise not to argue their side of the issue. Instead, they discussed which stereotypes they would like to dispel. Among other things, pro-life participants did not like to be seen as religious fanatics who took orders from men, nor as being indifferent to the needs of women who were in crisis. Pro-choice participants objected to being seen as anti-family, anti-men, and immoral. They explored what had brought each of them into their work and gained respect for each other's deeply held convictions. The initial four sessions they had agreed to were extended.

As their mutual understanding grew over time, the dialogue participants—all leaders in their field—began to model much less inflammatory rhetoric. One participant told the *Boston Globe* that she was hearing fewer instances of name-calling like "baby-killer, murderer, Nazi," while a pro-life participant told a reporter that she used the term "pro-choice" "because that is what they want to be called. I have a basic respect for the person, even though I don't agree with or respect the position." However, one pro-choice participant noted, "I was struck by the media's desire for conflict. One host of a radio talk show actually encouraged me to attack my opponent personally."

Ultimately, the dialogue process included over 150 hours of talks over the course of five and a half years, finally concluding with an article coauthored by participants and outlining their dialogue process—"an experience," they wrote, "that has astonished us." In the article, while participants admitted that their differences remained profound, all agreed that the dialogue had stretched them intellectually and spiritually, altered the way they did their work, and changed their lives.

Noted one participant, "In this world of polarizing conflicts, we have glimpsed a new possibility: a way in which people can disagree frankly and passionately, become clearer in heart and mind about their activism, and, at the same time, contribute to a more civil and compassionate society."

Banking a Community's Social Capital

As these stories of dialogue reveal, dialogue processes can build trust and understanding between groups. In some cases, the civility built by dialogue can help transcend differences; it can also bring down the temperature on public issues, which in extreme cases such as the abortion example may even help reduce the likelihood of bloodshed. Such formal processes are especially critical when issues are deeply divisive and nerves are frayed. But in small neighborhoods and communities, long-standing relationships between residents often serve a similar function. Over the years, in a variety of roles, they come to know and understand each other's perspectives. In a sense, a strong community has some of the key elements of dialogue woven into its daily interactions. Some people call it neighborliness—that quality that turns a "town" into a "community," and "abutters" into "neighbors." Social scientists call it social capital.

Every community has a variety of forms of wealth, or "capital," that it can invest in and sometimes draw from:[6]

- **Natural capital**, a community's water, air, forests, fisheries, and so on, can be nurtured for health and can also be extracted.

- **Built capital** includes a community's buildings, roads, and infrastructure; we invest in these, while calculating our payback based on the many ways we use them.
- **Human capital** encompasses the people who live in the community; we invest here through, for example, education and health care programs, and reap the rewards in the form of a healthy and well informed citizenry.
- **Social capital** comprises the human connections that weave us together, measured by such factors as trust, reciprocity, social networks, and community norms and expectations. Like all forms of capital, it can be invested in—or not—and drawn from.

Some of these forms of capital are highly visible and easily factored into our everyday decision making. But others, like social capital, are less obvious. Indeed, social capital is too often taken entirely for granted.

Harvard political scientist Robert Putnam made the term "social capital" a household word, or at least one that is commonly used in community planning circles, in his landmark book *Bowling Alone.*[7] Here, Putnam sounded the alarm that Americans' fund of social capital was on the wane. Participation in civic organizations, churches, political groups, and voting, and even our engagement in group activities like singing clubs and yes, bowling leagues, was declining. Putnam offered a wealth of data showing that, increasingly, we are so busy in front of our television/computer screens or commuting that we make less time to enjoy each other's company, exchange views, and create community connections.

Social capital is divided into two types. "Bonding" social capital is inward-looking; it holds similar people together. Putnam calls bonding social capital a sociological "superglue," valuable in clubs and groups; with too much of it, though, our communities become a collection of exclusive, sectarian pods. "Bridging" social capital, meanwhile, is outward-looking. Putnam calls it the "sociological WD-40" of communities, easing social relationships and helping us make connections across our usual boundaries and interest areas. Bridging social capital is notoriously difficult to create, but research suggests that it is built through repeated, long-term connections over time. It is rarely created for its own sake, but more often through collaboration on other meaningful work.[8]

Perhaps most importantly, Putnam and other social capital researchers have made the compelling case that this trust and reciprocity are critical to our communities' health. Social capital is not just a "feel-good" concept; data shows clearly that these networks strengthen our political systems, our local economies, and the long-term viability of the democratic decisions we make.

Strengthening social capital and community understanding—whether through democratic deliberation, arts festivals, budget meetings, historical societies, potluck suppers, discussion groups, or neighborhood heritage days—is not just a nice idea. It is part and parcel of slow democracy.

Public Spaces, Free Spaces

Almost none of us take our first steps into public life by making a speech or running for office. In fact, we usually don't begin at a meeting at all. We associate with friends, neighbors, colleagues—and their ideas—in public spaces. Communities' public spaces—their places of worship, eateries, community centers, concert bandstands, and even online gathering spots— are critical to inviting people into public life and strengthening community.

Building social capital and social movements depends on what civic scholars Sara Evans and Harry Boyte call free spaces: informal settings where people can meet, share ideas, and make connections. As an example, Evans and Boyte cite the civil rights movement, which found its earliest cohesion through a network of community churches that became a training ground for civic engagement.[9]

When citizens are involved in creating public spaces, these spaces are all the more inclusive. Especially given today's strapped local budgets, cities and towns are embracing small-scale, citizen-based projects that make the most of public space.

Urban planners have embraced the concept of placemaking, based on the work of urban writer and activist Jane Jacobs and planner William "Holly" Whyte. As the nonprofit planning group Project for Public Spaces explains,

> Making a place is not the same as constructing a building, designing a plaza, or developing a commercial zone. When people enjoy a place for its special social and physical attributes, and when they are allowed to influence decision-making about that space, then you see genuine Placemaking in action.[10]

Not all public space has to come at great cost. These planners advocate taking small steps to invite people to the commons. A temporary art installation, a bench, and a coffee cart placed together strategically will draw more people than if they were strung out separately, and, as Holly Whyte noted, such thoughtful placement "provides a linkage between people, and prompts strangers to talk to other strangers as if they knew each other."[11]

While their approach sounds straightforward, it is not simple. It is critical to know what local residents value and how they are likely to come together to use a space. If planned and created inclusively, however, public spaces will in turn strengthen a community with every new day they're used.

Online Tools to Build Place-Based Communities

Public spaces do not have to be physical. Organizers are also finding surprising ways to use cyberspace to connect neighbors.

When we think of online social media, many of us think of Facebook, LinkedIn, MySpace, or Twitter—tools that have questionable value for strengthening local communities. A recent survey showed that of the typical Facebook user's "friends," a mere 2% are neighbors, an average of only five actual people.[12] But a different kind of online connection is also happening, one that is based on place. A growing number of "hyper-local" forums are popping up across the nation, connecting neighbors on a range of everyday issues.

In the Minneapolis–St. Paul area, BeNeighbors.org is connecting area residents to discuss community topics and share announcements. Steven Clift, executive director of e-Democracy.org, noted in a blog about the project:

> In just the last few weeks, we sent deep dish pizza sales through the roof at a new pizza delivery place struggling to get established, generated local elected officials' help to take on the FAA over surprise airplane route changes rattling windows, directed neighbors to local Girl Scouts for cookies, and helped a mom find out how to request a new stop sign at a dangerous intersection.[13]

The nonprofit e-Democracy.org has also launched local issues forums across St. Paul, with several dozen additional forums across the world. With the objective of giving all residents a stronger voice in local decisions and policymaking, the sites are citizen-driven; residents subscribe and post their ideas, and community hosts manage the online conversations. The focus is not on local people discussing national issues (organizers direct participants to other online forums for that); it is local people discussing local issues.

Another well-established tool is Front Porch Forum, an electronic mailing list and online bulletin board now in seventy Vermont cities and towns. Front Porch Forum (FPF) offers a way to share opinions on issues, announce a yard sale, or borrow tools, and rarely does a week go by without a posting about a lost cat or dog. These are the concerns that are real to neighbors on an everyday basis. FPF founder Michael Wood-Lewis points out that Facebook's business model relies on enticing you to stay in front of your computer for as long as possible. FPF is just the opposite: it's intended to get you out into your neighborhood.

To help ensure civility, FPF and the issues forums require participants to give their names, and to different degrees, comments go through moderators. Just as face-to-face deliberation tools must be well matched with the issues and political situation, FPF has struggled with some users' impulse to use the electronic mailing list and bulletin board as a way to engage in dialogue or debate on controversial issues, which FPF organizers argue is not the right tool for the job.

"FPF is fine for pre-election statements and issues questions, but it's not the right place for ongoing political discussion," notes Wood-Lewis.[14] Like facilitators who sometimes need to step in at public meetings, at times FPF moderators have had to reject postings or even, rarely, shut down overheated topics. In these cases, the staff encourages communities to host a face-to-face meeting about that issue or steers citizens to an online forum dedicated solely to that issue.

These online tools are designed to build community, and participants indicate that they're working. In one city survey, 60% of respondents felt that FPF made local government more responsive to neighborhood needs, 78% felt that FPF made their neighborhood more neighborly, and 93% felt more civically engaged since joining FPF. The comments from survey respondents filled in the numbers with stories that are similar to those from FPF communities across the state:

> "Seemingly everyone casually talking in the locker room one day
> at the YMCA had read the dialog [sic] about the . . . [electric] plant

development and everyone from lawyers, advocates, and run of the mill guys were able to have a qualified discussion and ask good questions."

"The most overwhelming thing was when my upstairs neighbors took in a refugee family for a few weeks. These people had arrived with only the clothes on their backs. I asked people if they could donate warm clothes and some toys for the family. . . . The generosity of the neighborhood was overwhelming."

"In the 24 years I've lived in this neighborhood, this is the only time I've ever been in such good touch with everyone."[15]

Although a number of such community forums are popping up across the country,[16] both Wood-Lewis and Clift agree that their success does not lie in technological bells and whistles. Online connections must be based on face-to-face community organizing; they take a tremendous up-front effort to garner diverse participation before they have a life of their own.

Online users tend to be in higher socioeconomic groups, and Clift says that the "change the world opportunity" is in including lower-income and underserved neighborhoods.

"Serendipity is at the center of our model," explains Clift. "We've found that if you get local enough, the relevancy of place in the 'common interest' can trump most people's tendency . . . to filter out and avoid stuff we would not click on. Meaning, at the neighborhood level we can have a shared community information stream with conversations that cut across all the silos of public service and community and cultural groups around us."[17]

"People belittle the 'lost cats' thing we do—they want to host discussions on huge global issues," says FPF's Wood-Lewis. But he argues that following up an FPF post, whether by attending a meeting or by calling a neighbor about a lost pet, can lead to new relationships. Notes Wood-Lewis, "These kinds of connections are the compost, the fertilizer of community engagement."

The Bonus of Strong Relationships: Strong Economy

Many researchers have noted connections between civic involvement and local economies. It turns out there is a surprising link between social capital and, well, capital capital.

In a 2011 study by the National Conference on Citizenship, researchers measured citizen engagement—things like volunteering, attending public meetings, working with neighbors to address community problems, and voting—and found a strong correlation between a community's participation rate and its resilience against unemployment. That is, places with a more engaged citizenry in 2006 experienced a smaller rise in unemployment between 2006 and 2010, even after adjusting for other economic factors such as housing prices and the proportion of white-collar workers.[18] Although the correlation cannot prove cause and effect, researchers posit that citizen participation may help us weather recessions and keep local economies strong. Some of the possible explanations:

- Being civically involved gives us transferable skills and confidence that can translate into jobs. Guiding productive small-group discussions, building consensus, and other leadership skills are all as critical in today's workplaces as they are in the public square.
- Civic participation enhances information flow. Whether we're at meetings, dishing food at the soup kitchen, or planting trees together, we talk, exchange news, and share information about job or training opportunities.
- Civic engagement creates social networks   connections that can lead to job opportunities.
- Working together, we learn to trust each other. Researchers have found an upward spiral: participating in groups increases trust, and trusting others encourages us to participate in groups. High levels of community trust are strongly correlated with economic success; after all, trust is critical to business associations, contracts, hiring, and investing.[19]
- As we engage in our communities, we may become more attached to them. Researchers have found a link between citizens' attachment to communities and economic growth. If we love our community, it stands to reason that we are more likely to invest here, both emotionally and economically.[20]
- A high rate of civic engagement in a community is a strong predictor of a well-functioning government. As the National Conference on Citizenship researchers note:

Active and organized citizens can demand and promote good governance and serve as partners to government in addressing public problems. States with more civic engagement have much higher performing public schools (regardless of the states' demographics, spending, and class sizes). American cities with stronger civic organizations are better able to make wise but difficult policy decisions. . . . In the current economic crisis, governments that benefit from better civic engagement may be able to reduce the scale of unemployment through more efficient and equitable policies.[21]

Widening opportunities for citizens to connect and engage not only taps residents' wisdom and skills but may strengthen our economies as well. We underestimate the value of building community understanding and social capital at our peril.

nine

DELIBERATION

It's just another public hearing. In front of the local auditorium, tired-looking members of a state wildlife board sit behind a table cluttered with documents, microphones, and tepid water glasses. The rest of the room is filled with rows of chairs, most of them empty; those citizens who have shown up sit with their arms crossed, facing the front, and one lone microphone stands in the center aisle.

New regulations are up for discussion, and when citizens first arrived for the 7 p.m. hearing, those who wanted to address the panel were required to sign up under "for" or "against." Some of the first people to testify began by asking panel members questions about the regulations but are told by the board chair, "We are required to listen; we are not required to respond."

An hour into the hearing, the questions have dried up, and testimony has become increasingly shrill and polarized, with tempers flaring. It looks like it will be another long night.

The Public Hearing: A Nondeliberative Legacy

This public hearing may sound all too familiar to many Americans, but only the strong-hearted will endure such a scene with any regularity. As former Montana governor Daniel Kemmis has noted, "A visitor from another planet might reasonably expect that at a public hearing there would be a *public*, not only speaking to itself but also *hearing* itself. . . . But this almost never happens."[1]

Sadly, "public hearings" are frequently neither.

Many government entities are legally mandated to use the public hearing format. In fact, from federal issues to state and local decision making, the public hearing is one of the most-used public participation processes in the United States.[2] But any public body that depends on hearings as its sole public engagement tool is courting disaster, in the form of a disgruntled citizenry and unsustainable decisions.

Most public hearings are publicized as per statutory requirements, with a formal notice in a newspaper of record, postings on two public bulletin boards, and that type of thing—hardly the welcoming outreach that's likely to bring in a crowd. Those who do attend are likely to represent not a broad cross section of the community but rather factions on either end of the decision-making spectrum.

Ordinary citizens who aren't accustomed to public speaking need only one intimidating experience with a squeaky microphone ("Please speak up, ma'am, your comments are going on the record!") to ensure that they won't be attending another public hearing anytime soon. Research backs up what participants already know: public hearings, although technically open to all, don't result in a broad or representative cross section of stakeholders.[3]

If inclusion is critical to a good public process, public hearings have already flunked the test. But their ranking on deliberative qualities is even lower. While the ideal public hearing can offer an opportunity for open-minded leaders to hear citizens' views, too often they fall far short of this goal. Scholars and practitioners agree: "In practice, public hearings routinely fail to resemble even a crude form of deliberation."[4]

The typical public hearing begins with a brief presentation by the convening body and then a public comment period, often with each citizen limited to a certain amount of time to speak. In general, citizens are not encouraged to ask questions, and leaders are not required to answer them.

Hearings usually have a predefined scope; collaboratively reframing issues and identifying middle ground are far from the agenda. Even the format of the room gives the feeling of adversity, with conveners typically lined up in the front of the room, emphasizing their separate status, and microphones arranged so that those testifying stand isolated, with their backs to the rest of the audience. The public hearing lends itself to recitation of arguments and pro/con entrenchment—almost anything except finding new solutions.

Too often, public hearings occur far along in a decision-making timeline—too far along to make a difference. Although they fulfill legal requirements regarding public participation, there is no obligation to incorporate public opinion into final decision making. This became particularly clear in the early years of the environmental movement. Embattled conservationists complained that rather than a civic engagement tool, public hearings were an element of the Army Corps of Engineers' "decide, announce, and defend" strategy for development projects.[5] By the time a hearing was announced, a strategy had already been determined and any battle against it was uphill all the way.

Today, in the eyes of some citizens trying to make themselves heard, the best use of a mandatory public hearing has been to garner media coverage for a staged public protest. This is a far cry from the original intent of public hearings, which was to ensure public participation. But this tool has probably done as much as any institution to frustrate citizens and push them away from civic engagement. The public hearing is an object lesson in the fact that effective civic participation isn't simply a matter of summoning and dismissing citizens whenever it suits leaders. True slow democracy begins at the grassroots and grows from the ground up.

For Meetings, It's Not Only Quantity, but Quality

As Frances Moore Lappé has noted, democracy is not something we are born knowing about; it's something we *learn* by doing.[6]

Many community leaders are open to genuine deliberation but don't know how to set it up. In a recent National League of Cities survey, almost half of all the city officials and top staff members polled admitted that they didn't have the training or skills to carry out effective citizen engagement processes.[7] Furthermore, they didn't think the public had the experience to participate effectively, either. Although almost all respondents (95%) said that they valued public engagement and knew it was beneficial for developing local solutions and building a sense of community and trust, many noted that some community groups, including the media, special interest groups, and citizens in general, were not effective in this work.

Revealingly, 81% of respondents reported using a variety of engagement techniques "often" or "sometimes," but the techniques ranged from surveys and "town hall" meetings to empowered neighborhood councils. In other words, different officials perceive participation differently, and deliberation with the power to influence is not a priority for all. For instance, although the majority of respondents used the Internet to communicate with citizens, only 14% regularly used online forums that were actually interactive.

The report's authors find hope here, however, arguing that the fact that most city leaders see participation as a priority suggests that the problem is not the quantity of engagement venues. Rather, they note, "the opportunity for improvement may be qualitative—to make the processes work better."

After all, poor public engagement practices are often as scarring for local leaders as they are for the citizens. As John Nalbandian, former mayor of Lawrence, Kansas, said, "What drove me to try structured, planned public engagement was my awful experience with unstructured, unplanned public engagement."[8]

Improvements can't come soon enough. We know that carefully designed, skillfully facilitated processes can have positive outcomes for both individuals and communities, but we also know that citizens are still often subjected to poor-quality public events where deliberation is incomplete or nonexistent. Such processes not only are ineffective in opening minds but can lead to even more retrenchment and calcification of views.

Simply convening people with opposing viewpoints in the same room to talk can do far more harm than good. In fact, it is a proven method for turning people off from political participation altogether.[9] For these reasons, communities need to plan for public deliberation conscientiously, tailoring processes to meet their needs while embracing rigorous standards for deliberative excellence.

Deliberative Decision Making

Not a negotiation, not a debate, and certainly not the shouting matches that have come to characterize many of our public issues, a healthy deliberative process is at the heart of slow democracy.

Defined by such refreshing practices as collecting useful and relevant information, considering all sides of an issue, and creating new solutions together, deliberation depends on citizens' reasoned argument and critical thinking skills to make public policy decisions. The key term here is "make decisions." Deliberation implies that, ideally, we will not only talk together, we'll decide together. And in an ideal deliberation, participants are not simply debating option A versus option B but co-creating C—inventing new solutions together.

Deliberative decision making offers a sharp contrast to the democratic method that comes to mind for most Americans: casting a ballot. In fact, democracy scholar Benjamin Barber has called voting "the least significant act of citizenship in a democracy." Rather than seeing it as the pinnacle of freedom, Barber compares voting to using a public toilet—waiting in line with others, then closing ourselves in a booth to do our business in solitude. While the comparison is harsh, it highlights the distinction between individual decision making and democratic deliberation. Notes Barber, "Because our vote is secret—'private'—we do not need to explain or justify it to others (or, indeed, to ourselves) in a fashion that would require us to think publicly or politically."[10]

Another familiar process that contrasts starkly with deliberative decision making is debate. As Sandy Heierbacher, director of the National Coalition for Dialogue and Deliberation, points out, the goal of dialogue and deliberation is to find common ground; the goal of debate is to win. Dialogue and deliberation aim for an atmosphere of safety, using agreed-upon ground rules and, if necessary, a facilitator to enforce them; in debate, the atmosphere is more threatening, with ideas under verbal attack. Whereas debate often focuses on one participant's presumably correct answer, dialogue and deliberation processes assume that "all of us know more than any of us" and that putting heads together can lead to new and creative solutions.[11]

Obviously, the boundaries between the various forms of communication are not always clear. In any given sit-down, deliberation may feature a hint of debate, or dialogue can merge into deliberation. Although the pathway may be varied, the role of the facilitator is to ensure that the general goals of the journey are met.

The field is still young, and there is still much research to be done.[12] But stories from real communities suggest that deliberative processes can be enormously valuable on a number of fronts.[13]

First, deliberation can make participants more open to new information, ideas, and perspectives and help us refine our attitudes about issues.[14] Deliberation may also help us recognize connections; there is some evidence that deliberation participants are more likely to view people and communities as interdependent. This more "cosmopolitan" viewpoint may be a result of looking at issues not only from a personal standpoint, but with consideration for the common good.[15] Deliberation often leads to more engagement; as we become more confident about grappling with complex issues, we are more likely to vote, volunteer, and become more involved in our communities.[16] And it can raise the bar: as we find success in deliberative processes, we come to feel a stronger sense of responsibility toward our community and expect ourselves, our communities, and our leaders to work together to find common ground.[17]

Democratic deliberation can strengthen community capacity, that is, a community's ability to communicate, collaborate, and solve problems.[18] Well-structured deliberative techniques can produce high-quality discussions, where even people with opposing viewpoints can discuss all sides of issues and find common ground. Well-facilitated deliberations can enhance our sense of community and mutual respect, helping us understand each other beyond the stereotypes we create for each other and reducing problems of marginalization.[19] Public deliberation helps increase public buy-in of decisions. Many communities have found that strong deliberative processes result in more just, sustainable decisions.[20] And in case after case, it is clear that if a deliberative process is well run and meaningful, people find it profoundly rewarding. In fact, they genuinely enjoy it.[21]

Montgomery County Public Schools

The case of the Montgomery County public schools is a classic example of how one community was able to use deliberation techniques to increase racial understanding, improve school climate, and make real gains in student performance.

Montgomery County in Maryland has almost a million inhabitants and stretches from Washington, DC, in the south to Baltimore in the northeast. It is one of the richest counties in the United States, ranking thirteenth as of 2008, with a median income of over $92,000. It is also racially diverse, with roughly 57% white inhabitants, 17% each black and Hispanic, and 14% Asian. Residents come from 164 countries and speak 134 languages.[22]

There are two hundred schools in the public school system. Many of them have good reputations, and the county's schools are known for their excellent AP scores and 90% graduation rate.[23] But there has been an achievement gap based on race, with white and Asian students populating the gifted and talented programs and graduating at higher rates, while black and Hispanic students have been directed to intervention classes and have dropped out more frequently. In one elementary school, two-thirds of Asian students and half the white students had been recommended for the gifted and talented program, compared to only 8% of Hispanic and 4% of black students—a particularly striking imbalance given the young age of the students.[24]

Racial issues dragged down student behavior and the schools' relationship with parents. As one elementary principal commented, "It is NO SECRET that our climate was horrible. It was common knowledge."[25] A middle school principal described frequent comments from parents: "[The school] is racist. The teachers don't care about our children. Our children don't receive the same opportunities as white students. The administration is targeting children of color and giving them unfair consequences."[26]

The school district implemented a "study circles" dialogue and deliberation program on a small scale in 2003 (the same process employed in Portsmouth, New Hampshire). The circles consisted of small groups of about fifteen participants, first with students alone and then with various configurations of students, staff, administrators, and parents. Trained facilitators started with trust-building exercises and open-ended discussion questions—for example, building a timeline of public events that had impacted participants' lives—and moved to develop action steps. Fifteen thousand people from all parts of the school district have participated, including 65% of staff.[27] Groups have suggested action steps including outreach to parents of struggling students, a Hispanic parent group, a diversity club, "Homework Help Nights," diversity training for staff, and mentoring programs for both students and new parents.[28]

By all accounts, study circles have had a big impact on the schools. Gifted and talented programs now make a conscious effort to incorporate students of all races. Schools have incorporated clubs and activities that draw students across racial lines. Administrators have been more careful about putting African-American boys in intervention classes. Teachers have used what they have learned in their classrooms; as one said, "We understand how to support students better."[29] In one middle school, suspensions decreased by almost 90%—which means, says the principal, "that students are in the classroom where they have an opportunity to learn."[30] On a high school level, black and Hispanic students take AP exams at record rates, compared to other schools.[31]

Some of the biggest changes have come in the parent-school relationships. Parents who participated in the study circles were far more comfortable at the schools, had more allies there, and were much more likely to be involved; seven out of ten reported that their involvement had increased. Three-quarters of principals surveyed reported a similar shift, not only in the numbers of parents but in their backgrounds. As one said, "The PTSA Board looks very different this year; it is not all white women."[32] And parents reported a much clearer sense of how to help their children succeed; there was a 25% jump in the number reporting that they knew which classes their children needed to take to get into college.[33]

The most lasting effects may or may not be quantifiable. As one principal described, "I don't have any hard data on [student achievement] yet, I must be honest. But teachers are working harder and more collaboratively than ever before. Students appear more focused on learning than ever before. We, as a staff, have been able to focus ourselves on our work building data and planning structures with ownership and commitment from all—that was never the case before."[34]

Horizons

Horizons is another program that used deliberation techniques for community problem solving. An antipoverty initiative, Horizons ran from 2003 to 2010 and funded community programs to get people talking about poverty and taking steps to do something about it. It was adopted in four hundred very small rural towns, places where poverty rates were over 10%. Most had fewer than a thousand residents, and 20% were on Native American reservations. Participating communities stretched in a band across the American Northwest from the lake country of Minnesota through the Dakota plains out and west to the Columbia River valley in Washington State.[35]

Horizons was implemented in various locations as an eighteen-month program with four distinct stages. It started with two-hour dialogues exploring the issues of poverty and how it appeared in the community. The second phase was a five-month leadership training for at least twenty-five participants, with the goal of identifying new leaders. Participants in the dialogues and leadership training then led the third phase, community visioning, in which at least 15% of the population came together to imagine the economic and social future of their town. And that vision then informed the fourth phase, the action plans: the concrete proposals for making that vision become a reality.[36]

Horizons is an interesting take on slow democracy because it had elements of a top-down effort: the Northwest Area Foundation provided facilitators, the central discussion topic of poverty, leadership training, and criteria and timelines for each step in the process, as well as funding to get everything going. But the structure seemed to work, at least for many communities. In South Dakota alone, participating towns have:

- Received over $1.3 million in grants
- Founded four new businesses
- Developed three new day-care centers and one after-school center

- Opened three youth centers
- Opened two new fitness centers
- Developed two farmers' markets and four community gardens
- Held a personal financial planning course, which reduced debt and increased savings for over thirty residents
- Started negotiating for a possible wind farm
- Started a community foundation to keep local money in town.[37]

One of the most common legacies of the deliberations was increased participation. More people now come to local meetings, including school board and town and city council meetings. And Horizons participants have run for elective office in over 35% of communities. Many of these roles are new; noted one participant, "We have new leaders in the community because of what we are doing here."[38]

One facilitator was initially skeptical about poverty discussions, admitting, "I couldn't figure out what would motivate people to give up their Wednesday nights to go to a community room and talk out loud about something that causes most people to whisper." But people did. As one participant described it, "It brings back the community connections they had long ago, when grandparents and their parents used to all come together and talk and organize things."[39]

And another wrote to Horizons organizers, "[Community members] are more eager to communicate . . . they're more positive. I think it's kind of like a swarm of bees that's kind of looking for their hive before you guys came along and everybody is flying out there doing their own thing but never found the hive. And now this Horizons thing is the hive and everyone is going to it with their ideas."[40]

Decision Making Made Easy (Sort Of)

As the field of deliberative democracy progresses, practitioners and scholars are working to define what constitutes a high-quality deliberative process. The standards that are emerging look less like a fixed recipe and more like a collection of inspiring cooking practices from across cultures. In the deliberative processes of slow democracy, every community is unique, and every decision-making situation is different. Community members will need to take stock and match techniques with their specific needs. Still, some elements are applicable in most processes.

Planning comes first. While public engagement does not need to be expensive, everyone pays a certain "price" for what may be an emotionally taxing and time-consuming process. In general, when decision making stretches over time, more intense deliberations run the risk of reducing participation. Effective planning will ensure that everyone's time is respected. If a decision-making process is going to be substantial, it is worth hiring a process consultant who is familiar with a range of deliberative techniques and can help choose and implement the right process for your needs.

Determining the goals of engagement will help communities avoid the mistake of choosing a particular technique before they've determined whether it is a fit with their real needs. The process of inclusion begins here; ideally, a cross section of community members with a range of interests will help set those goals.[41] Patience is a virtue. Decision making is often iterative, so communities need to work in some time for back-and-forth; that is, opportunities for information gathering will be followed by time for deliberation to refine research questions, and then it may be time to go back for more factual research.

Communications scholar John Gastil has created a comprehensive description of the key elements of a high-quality deliberative process.[42] These include what he calls the analytic process:

- Finding sound, unbiased information
- Identifying the community's underlying values
- Determining a variety of viable solutions
- Evaluating the pluses and minuses of each solution
- Making the best decision possible.

Gastil notes that we must examine deliberation with another lens as well, that of the social process:

- Making sure everyone gets a chance to speak
- Ensuring that participants understand each other
- Considering a variety of ideas and experiences (from experts as well as the general public)
- Ensuring mutual respect.

We've already considered the social process in our discussions of inclusion and trust; here, we'll highlight the considerations of the analytic process that are most relevant at the neighborhood or community level.

Start with a Foundation of Information

Just as in any healthy relationship, good communication within communities is critical. Ideally, deliberative communities will establish methods, such as standing citizen committees or regular meetings between local leaders or candidates and citizens, to reassess their progress and get a sense of emerging issues throughout the year. Rather than collecting information only in advance of a deliberative "event," these communities are continually in learning mode.

When a specific deliberative process is in store, more detailed information gathering will be necessary. Ideally that information will be a combination of both organizer-compiled and participant-compiled materials. Deliberative models such as the National Issues Forum process and study circles have professional researchers and writers who put together balanced materials for their issues deliberations, which are valuable if they are related to the issue your community is addressing.[43] At the local level, resources are limited, and communities may not be able to hire a professional to pull together a briefing book specific to their issue.[44] However, every community has people with knowledge, curiosity, and passion about the issue. Informational materials can be crowd-sourced, with information for the various positions provided by anyone interested in the topic. Citizens can play a number of roles, including researcher, fact-checker, interviewer, and editor. In any case, creating a sound information base can and should be a collaborative inquiry. Materials should include a range of perspectives and research from a variety of sources, and they should include both expert research and local wisdom such as local stories, knowledge, and experience.

As information becomes available, it makes sense to communicate it regularly to the community, whether through the local media, newsletters, e-mail alerts, websites, or communication vehicles unique to your community. Keeping the community up to date on research will help them participate more intelligently and allow them to suggest additional research directions, while also reassuring them of the transparency of the ongoing process.

Information will inform deliberations, and then those deliberations will clarify the need for more specific information. Obviously this can't go on forever, but when planners and participants anticipate and leave time for some of this back-and-forth, the deliberative process is much richer and more effective.

An example of this virtuous upward spiral, from information to deliberation to action, comes from our friends in Portsmouth, New Hampshire. In their deliberative process about whether to renovate or relocate their middle school, Portsmouth residents proved that a wide-open process encouraged participants to keep their minds wide open to new information. Curious, empowered citizens threw themselves into seeking information with a passion. After the deliberation process, 92% of those who completed exit surveys reported that they had done independent research. Meanwhile, 84% got information from the Portsmouth Listens online database more than twice, and half used it more than four times. The overwhelming majority of participants spent more than two hours per week gathering information, in addition to the hours they spent in the study circle meetings.[45]

In a related story, Portsmouth city council member Chris Dwyer recalled that through small-group deliberations on sustainability and transportation, she gained new insights that were critical to her work as a policy maker. In its research, her study group came to the realization that the city needed to fundamentally restructure the way it addressed transportation issues. "You're never going to get bicycle and pedestrian and alternative stuff talked about seriously," said Dwyer, "if your committees are about 'Traffic' and 'Safety' and 'Parking'—if you don't change the whole conversation."[46]

The transportation professionals in her study group morosely predicted a stalemate: the city would never agree to change Portsmouth's long-standing committee structure. However, armed with the information and thoughtful analysis gained from her study circle, Dwyer was able to make the case to her fellow city council members, and the city now has a single transportation policy committee. "It took me a year," she laughed, "but I did it."

"To me that's the essence of the 'study' part of the study circle," noted Dwyer. "I was able to speak to it articulately, because we had studied it together for six weeks, and I learned a lot. It enabled me to take action, and to speak to that action. Whether it's a citizen or an elected official, that's when it's really working."

Identify Community Values

It is important that communities come to understand their key values. Here, communities work together to recognize not only the values that get expressed the most regularly or the loudest, but all elements of a sustainable community that they hold dear, which are likely to include environmental, economic, and social values.

When Portsmouth parents and community members began determining how to redistrict their schools, they were divided into opposing factions. They had preconceived ideas about the "type of person" who lived in different parts of town, and each identified the needs of their own school as the top priority. However, as they worked through the deliberative dialogue of the study circles, they came to identify more with the interests they held in common—among them, high-quality education for Portsmouth's children, at a price that the community could afford—which allowed them to move forward in a less adversarial manner.

The extent to which we can name our common interests will determine which type of decision-making process we will use. When most of us think of "democracy," we think of voting booths and majority rule. These democratic traditions, however, represent only one type of democracy. In her groundbreaking book *Beyond Adversary Democracy*, Jane Mansbridge clarifies that another kind of democracy exists. "The West believes that it invented democracy, and that institutions like Parliament, representation, and universal suffrage are synonymous with democracy itself," Mansbridge notes. However, "every step in this adversary process violates another, older understanding of democracy," which she calls unitary democracy.[47]

Adversary democracy, Mansbridge explains, assumes that citizens are in conflict. It features electoral representation and winner-take-all voting and has many similar attributes to laissez-faire economics. Unitary democracy, based on common interest and equal respect, features consensus and face-to-face decision making.

The tensions between these concepts of commonality and competition are at the heart of every discussion about citizen participation. Every time people get together to make decisions—whether it is a couple deciding which restaurant to go to, or Congress deciding on spending allocations—unitary and adversary systems are in tension. Notes Mansbridge, "Both couples and large polities can and should shift from one system to the other, depending on the context to which individual interests are actually in conflict."[48]

The work we do to recognize common interests will lay the groundwork for our deliberations, affect which decision-making processes we choose, and determine how effective unitary, versus adversary, democracy decision-making techniques will be.

Facilitate Solutions and Trade-offs

In identifying solutions and trade-offs, the role of an objective, skilled facilitator or moderator cannot be overemphasized.[49] Facilitators play a neutral role as far as the content of the discussion is concerned, and instead they focus entirely on the process. Part gracious host, part traffic cop, and part referee, an effective facilitator can make the difference between a productive, solution-oriented deliberation and a pointless free-for-all.

The facilitator ensures that all participants get to speak their minds, which means not only bringing out the thoughts of less talkative members, but also maintaining a safe environment for participants to voice unpopular views that are important for the group to consider. He or she continually refocuses the deliberation, making sure comments address the key issues rather than the personalities involved, and helping the group hone in on its work. A master of understanding nonverbal communication, the facilitator helps gauge the energy of the group and keeps the process on task and on time.

Evaluation of the trade-offs should be systematic, looping back to recall the values identified at the beginning. Professional facilitators use a range of tools that help participants weigh the impact and feasibility of each option and determine where more information is needed. A good facilitator will encourage people to look at the downsides as well as the upsides, and to make a realistic assessment of what *won't* get accomplished—and the costs of not accomplishing it—if they move forward with their selected priorities. Katherine Cramer Walsh, in her study of interracial dialogues, notes the importance of the facilitator in allowing uncomfortable issues to surface. She calls for "a good dose of provocativeness" in a facilitator, noting that while facilitators must be fair, it is also their job to ensure that key issues do not go by unexamined.[50]

Facilitators are expert listeners, helping ensure that participants express themselves to their own satisfaction. Listening is one reason facilitators often work with flip charts or some kind of electronically projected group record. Recording notes for everyone to read at the front of the room is a form of active listening, reflecting back comments so that each speaker can have no doubt he or she has been heard. Facilitators know this is a valuable tool to keep a group moving ahead, too—people feel less need to repeat themselves and dominate the conversation when they can see that their point has been acknowledged and recorded.

Many deliberative processes train, and then rely on, citizen facilitators to run their small-group processes. Facilitation training is an excellent capacity-building investment for neighborhoods and communities, with both short-term and lasting advantages. For instance, in a multiyear dialogue and deliberation project focused on improving education in Bridgeport, Connecticut, a diverse group of at least twenty-five people was trained in moderating and recording. Marge Hiller, director of the Bridgeport Public Education Fund, noted, "We use the parents who have been trained to be our moderators and facilitators when we have other conferences, and their leadership skills have expanded dramatically. When they're the ones that are in front of the group, everybody else is much more comfortable speaking and taking responsibility."[51] Communities that have a critical mass of people with these key deliberative skills are more likely to turn to deliberation as a decision-making tool.

In the work of identifying a range of solutions and the trade-offs among them, the value of "local" comes to the forefront, since in small communities solutions may come from any sector. The group may generate the types of solutions we expect from government, or they can be citizen-based innovations. Increasingly, citizens are coming together not simply to make decisions, but to carry them out themselves.

The range of online deliberation tools is growing, and their quality is improving quickly. No longer simple surveys and chat rooms, deliberative software can offer citizens the ability to prioritize values, weigh options, and share relevant stories. While slow democracy depends on face-to-face communication, online elements can be a valuable addition to broaden participation and help new ideas surface. (For more on online deliberation tools, see chapter 7.)

Decide How to Decide

Ultimately, the group will need to select the solution (or combination of solutions) that best suits their needs and values. Before they do so, it is critical for them to choose some form of decision-making model. Whether it is a form of parliamentary procedure like in *Robert's Rules of Order*, a consensus model, or some other process, it is critical to get clarity up front about how the group will move forward.

In her aptly named book *Freedom Is an Endless Meeting*, Francesca Polletta studied social movements that have governed themselves through participatory democracy, from pre–World War II pacifist efforts to civil rights to the women's movement and other causes of the 1960s and '70s.[52] Polletta observed that many social change organizations made the mistake of thinking that because they came together around a common cause, they could move forward as friends, making decisions the way friends make decisions. But deciding on which movie to go to is a very different process from committing to long-term organizational strategies, and many groups foundered for lack of a workable democratic model. While their decisions were based on respect, trust, and consideration, many groups were vulnerable to the downsides of close association: exclusivity, a lack of openness to new thinking, and an inability to hold participants accountable.

In communities, we may be lulled by long-standing relationships into thinking that we can make decisions through informal conversations and assumed consensus. However tempting it is to skip the decision *about* decision making, it is wiser to decide in advance on a structure and specific rules; depending on the organizational level, groups often formalize these in bylaws. Many models exist that can ensure inclusive participation, foster an atmosphere that helps incorporate new ideas and sort out disagreement, and create a balance between trust and accountability. The trick is to choose the tool that is right for your group's work.

The two most common processes at the community level are majority rule and consensus, but there are other choices as well.

Majority Rule

Majority rule is often quicker than other decision-making processes in the short term, but as we have noted, it can result in a disgruntled minority (as large as 49%) that can slow the process down later. Formal parliamentary procedures such as those found in *Robert's Rules of Order* describe in daunting detail the process of getting proposals moved, seconded, discussed, amended, and voted on. Those who criticize Robert's Rules for being linear and stifling the free exchange of ideas won't be surprised to learn that they were created by not only an engineer, but a general. Just after the U.S. Civil War, Army Corps of Engineers Brigadier General Henry Robert created the rules to standardize and demystify democratic decision making. At the time, Americans were increasingly involved in civic groups and grateful for a consistent process for majority rule while respecting minority viewpoints. Based loosely on the rules used in Congress, and used in many New England town meetings, Robert's Rules are perhaps best suited to large assemblies making multiple decisions, where order is at a premium. However, any group can select elements of a majority-rule process or readily amend Robert's Rules to suit their needs (Robert's Rules has a rule for everything, including how to change the rules). When groups have experienced an inclusive, deliberative process throughout, a majority vote can be a sensible method to confirm final group approval.

Consensus

Some citizens have been burned by overzealously (or unfairly) applied parliamentary procedure and are more enthusiastic about consensus decision making.[53] Consensus is perhaps best known for its long-standing use by the Religious Society of Friends (the Quakers), and its goal, as its name implies, is to find a solution that is "consented" to by all. Achieving consensus doesn't necessarily mean that everyone likes the solution, but at least no participant believes that the solution is so far outside of the group's best interest that it is necessary to block it. Consensus has the advantage of allowing multiple, conflicting solutions to be considered simultaneously. Since consensus focuses on shared understanding and can take more time, it stands to reason that it is most worthwhile when the decision is difficult, will have long-term impact, or will affect many people. Groups choosing this method, which has many forms, also need to identify a fallback if consensus cannot be reached—will they take no action (which favors the status quo), or will they resort to a majority vote (perhaps moving forward only if there is a two-thirds or three-quarters majority)?

Dynamic Facilitation

Less common but increasing in their use are newer techniques that attempt to address the limitations of more traditional processes. For instance, consultant Jim Rough created the dynamic facilitation technique, also called "choice creating," to handle "impossible issues" and difficult-to-manage participants.[54] Designed to encourage outside-the-box thinking, the process invites the assembled group to define (or redefine) the problem statement, helps underlying and previously unrecognized issues to emerge, allows multiple (potentially conflicting) solutions to be considered, and continually seeks additional options. Rather than trying to reconcile disagreements, a dynamic facilitator works to enlarge thinking to include all perspectives as valid. Ideally, rather than being a decision-making process, dynamic facilitation winds up with a "collective breakthrough."[55]

Whatever the method, decision making becomes easier as participants come to understand the processes involved. As mentioned above, a neutral facilitator—ideally one who has studied the chosen process and is familiar with its possible complications—is critical to the success of any of these processes. In rule-driven processes (e.g., Robert's Rules) a moderator may succeed with a simple working knowledge of procedure. Facilitating a more responsive technique like consensus requires more experience, and an intuitive technique like dynamic facilitation is almost its own art form. A growing number of trainings and guides are available on group decision making. Whichever decision-making model is chosen, leaders should seek and actively consult resources to guide their process.

Deliberation on the Rise: Oregon's Citizens' Initiative Review

Respect for deliberation inspired a recent change in the direct democracy process in Oregon, one that has allowed a much more thoughtful examination of ballot initiatives. The initiative and referendum system, used in two dozen American states and many cities, allows voters to create public policy through ballot measures. Many western states adopted this system in the early twentieth century, in a sweep of populist political reforms intended to wrest control back from a system they saw as corrupted by big oil and railroad money. Supporters of the initiative and referendum process argue that it keeps power close to citizens, and in this era of deep skepticism about government, the process remains popular with voters.

However, while citizens can do their own research or talk with neighbors, there is no built-in forum for discussing ballot initiatives before voting. Critics argue that well-funded, high-stakes campaigns frequently offer only polarizing slogans rather than detailed, balanced information, and voters often are not well informed before they vote. Surveys seem to back them up. In 2003, for example, researchers surveyed four hundred active voters in Washington State, 90% of whom said they had either already voted or intended to vote on statewide and local ballot measures. Over half of these voters, however, were unable to name a single measure on the ballot. Once reminded of the measures, most could not give pro or con arguments on the issues.[56]

Oregon's Citizens' Initiative Review (CIR), created in 2011, is an effort to strengthen decision making by incorporating citizen deliberation into the initiative process. Through the CIR, a random, demographically balanced sample of twenty-four voters examines statewide ballot measures and deliberates on their merits. The group calls on policy experts and hears from campaigns on both sides of the issue. They draft a "citizens' statement" that highlights what they consider to be their most important findings and notes how many of the citizen panelists support or oppose the measure. The state then publishes the results of their review in an official voters' pamphlet, which is distributed to every voting household in the state.

Oregon representative Nancy Nathanson explained, "When you have regular voters researching and questioning panelists and experts in the field, able to ask and probe over a number of days, that's a lot more time than any of us would have as a regular voter."[57]

Elliot Shuford, codirector of the Healthy Democracy Oregon group that pushed the CIR legislation, noted, "We think voters are the exact group who should be doing an evaluation for their peers."[58]

A Gift to Future Generations in Virginia

Hampton, Virginia, a historic city of over 150,000 people on Chesapeake Bay, is making new history. Hampton's work in increasing deliberative democracy has earned it the Innovations in American Government award from Harvard's Kennedy School, as well as accolades from many researchers for its exceptional efforts in empowering citizen decision making.

One of Hampton's most striking projects is the Youth Civic Engagement initiative.[59] Here, the city's youth are invited to discuss the public issues most relevant to their own lives. While receiving hands-on training in research, collaboration, and deliberation skills, the young participants host candidate debates and are actually involved in some of the city's decision making. Hampton leaders see the youth initiative as an investment in their future, to create citizens who will continue to contribute to Hampton's community life.

In a second Hampton initiative, a city-run "Neighborhood College" offers classroom sessions on facilitation, budgeting, and other process and policy topics. An early inspiration for the civic trainings offered in Austin, Texas, as well as a growing number of other cities, Hampton's adult education program builds community members' capacity to engage in the research, prioritization, planning, and other skills necessary for successful deliberative decision making. Several hundred residents have graduated from the program so far, with many moving on to run for office or lead community boards or organizations.

Hampton values public deliberative governance so highly that it has created the twenty-one-member Neighborhood Commission, with representatives from neighborhoods, schools, local organizations, and youth. Its deliberative format allows conflicting opinions to emerge and be addressed and offers the opportunity for citizens and the city institutions to find consensus. The commission not only makes neighborhood-related recommendations to the city council but also has its own projects and budget.

As Hampton and many other communities are discovering, linking inclusive deliberation to real power is what keeps citizens coming back to the democratic process. Indeed, as we will see in the next chapter, power— although it's a word some of us would rather not talk about—is the final, critical element of slow democracy.

ten

POWER

In the end, once we've done all of our talking, who will make the final judgment? Who holds the power?

Some people are not comfortable talking about power. While power may be the currency of political activists, to others it is a dirty word—like "money," it is not mentioned in polite company. But listen for words like "influence," "impact," "authority," or "control" and notice how often they come up. Ultimately, power is a crucial element of democracy and something we need to discuss.

It would be helpful if every decision-making process came with its own "power gauge." We imagine a dial like an old-fashioned speedometer that would tell us how leaders answer the question, "Who makes the decision?" At one end, the dial reads "Me"—the leader holds all the power. In the center, "We"—decisions are made together. At the far end, "You"—citizens are the decision makers. Exactly where the needle quivers on this dial should be clear to every leader who plans to engage the public, and to every citizen before he or she commits time to the process.[1]

Social change analysts have been fooling around with some version of this gauge for over fifty years, offering a variety of advice on where to set the needle. From the perspective of community leaders, setting the dial on "Me" allows for speedy decision making; as long as leaders make arrangements for the decision to be well informed and implemented, avoiding public involvement will save time.

However, if a community ranks other values as highly as, or more highly than, speed—for instance, such priorities as keeping the public informed, strengthening citizens' democratic skills, building a sense of community and teamwork, and tapping public opinion and wisdom—then leaders would do well to set the dial toward the other end.

In other words, shutting citizens out of the process causes problems. But there is something worse: inviting them in, but then wasting their time by ignoring their input. Leaders have been getting this one wrong for decades. Back in 1969, activist Sherry Arnstein noted that public hearings were anything but empowered. Instead, she observed caustically, "what citizens achieve in all this activity is that they have 'participated in participation.' And what powerholders achieve is the evidence that they have gone through the required motions of involving 'those people.'"[2]

When Arnstein wrote these words in 1969, civil rights issues were at the forefront of the American psyche, and the economic and racial conflicts prevalent in urban renewal efforts were fresh and raw. Arnstein's experience as an advisor in the U.S. Department of Housing and Urban Development's Model Cities program and other federal positions had left her cynical about the value of citizen participation mandates.

She paid keen attention to where power lay. In her now classic paper "A Ladder of Citizen Participation," she created a matrix of public processes that clearly indicated her disdain for any public engagement effort that was less than fully empowering for the citizens involved. Now, over forty years later, the International Association for Public Participation (IAP2) has developed a "spectrum of public participation," without Arnstein's activist stance but with similar questions in mind.[3]

By combining insights from Arnstein's ladder and the IAP2 spectrum, we can get a clear picture of what our "power dial" might look like. (For the purposes of this analysis, we'll assume that the "Me" is the leader and the "You" is the citizen.)

- At the edge of the "Me" spectrum is a zone that doesn't even count as citizen engagement but needs to be considered: **manipulation** and **therapy**, where citizens serve on "rubber stamp" advisory committees or, just as painfully, see their energies co-opted in a patronizing attempt to change their views or to distract them from more important decisions.
- As we move into the "Me" zone, we come first to **informing** citizens. Whether citizens are offered fact sheets and web addresses or invited to an open house, communication is generally one-way.
- The next stage is **consultation**. Public hearings and comment periods, surveys, and focus groups can give leaders access to citizens' ideas,

although citizens need to understand that there is no guarantee that their input will be put to use. Ideally, leaders will at least provide feedback about whether and how citizens' ideas influenced their decision.

- We arrive in the central "We" zone with **involvement**. Here, citizens are invited to workshops and the like, and leaders commit to reflecting citizens' ideas in proposed decisions and being accountable to their input. As far as Arnstein is concerned, since no binding decision-making power has been conferred, the dial still has not budged beyond "tokenism." Beware symbolic advisory committees with no authority, Arnstein warns, labeling them **placation.** However, as today's deliberative tools become more sophisticated and leaders become more interested in ideas from the public, involved citizens have the potential to influence the outcomes of public decisions, especially at the local level.
- Inching toward the "You" zone, **collaboration** or **partnership** is represented by participatory decision making and empowered citizen advisory committees. Here, leaders commit to incorporating citizen recommendations as much as possible.
- At the far end of the dial, we have fully arrived in the "You" zone of **citizen control**, a.k.a. **empowerment**. Here, voting puts citizens squarely in the driver's seat of power: citizens' decisions are binding. But citizen-controlled processes that are also deliberative are more rare, most commonly found in juries, the traditional New England town meeting, and recently, participatory budgeting.

All Talk, All the Time?

Slow democracy encourages inclusive, deliberative, empowered participation in local democracy. But does everyone have to have power over every decision? It stands to reason that decision-making power is most important on issues that are most relevant and meaningful to the citizens involved. Offering citizens full-bodied control over tiny, unimportant decisions is as disingenuous as the participation activities at the "manipulation" and "therapy" end of the power gauge. So, practitioners on the ground have added practical nuance to the spectrum we describe above.

Jennifer Hurley, an urban planner in Philadephia, applies an overlay to the power matrix to help determine when to use processes that are at the leader-centric "Me" end of the spectrum and when to use tools that are closer to the citizen-empowerment end.[4] As Hurley observes, most citizens don't care which route the city garbage trucks take. As long as our trash is collected in a timely manner, the route planning meeting is one we're delighted to miss. But ask us what type of economic development is needed in our neighborhood—its character, its density, its impact—and we will generate opinions that are not only impassioned but imbued with valuable local knowledge.

To determine which kind of decision-making situation is which, Hurley and her colleagues suggest that leaders consider additional elements:

- *How complex is the situation?* Decisions that are controversial or that are values-based require more participation.
- *Who will influence or be influenced by the project?* If the stakeholder groups are not yet known or comprise an especially large or diverse group, it's time to put out the welcome mat. Likewise, if there is a clear imbalance in power and resources, or if there are stakeholders who are outside of the traditional structures and need to be drawn in, then more inclusive engagement techniques are called for.
- *Are there concerns of legitimacy and buy-in?* If citizens have the sense that leaders are acting outside of their mandate, it's time to slow down and listen.
- *Where does the proposal sit on its decision-making timeline?* Early tasks like goal setting, idea generation, and prioritizing alternatives are ideal times for citizen engagement. But never, ever try to "include" the public in a decision that has already been made. As Hurley notes, "Fake engagement is worse than no engagement."

Like Hurley, the city of Portland, Oregon, has applied a similarly nuanced approach in its parks and recreation department. Here, the staff begins every project with a quick public-involvement assessment to evaluate such elements as the project's potential for public impact, public interest, and controversy. They take the time to look at these from the perspective of both the city government and the citizens and other stakeholders. Planners then work to match the participation need with the appropriate tool, from educational publications (to announce the use of new light bulbs) to community-run meetings or deliberative forums (to discuss a new ice rink proposal).

The process was developed in collaboration with community members. According to Elizabeth Kennedy-Wong, the community engagement and public involvement manager at the parks department, it "has actually relieved a lot of angst on the part of project managers to see that public involvement can be focused and strategic and thoughtful."[5]

Democratic Impact Statement

While we are making sure our policy-making processes are empowered, we must consider what effect any resulting new programs will have on the power of local democracy itself. As we saw in the case of West Virginia's school consolidation, for instance, shuttering schools not only affected students but weakened community members' ability to engage democratically with education-related decision making. And when community schools closed, towns also lost a gathering place where they could strengthen community bonds, hold public events, and even vote.

You may have heard of an "environmental impact statement"—the form that developers must fill out to show the effect their proposal will have on the local wildlife, and water and air quality. New development proposals are also often assessed on how they impact historical resources, traffic, and aesthetics. In the case of educational programs, we ask about effects on student learning, program efficiencies, and, of course, spending. But rarely, if ever, do we inquire what impact a policy will have on our local democracy.

It's a question worth asking. While a "democratic impact statement" hasn't been invented yet, with every new policy under consideration, we can all ask ourselves: How will it affect citizens' decision-making power and the likelihood that people will engage democratically?[6]

As both community leaders and citizens get better at sharing power, they are discovering a variety of ways to make their collaborations more manageable. Here, we offer a series of examples of the progress being made at various levels of government to share decision-making power.

Power Outside of Power: Public Land Collaborations

Some deliberative processes have grown up outside of existing power structures. In Idaho and Montana, environmentalists and loggers have been fiercely at odds for decades over issues like timber sales on public lands managed by the U.S. Forest Service. There, conservationists' alarm about the devastation of trout and grizzly bear habitat has been pitted against the realities of shuttered sawmills and struggling local economies. But decades of polarized hearings have made both sides lose faith in the public process. In recent years, the antagonists have begun to meet privately, in the hope of finding more common ground than in the Forest Service's proposals.

In a study for the Kettering Foundation, Daniel Kemmis (the former mayor of Missoula, Montana) and Matthew McKinney describe the growing trend of multiparty collaborations around public lands issues in the American West. Far from being organized by the government, these conservationist–timber industry talks have grown naturally over time. Kemmis and McKinney describe the conversations as "emerging," "organic," and even "feral."[7]

A natural tension exists between the empowered federal government and these citizen-based initiatives. In the case of public lands, both entities have some element of the common good in mind, but only one side holds the power. As one environmental law pundit argued, "The federal government is the only federal government we have. It owns the federal lands and resources and must be responsible for allocating them in the fashion that a national majority—not a local group or partnership—deems appropriate."[8] However, many citizens feel disconnected from what they see as an unresponsive, over-bureaucratized system. Kemmis and McKinney note that especially in states where vast tracts of land are owned and managed federally,

> more and more Westerners on both sides of the political fence have come to believe that they can do better by their communities, their economies, and their ecosystems by working together outside the established, central-ized governing framework than by continuing to rely on the cumber-some, uncertain, underfunded, and increasingly irrelevant mechanisms of that old structure, which had only taught them how to be enemies.[9]

Kemmis and McKinney describe a variety of efforts in which former adversaries have found mutually beneficial agreement, and they argue that although the process is still emerging, it is important enough to notice. Solutions from these multiparty collaborations have worked their way, undirected and unsanctioned, into policy and legislative proposals.

"If it were not for the persistence and the frequent productiveness of these collaborative efforts," the authors note, "they might simply be dismissed as extraneous and corrosive to the established democratic system. But they do persist, and they persist largely because they work."

Power Given by Power: High Guidance, Local Reins

When higher levels of government have identified specific goals they'd like to encourage, they can offer tools and incentives to local communities to help them reach those goals, letting the citizens apply them as they see fit for their local needs. For example:

- In Massachusetts, the Community Preservation Act empowers municipalities to offer a referendum to voters on whether to add up to 3% to the property tax to create a local community preservation fund.[10] The state kicks in an additional percentage of the dollar amount raised by the local fund, and the town allocates the funds toward historic preservation, affordable housing, and open space or recreation land. Now over ten years old, the act has been adopted in 148 communities (42% of cities and towns), and the state has allocated some $387 million toward the community funds. Although the state contribution, which began as a 100% match for the dollars raised locally, has declined to less than a third with the economic downturn, community participation has continued to increase.[11] Perhaps most importantly, towns have the power: communities have identified, prioritized, and supported the 15,000 acres of conserved open space, the nearly 2,500 historic preservation projects, and the more than 5,000 affordable housing units created through the program.[12]
- In Connecticut, the state-financed Clean Energy Finance and Investment Authority has fostered the creation of over eighty community-level clean energy task forces. These citizen groups work to convince their communities to commit to clean energy use, such as for powering town and school buildings, and then go on to take up additional energy-related efforts according to their local interests. The citizen task force in West Hartford coordinated a comprehensive energy plan, got solar panels installed on local school and town buildings, hosted a school energy competition, and even hired a town energy manager. Activist Roger Smith notes that town efforts are as varied as the communities themselves: "Other towns are working on

large-scale renewables like hydropower, some focused on educating residents about green buildings, energy efficiency, and clean energy, others [are] into electric vehicles and alternative fuels, climate plans, and even local food. There is a lot of diversity around the state."[13]

Power within Power: Chicago Conservation Corps

Chicago is among a growing number of cities finding ways to engage and train citizens, empowering them to take direct action on the issues that are most important to them. When Chicago residents and nonprofits expressed interest in helping out on environmental issues, the Chicago Department of Environment (DOE) saw an opportunity. Rather than feeling threatened by a public horning in on its work, the DOE created the Chicago Conservation Corps (known as C3). The group motto is simple: "You Care. Do Something. We'll Help."[14]

Conservation-minded residents can contact C3, which recruits and trains volunteers and then supports the resulting projects. With the help of C3, one local group assembled and distributed three hundred weatherization kits to neighborhood residents in need. Another created a multilingual presentation in Chinatown on energy efficiency. Workshops on simplifying home recycling, composting, reducing carbon footprints, greening an office, disposing of household hazardous waste, and dozens more have sprung up all over Chicago, and they're all run by community members.

Today, these volunteers are essential to the city's environmental programs. For instance, through community action teams, volunteers train residents in energy efficiency. "The City previously used the funding for this program just to distribute kits at large, city-run events," notes Kristen Pratt, C3 project coordinator. "However, they have now redirected that funding because they see the value in community engagement and more one-on-one interaction."[15]

Similarly, C3 volunteers have been an important part of Chicago's Sustainable Backyards Program. The program focuses on issues like stormwater management, waste reduction, and air quality improvement, and to this end it offers rebates to residents who purchase compost bins, rain barrels, and native plants and trees.

C3 has grown over the years and now actually trains citizens in a rigorous twenty-hour course twice a year that covers water, air, land, and energy issues. The course also strengthens skills in areas such as recruiting volunteers and managing a budget. And, critical to ensuring that community projects endure over time, it teaches participants to map the assets of the community, to help them tap into the networks of individuals, organizations, and resources in their neighborhood that could serve as allies. Course graduates submit proposals that in turn can receive mini-grants and C3 staff support.

"I think the fact that our staff is very attuned to environmental justice issues causes us to reflect frequently and seriously upon engagement in our program," Pratt says. "We spend a lot of time providing one-on-one support to our volunteers, helping them move forward at their own pace, and building capacity where needed. We work with a lot of people who are un- or underemployed, who are not college graduates, and who are not your 'typical' environmentalists."[16] Although C3 is more culturally diverse than many other volunteer environmental programs, Pratt feels that there's always more that they can do to broaden participation in the group. She would like to see C3 education programs offered in more languages than just English, for instance.

Since the program's inception, C3 has trained over three hundred volunteers, and Chicago has had the benefit of over 350 community-based projects with representation in each of Chicago's fifty wards. C3 also supports after-school conservation clubs in eighty Chicago public schools. In these ways, C3 not only shares the power of the DOE but trains citizens to use their own power to act locally on the issues they care about most.

Power to the People: Participatory Budgeting

With communities across the United States facing deep budget cuts, leaders are looking for ways to target their spending decisions ever more precisely. They may have found it with a fast-growing technique called participatory budgeting, a process through which citizens deliberate on how to spend certain public funds, typically the discretionary portion of a city budget.

Every city needs to weigh decisions about street lighting, road resurfacing, sidewalk repairs, bike lanes, and community gardens. In participatory budgeting, rather than having the city council make the call on these and similar issues, the binding decision is made directly by the citizens.

Pioneered in 1989 in Porto Alegre, Brazil, participatory budgeting has caught on in more than 1,200 cities and towns across the world. The system has been instituted at the local level across Europe, Africa, Asia, Latin America, and Canada and has been proclaimed a "good governance practice" by the United Nations. While the United States has been comparatively slow on the uptake, the 49th Ward of Chicago adopted the process in 2009, four New York City council districts adopted it in 2011, and participatory budgeting is now being considered or implemented in a number of American cities including San Francisco, New Orleans, Providence (Rhode Island), Greensboro (North Carolina), and several communities in Massachusetts.

As participatory budgeting is typically applied, neighborhood assemblies of citizens (open to any residents in that district) take part in a gathering to discuss the city's discretionary funding options. Fixed costs like labor contracts, infrastructure responsibilities, and debt payments take up the bulk of most U.S. cities' budgets, so discretionary funds generally don't exceed 20%. However, this sum is still plenty to change daily life in a neighborhood—in many cities, it equates to millions of dollars—enough that it's well worth citizens' time to come to a meeting.

After the initial deliberation, the neighborhood assemblies choose delegates to create specific budget proposals based on their wishes. After several months of committee work, the public gets to vote on the proposals. As with traditional New England town meetings, decisions by the citizens are binding.

While far from perfect—for instance, a World Bank report notes that low-income people are empowered by the Porto Alegre process, but the very poor are still not well represented[17]—most cities report positive experiences with the process, and its use is on the rise. In San Francisco, proponents of participatory budgeting say that they prefer it to the existing dynamic, which activist Oscar Grande refers to with terms like "battles," "a lot of begging," and "deals made in the back room." Says Grande, who is with People Organizing to Demand Environmental and Economic Rights, participatory budgeting is about "opening up governments, reconnecting people with decision making, and giving them real power to make real decisions with real money, which is a fundamental break from how democracy has been run."[18]

Power Struggles, Power Clarity

The slow food movement urges us all to see ourselves as part of the food production system. As a locavore T-shirt proclaims, "Eating is an agricultural act." When we recognize our empowered role in the system, we will make more thoughtful, responsible everyday choices.

Similarly, in order for citizens to feel ownership and responsibility for democratic decisions, we need to see meaningful connection to power structures. Leaders cannot remove citizen power on the one hand and then bemoan citizen apathy on the other. When a state centralizes school boards and drains decision making from communities, that policy is about more than education; it's about power. When a state refuses to allow a city to generate its own electricity, that policy is about more than energy, or even money; it's about who decides. These policies send strong signals to citizens about their role in democracy: you are not active producers of decisions but passive consumers of policy.

Citizens hear these messages and act on them. As New England town meeting data proves, when a meeting loses its power and becomes "informational," attendance plummets. If our opinion will not be valued, we will find alternative places to spend our time. Or we may fight back.

Citizens should not be in endless combat with their elected officials. Likewise, community-based processes and state and federal representative government do not need to be continually at odds. Indeed, they should be connected, so that they support each other. Slow democracy calls for not the dissolution of existing power structures but for a reimagining—or perhaps a reminder—of their intended roles.

In a slow democracy, centralized government's job can shift from direct problem solving to supporting the decisions made by local deliberations. They can help communities coordinate with each other and play a critical role in strengthening, rather than weakening, the integrity of local decision making.

Meanwhile, citizens can be an active, savvy political base. With its energetic, oxygenated activism, such a public strengthens and legitimizes the mandate of elected officials. Local citizens can discern critical differences that distant lawmakers and bureaucrats might not pick up on, whether issues are as huge as the forests of Idaho or as small as a rainwater barrel in Chicago.

PART IV

reflections
on slow democracy

eleven

THE JURY, TOWN MEETING, AND SLOW DEMOCRACY

Many of the slow democracy practices we are describing have been in place for only a decade or less. But slow democracy is certainly not new in America. At least two deliberative institutions of direct democracy have been in place here since before the United States became a nation. These are places where citizens are not electing representatives or "advising" government but are, in fact, the government themselves. They are the American jury system and the New England town meeting.

Alexis de Tocqueville singled out both institutions for praise, not necessarily for their decisions but for their profound effects on creating good citizens. On juries, he wrote, "I do not know whether the jury is useful to those who are in litigation; but I am certain it is highly beneficial to those who decide the litigation; and I look upon it as one of the most efficacious means for the education of the people which society can employ."[1] And on town meetings: "Town meetings are to liberty what primary schools are to science; they bring it within the people's reach and teach men how to use and enjoy it."[2]

Both the jury and town meeting systems have their passionate defenders and ardent detractors. Both have received surprisingly scant attention in political deliberation studies. Both, to varying degrees, are under attack and in decline. And both are well worth a hard look in terms of what they can teach us about slow democracy.

Lessons from the New England Town Meeting

Town meetings have been taking place in New England since colonial times. These citizen assemblies that were first developed in ancient Athens sprang up again 2,300 years later along the chilly North Atlantic. By the time of the Constitutional Convention in 1787, New Englanders had been practicing town meetings for over a century.

While many governments convene citizens to hear their views, town meetings are unusual because the citizens who participate in them take binding action. Here, voters discuss, amend, and approve (or reject) budgets and policies. Like the initiative and referendum systems used in many states, voters are making policy directly; unlike these systems, they are doing so in a face-to-face assembly.

Hundreds of towns in the six New England states govern themselves with some form of town meeting.[3] However, when America moved west, town meetings did not go with it—perhaps due to more dispersed populations and geography, and also because some preferred a system of elected elites.[4]

Those unfamiliar with town meetings are often surprised by the power they afford to citizens. For years, the Vermont secretary of state's office invited secretaries of state from other parts of the United States to observe Vermont town meetings. "[I]t was as if they were viewing some curiosity," recalls former assistant secretary of state Paul Gillies. "Their reaction was fascinating. One said, 'You mean you let the people vote on the budget?' with a kind of horror, as if we aren't qualified, or at least that in other states this is simply for elective officials to decide."[5]

Town meeting research is notoriously difficult as political studies go, since rather than simply crunching voting numbers, it requires on-site observers to attend meetings that are, in many states, happening in dozens or hundreds of towns simultaneously. In 2004, University of Vermont political science professor Frank Bryan published a remarkable twenty-eight-year study of the Vermont town meeting. With the help of students who spread out across the state each year, Bryan collected and analyzed data from 1,435 town meetings held in 210 Vermont towns between 1970 and 1998. He had students observe how many men and women attended, who spoke and how often, the length of their participation, and a variety of other elements. He then compared his findings with socioeconomic data about the communities and wove meeting observations into his analysis.[6]

Bryan found that a wide variety of citizens attend and participate in town meetings. While Vermont is among the whitest states in the nation, its residents come from a range of educational, income, and cultural backgrounds. However, Bryan found no link between a town's socioeconomic indicators and its citizens' attendance at or verbal participation in its town meeting.

(This stands in stark contrast to national voting data that shows a strong socioeconomic link.) He also discovered no link between towns' socioeconomic diversity and attendance at town meetings. In addition, women (who are typically underrepresented in elected legislative bodies) made up nearly 50% of attendees. This is aggregate data, of course, and experiences differ from town to town, but Bryan's data indicate that we can be hopeful about diverse groups being willing to participate in face-to-face decision making.

The single most reliable predictor of good town meeting attendance, Bryan found, is town population size. Town meetings work better—dramatically better—in small towns than in large towns.[7] "The logic is clear," he wrote. "In a small town, your presence at town meeting counts for much more than it does in larger towns. Also, small-town people feel more responsibility to participate: Since their lives as citizens are more visible, they are better connected with each other, and they feel more needed by the community."[8]

Besides town size, the most reliable predictor of high town meeting attendance is having issues of real importance on the agenda. Bryan's town meeting data shows clearly that if citizens know that they can make a difference, they are willing to brave potentially difficult conversations.

Bryan also found that the vibrancy of the institution depended on its power. When towns switch from floor voting on money and issues ("all those in favor say 'aye'") to preprinted ballots, the meetings themselves become merely informational. Many people see no need to deliberate if they can skip the talking and simply cast a ballot. While some towns are able to maintain good participation rates even with ballot-box voting, far more see results like those of the town of North Hero. According to Bryan's research, North Hero was for years among the towns with the highest per-capita attendance and most vibrant discussions. However, the town recently voted to switch to ballot-box voting for its money issues. Voters liked the efficiency of the ballot box, and many assumed that their meeting would still retain its vibrancy. They underestimated the power of power. The following year, their attendance dropped by half, and the number of people who actually spoke dropped by two-thirds. If North Hero follows the pattern of other Vermont towns that have drained power from their deliberative process, attendance numbers will continue to decline until the meeting is meaningless.

So, town meetings feature key elements of slow democracy, in that they are local, inclusive, and empowered. How deliberative a town meeting is, however, may depend on the town and the meeting. New England town meetings are often portrayed in the national media as a warm, slow, friendly community gatherings—a Normal Rockwell-esque festival of plaid flannel and casseroles.[9] A CNN blog even recently observed, with comical inaccuracy, that "Vermont's government traditionally rules by consensus."[10] Actually, the majority still rules at town meetings. And town meetings' greatest shortcoming, according to some observers, is the quality of their deliberations. Political scientist Jane Mansbridge studied the institution in Vermont in 1983. She concluded that town meeting debate was often closed prematurely, due to deference to prominent citizens, experts, or majority opinion. In town meetings, Mansbridge did not see towns acting as "unitary" democracies based on common interests and consensus, but as "adversary" democracies, where majority rule prevailed and the interests of the less powerful were suppressed.[11]

Town meeting deliberation can certainly be improved, with a particular focus on ensuring that all voices are heard. In addition, towns can apply (and in many cases are already using) innovative deliberative techniques to engage citizens with the issues in preparation for the annual gathering. Likewise, towns need to address population growth honestly; some are simply too big for this form of government, and carrying on with it is probably doing more harm than good to the institution and its waning number of participants.

However, even with town meetings' imperfections, five out of six of the New England states (the only states where town meetings are fully practiced) rank among the top ten nationally for social capital or civil society. Vermont, where the town meeting tradition is among the strongest, usually ranks in the top three, and often first.[12] It seems possible that the way communities make decisions, year in and year out, for centuries, has a powerful effect on social capital and citizenship.

With no payment for participants (indeed, many lose a day's pay to attend), no community organizers, a publicity campaign that consists of a bulk-mailed town report with a photo of a snowplow on the cover, a volunteer facilitator with (hopefully) a few hours of training, and topics that, on average, hover around the interest level of how much to pay for gravel, town meetings still bring out hundreds of participants, in hundreds of towns across New England, *every single year.* What is going on here, and what can we learn from it?

It is worth paying special attention to the link between citizens and power. By one estimate, during a four-year presidential cycle, the citizens of a typical

Vermont town will spend an aggregate of 908 hours of their personal lives voting in elections. In contrast, that same population will spend 2,240 hours at their town meetings. Revealingly, citizens devote nearly two and a half times as many hours to governing themselves as they do to choosing others to govern them.[13] When the issues the citizens are voting on are compared (a town budget compared to electing presidents and senators—some of the most powerful people in the world), the contrast is even more intriguing.

Successful town meetings are woven into a tapestry of year-long participation. In small towns, much of the deliberative policy making is done in citizen committees—planning commissions, conservation commissions, and many other volunteer groups that meet throughout the year. The town report offers voters a year's worth of research and analysis written by their neighbors. In addition, the mutual respect people need in order to communicate well is often facilitated by long-standing, densely woven community relationships.

In tiny Belvidere, Vermont (population 340), a vibrant political exchange is often happening at Tallman's Store. As co-proprietor Myrna Tallman remarked, "Town meeting is only one day. But here at the store, it lasts at least two weeks. The week before, it's 'What I'm going to say . . .' and then the week after, it's 'What I should have said!'"[14] Myrna was only partly joking. In a town meeting culture, conversations go on all year, with a continual cycling of information and opinion. "What I should have said" at last year's town meeting becomes "what I'm going to say" the next time I see one of my local leaders, which will have an impact on what issues I'll be voting on at next year's town meeting.

Many modern dialogue and deliberation processes, with their multiday trust-building exercises and small-group discussions, seem to be an effort to substitute for 250 years' worth of barn raisings and chicken pie suppers. In a well-functioning, human-scale community, dialogue and deliberation work happen all year. Here, residents have already put their time in, and they are, as Robert's Rules says, "ready for the question."

What lessons can town meetings teach us about slow democracy?

First, size matters. Small, local deliberations are the most successful, and small communities (neighborhood-size, by many states' standards) are an ideal place to invite citizens into decision making. The burgeoning participatory budgeting movement takes a page from the town meeting book.

Power also matters. Town meeting data offers evidence that citizens will turn out regularly, year in and year out, as long as deliberations are on important issues and as long as they end in real decision making. (Merely informational meetings with no link to decision-making power—like their cousin the public hearing—have little intrinsic interest.) The data offers hope that if there is real power at stake, a range of people—not just the elite—will come.

The town meeting halls of New England offer us food for thought. And, in fact, so do the courthouses across America. Here citizens of all walks of life offer us another lesson relevant to slow democracy.

Lessons from the American Jury Experience

The origins of the American jury system date to a time when the line between church and state was just beginning to appear in England. Before the Norman Conquest in 1066, priests were assumed to be the diviner of God's will, and the only judges society needed. Over the centuries, the crown gained more authority.

However, judging individual citizens is a tricky business. The entity with the decision-making power is also a potential target of blame and rebellion. Local officials were glad to pass the buck and give citizens authority to make legal judgments. This way, notes communications scholar John Gastil, "poor judgments could now only raise doubts about the wisdom of one's fellow subjects—not judges or priests."[15] In 1671, English law gave the jury the power to render a verdict, independent of a judge, and the pendulum of power did not stop there. Over time, the jury gained enough power that it could actually oppose the state: citizens, for example, can sue the state via the jury system.

Thus, the jury system offers citizens the remarkable opportunity not only to see the judicial system up close but to be an actual, power-wielding part of it. Again, recall that most of the time, our engagement in democracy involves electing other people to govern us. When sitting on a jury, we *are* the government.

The Seventh Amendment of the U.S. Constitution ensures the right to trial by jury. Much has been written, both positive and negative, about the American justice system, but very little has been written about the experience of the juries themselves. Jurors are summoned at random, and an estimated one-third of all Americans will serve at some point in their lives. From the perspective of our democracy, what effect does this system have on the participants?

In a recent multiyear study, scholars John Gastil, E. Pierre Deess, Philip J. Weiser, and Cindy Simmons set out to evaluate citizens' experience on American juries. The researchers conducted in-depth interviews with people who had participated in juries across the United States. They paired the interview data with before- and after-trial questionnaires and surveys of thousands of jurors, and they followed up with scrutiny of voting and court records.[16] Their findings are both fascinating and heartening.

First, jury deliberations themselves seem to be of high quality. Although jury deliberations are done in private, the researchers examined jurists' recollections, the quality of their verdicts (including how they compared with those of the presiding judges), and a number of other factors. On the whole, jury deliberations received high marks. In multiple studies, participants overwhelmingly report that they had enough chances to speak, that others listened respectfully, and that they thoroughly addressed the key issues. Indeed, Gastil wrote, the jury is "perhaps the most explicitly deliberative public institution in American government."[17]

In addition, and perhaps most importantly for our democratic future, the jury experience has important impacts on participants. For instance, jury service raises voting rates. Researchers found that the aspect of jury service most related to voting rates was the deliberation. The complexity of a trial and its deliberation, rather than daunting jurors, actually increased their likelihood of voting.

Jury service proved to have a number of other valuable impacts related to slow democracy. While there were many complexities involved in these measurements, and some factors affected some subgroups more than others, researchers could say with confidence that elements of jury service often:

- Increase participants' political activity (such as in political groups, contacting officials, and campaigning)
- Improve participants' self-confidence in their political abilities
- Increase participants' faith in public institutions, including the jury system, but also the responsiveness of the political system
- Strengthen civil society by increasing participants' discussions at the local level, both political and otherwise, as well as their involvement in local community groups
- Build an informed electorate by increasing the likelihood that participants follow politics through public affairs media
- Increase participants' civic pride in themselves, as well as their faith in fellow citizens.

While the jury system has been wrought with the same forms of discrimination that the rest of the American democratic system has suffered over the centuries, it has also made similar legal advances.[18] Juries are now far more diverse than they were historically, which means a broad cross section of the public is serving as jurors, and reaping the benefits.

Studies of jurors' experience present powerful evidence that deliberative decision making makes us better citizens. From de Tocqueville to the present, defenders of democracy have claimed that democratic engagement educates us and fosters further engagement. The experience of the jurors studied here offers proof of that claim.

Perhaps the best summary came from one of the jury participants surveyed in the study:

> I truly felt that Jury Duty was the best civics lesson I've ever had. In no other way that I can think of are citizens so equally involved in the state's affairs. In daily life, our conversations and opinions rarely have serious consequences. For example, our sphere of concern may include communist China, but as joe citizen, we have zero influence. In the trial, our sphere of concern overlaps our sphere of influence and our involvement produces very real consequences. Thus, as Jurors and as citizens, we become more aware of the weight and responsibility of our decisions.[19]

All Those in Favor . . .

From town meetings, slow democracy takes a lesson on the value of "local." From jury studies, slow democracy takes a lesson on the value of deliberation. And the importance of truly empowered decision making is a lesson from both. It is no wonder that some of the most prominent new deliberative tools, like Citizens' Jury and 21st Century Town Meeting, crib their names from these venerable institutions.

But the institution of the town meeting is in trouble. As towns grow in size, many are switching away from the face-to-face floor meetings to other, more "efficient" forms of governance. Some switch to representative town meetings or a city council form of government, which at least retains deliberation among representatives.[20] Some, however, make the mistake of substituting their floor vote for a paper ballot system, eliminating deliberation altogether.

The jury system is also on the wane. Gastil notes that many countries have reduced or eliminated their use of juries; indeed, over 90% of the trials in the world are held in the United States. Meanwhile, "in the name of procedural efficiency, many U.S. courts have reduced the size and frequency of jury trials," and the percentage of criminal and civil cases that are resolved by juries is plummeting.[21] While there is much to be said for some alternative dispute resolution methods, "efficiencies" such as plea bargaining and other workarounds are, like so many "efficiencies" before them, having unintended consequences. Certainly we should consider whether this era of citizen disillusionment is a time to shut down a system that is, as Gastil writes, "a quiet engine of public engagement."[22]

Lessons from these mature democratic institutions reinforce the conviction that is already taking hold in communities across the nation: in order to improve our democracy, we should increase the number of opportunities for citizens to make meaningful deliberative decisions. Despite their flaws and restrictions, these institutions give us great reason for hope and offer inspiration for what slow democracy can look like in the decades to come.

Over and over, we hear that people are moved and transformed by taking part in these long-standing democratic practices. Perhaps it's because these institutions remind us that we are part of a community, one that stretches not only laterally, to the people seated around us, but backward in time, to a common memory and heritage that predate the republic. The solemnity and grace of the traditions remind us that democracy is inherited from our forebears, but it is up to us to pass it on, intact and even strengthened, to our descendents.

twelve

WHEN ADVOCACY MEETS
SLOW DEMOCRACY

So, inclusive, empowered deliberation is a cornerstone for sustainable communities. But what happens when community members face off with truly irreconcilable differences?

In some highly polarized situations, mediation by a neutral third party can help people with profound differences hear each other and reach settlement. Negotiation is another technique that allows disputing parties to identify some interests in common. But even these rigorous methods can't solve everything. Sometimes, when a situation is beyond talking, advocacy is the only conscionable response.

Sometimes it's a matter of time. In Gloucester, Massachusetts, Rosalyn Frontiera realized that if she didn't take immediate action, her town's water supply would be sold and irrecoverable.

Sometimes it's a matter of money. The California counties that outlawed genetically engineered seeds experienced the extraordinary resources corporate agriculture wielded as a weapon; radical political action was their only recourse.

Sometimes it's a matter of power. When state governments consolidate schools, small towns that want to keep their schools are pushed up against a wall. And cities like Boulder, Colorado, who want to create their own electrical utilities in response to climate change, have had to lobby and in some cases enter into legal battles to defend their right to do so.

And all too often it's a matter of justice. There must be some measure of equality in order for dialogue, let alone decision making, to make progress. If fundamental racial, socioeconomic, or other inequality is systemic, the system must be changed before deliberation can ever be workable. Whether through civil disobedience, litigation, polarized organizing, or other techniques, citizens need to level the field before community building can begin.

"When a people are mired in oppression, they realize deliverance when they have accumulated the power to enforce change," advised Martin Luther King Jr. ". . . The powerful never lose opportunities—they remain available to them. The powerless, on the other hand, never experience opportunity—it is always arriving at a later time."[1]

When to Talk, and When to Fight

Understandably, some activists view dialogue and deliberation methods as too "soft." Scholars Peter Levine and Rose Marie Nierras interviewed some sixty activists from at least fourteen countries about their views on public deliberation.[2] These activists' primary concern was justice.

In cases involving oppression and poverty, they argued, organizing and gaining political power had to be the first priority. Some were skeptical that the populations they worked with were ready to join in unified discourse, worrying that deliberation can favor compromise when more radical measures are necessary. As Filipino activist Joel Rocamora noted, "Deliberation privileges reasonableness."[3]

Others were concerned that the deliberative processes themselves could be set up to work to their disadvantage. This may be done inadvertently, for instance when citizens with no public deliberation experience are intimidated by the process. Or inequality may be purposefully built into the system, via manipulation by the conveners or biased agendas and information.

In some cases, deliberation is so controlled that it seems only a half measure. Jose Benedito de Oliveira of Porto Alegre, Brazil, complained that in the government's participatory budgeting process, "the people in power want to establish limits. It is like there is a party inside the house but the citizens are only in the hallway, not inside the main room where the party is being held."[4]

Many activists consider other values more dear than deliberative democracy, such as environmental conservation, economic growth, equity, or liberty. And a truly fair, deliberative democratic process has, by its very nature, an unpredictable outcome.

Each citizen will weigh for him- or herself whether it is time to talk or to fight. Each community will do the same.

Appropriately timed direct action is invaluable. But it is impossible to maintain the ecstatically intense engagement necessary for this type of intervention over the long haul. Even the strongest supporters of adversarial techniques have to ask themselves, What happens after we win? We need models for democratic engagement that will sustain us at the pace of everyday life. Here is where the investment in slow democracy—building trust, developing citizens' skills, raising expectations about the value of public problem solving, and developing civic infrastructure that will outlast any individual incident—pays off.

Keep in mind that in a balanced, functioning democratic setting, deliberation is the forum most often chosen by the underdog. It is always the feisty challenger, not the comfortable incumbent, who proposes that the candidates debate; that's because the challenger has nothing to lose and everything to gain from shaking up opinions and exposing the public to new ideas.

Likewise, citizen participation and deliberation are critical tools for heightening political equality. As political scholars Joshua Cohen and Archon Fung have argued, deliberation "blunts the power of greater resources with the force of better arguments," and participation shifts the basis of the political contest "from organized money to organized people."[5]

In almost every community, there will be a time and a place for slow democracy. Slowly but surely, people's confidence about how decisions can and should be made will improve. As society embraces higher expectations for transparent, inclusive decision making, it is our hope that slow democracy will reduce the circumstances—inequality, injustice, environmental crises—that make advocacy necessary.

One of the best examples of the dynamic balance between slow democracy and advocacy lies in the mountain ranges of the American East. Here, conservationists have built one of America's most extraordinary natural heritage icons: the Appalachian Trail. In creating and defending the trail, environmental organizers collaborated with government powers to become an irresistible force for land conservation. Their advocacy conserved an exceptional resource, but at a considerable cost to community relationships.

Then organizers made some unusual choices. Their story shows how big government can embrace a decentralized, community-based structure, and how advocacy can shift toward cooperation. It offers a glimpse of slow democracy's future.

The Appalachian Trail: A Study in Fast *and* Slow Democracy

The climb to the top of Stratton Mountain, Vermont, takes a hiker into dense woods, around rocks and brush, and, depending on the season, through mud and black flies. But climb the fire tower at the top and the view is worth it. Here at the summit on a clear, breezy day in July of 1900, a young man climbed a tree to see the blue-green mountains in the distance—and the vision for the Appalachian Trail was born.

"I felt as if atop the world, with a sort of 'planetary feeling,'" recalled the hiker, a young adventurer named Benton MacKaye. ". . . I seemed to perceive peaks far southward, hidden by old Earth's curvature. Would a footpath someday reach them, from where I was then perched?"[6]

Over 110 years after MacKaye's summit experience, much of his "planetary" vision has been realized. The Appalachian Trail, known more familiarly as the AT, now reaches from Springer Mountain in Georgia to Mount Katahdin in Maine, an extraordinary 2,180-mile footpath. The hikers who follow the trail's white blazes traverse rocky peaks and fertile valleys, agricultural and logging regions, rivers and roads. The trail passes through fourteen states, six national parks, eight national forests, and dozens and dozens of towns. Skirting America's most densely populated regions, the AT now hosts approximately two and half million visitors per year.

The Appalachian Trail, sometimes fondly referred to as America's longest, skinniest national park, is beloved as a natural oasis, a thrilling physical challenge, even a hand-hewn work of folk art. But the history of the AT is also an unlikely tale of what happens when David becomes Goliath. It is a travelogue that begins with human and natural partnerships, moves through fast democracy's world of win-lose advocacy, and then begins the surprising, slow trip back again. Here, human vision, economic need, and natural resource protection have converged, and those who love the AT are blazing a new path of slow democracy.

A Giant's Perspective

A Connecticut-born, Harvard-educated forester, Benton MacKaye spent his youth rambling the land around his family's cottage in rural Connecticut.[7] Even as a child he preferred country to city, and by age fourteen he had mapped eleven "walking expeditions" in the countryside around his house. But his vision for the Appalachian Trail would go far beyond a recreational footpath. MacKaye was an idealistic, some would say eccentric, visionary. His outdoorsman's passion for wilderness was matched by a strong socialist streak that made him fume about labor problems, overindustrialization, and militarism.

In his 1921 essay that launched the Appalachian Trail concept, MacKaye proposed a skyline path that would connect self-sufficient community farm and forest camps. Here, Easterners would come to appreciate their place in the natural world. At a moment when America's urban population had eclipsed its rural population for the first time, and city dwellers were increasingly exposed to painful realities like overcrowded tenements and factory fires, MacKaye presaged the back-to-the-land movement by some fifty years. He pushed for a "counter migration from city to country."[8]

MacKaye's sensitivity to the human condition and conviction that humans need to connect with nature were especially acute given recent events in his life. MacKaye launched the AT proposal only months after his wife of four years had committed suicide. Jessie Hardy Stubbs MacKaye, known to all as "Betty," was a well-known peace and women's rights activist. However, she had long suffered from depression, and the MacKayes often spent time in the countryside where the air, they believed, could help restore health. Tragically, a reviving trip to the country came too late; the couple was in Grand Central Station headed for the country when Betty broke away, ran to the East River, and leapt to her death.

In the 1921 essay, Benton MacKaye asked readers to imagine a giant walking along the ridgeline of his proposed route. MacKaye's giant admires the landscape and counts on his long fingers the rich natural-resource-based opportunities. From the waterways of Appalachia to the Carolina hardwoods, the giant sees potential for recreation, employment, and fresh mountain air to cure the physically and mentally ill. This giant "discerning spirit" also takes the time to look into the faces of the rugged, exhausted, and sometimes homeless workers along the way and observes that the agricultural and forest economy must be better tuned with both natural cycles and the human spirit. He envisions a trail connecting natural-resource-based communities as part of the solution.

For MacKaye, oxygen and optimism were one. He was convinced that even two weeks per year breathing fresh air on the Appalachian skyline would enrich all Easterners' understanding and create profound societal change. "Industry would come to be seen in its true perspective—as a means in life and not as an end in itself," he wrote.[9]

MacKaye's essay, and his subsequent high-level networking with professional groups and government, created excitement about his idea. In 1925, the first Appalachian Trail Conference (ATC) gathered, and an organization of the same name was established to pursue the trail concept.[10]

But constructing a footpath and creating social change are two different things. As MacKaye wrote prophetically to a friend, "It will be comparatively simple to push on the trail proper portion of our program. The main problem will be how to handle the community feature."[11]

Make Way, Coming Through

Like many visionaries, MacKaye had the ability to inspire, but only limited skills in practical organizing.[12] Eventually, other volunteers took up the AT cause—or at least the trail-building part of it. The best known was the ambitious, brilliant Myron Avery.

Avery was a hard-driving lawyer who took his hobbies as seriously as his work. He helped found the Potomac Appalachian Trail Club, in 1928 organized the second AT Conference, and by 1931 was at the ATC's helm. A stickler for standards, Avery eventually walked every mile of the Appalachian Trail, often rolling his trademark measuring wheel.

Avery continued MacKaye's networking at high levels. He also worked at the local level, but he did not favor the slow social-change tools of community mobilization or education. His efforts focused on rallying like-minded hiking enthusiasts to get the trail built. Their numbers were tiny—there were no more than two hundred working volunteers, by some estimates—but these small bands combined their local knowledge and arduous manual labor to extraordinary effect.[13] In August 1937, a mere six years after Avery became ATC chairman, the physical trail from Georgia to Maine was completed.

Avery had a reputation as a single-minded leader: one AT historian described him as getting along with everyone, as long as they agreed with him.[14] His win-at-all-costs intensity created some ill will. But for Avery and many recreationists who worked with him, the trail agenda was not ideological but practical. The goal was to construct and protect a trail, not to improve the lives of the working poor or tilt at conservationist-inspired windmills. They built the AT with the long-range vision supplied by MacKaye's "giant," but perhaps without the accompanying inclination to bend down and look into the faces of those communities whose lives they touched.

During the early days of the AT, backpacking or "tramping" was becoming popular in the Northeast. The Southeast, however, was a different story. When MacKaye made initial inquiries on behalf of the AT concept, one district forester cautioned that it would "be particularly difficult in the Southern States to popularize the idea as the recreationists are not given to hiking as a means of recreation."[15] Although southern forest supervisors promised their cooperation, the AT idea was foreign to most local communities.

While MacKaye's vision had included local and sustainable communities anchoring the trail, efforts now focused on simply securing the trail itself. The work was intense: "I don't think anyone had the capacity to think about communities at that time," says Rita Hennessy, now the assistant park manager for the Appalachian National Scenic Trail.[16] Supporters of the AT concept "loved the idea of the trail," notes Hennessy, and many were inspired by MacKaye's original vision of an "Appalachian skyline" connecting people from all walks of life with nature. But Hennessy notes that the AT boosters had little time for developing local support; they were too busy worrying about threats to the trail. While their omission may have seemed expedient at the time, it would later prove to have unintended consequences.

At that point, some 875 miles (about 40%) of the AT was protected on federal land, but other sections crossed privately owned parcels, with right-of-way secured with mere handshake agreements with the landowners. The automobile-spawned "motor slums" (now known as suburban sprawl) that MacKaye predicted were already beginning to consume the countryside. "Skyline parkway" road proposals from Congress, ski resort and second-home development, communications towers, mining, and timber extraction all threatened the AT. Over time organizers relocated multiple sections of the trail in an attempt to outrun development. But eventually, leaders realized that they needed a better-protected, broader greenway.

After several decades of advocates' pressure, Congress officially designated the Appalachian Trail as the first "National Scenic Trail" in 1968. By that point, roughly half of the AT was located on private property or on roads. The new law included a provision for states to acquire that private property; if they did not do so, the National Park Service was authorized to protect the AT in any way it deemed necessary, whether through land acquisition, exchange, donation, or eminent domain. Still, land protection moved slowly. In 1977, with about 59% of the trail protected by virtue of being on public land, AT advocates won congressional authorization for $90 million in land acquisition funds. Congress also multiplied by five the number of acres per trail mile the U.S. Department of the Interior had the authority to protect; and it required that the trail acquisition be substantially complete within a wildly ambitious three years.

The new federal power and money transformed the role of AT supporters almost beyond recognition. Paradoxically, what had begun with a rustic visionary and a tiny band of ax-wielding trail-builders was now a polished, well-funded land acquisition machine. The National Park Service trail acquisition office (which today has eight staff) grew to include three different offices and forty-five employees, plus two to three times that many additional surveyors, appraisers, and other private contractors.[17] The National Park Service team acquired or negotiated easements on some 2,500 parcels. Although the original deadline proved unrealistic, by 2000, 99% of the designated land had been protected.[18] The AT and its buffer corridor now encompass a quarter of a million protected acres.

From the perspective of the organizers, the Appalachian Trail is one of the most successful single-park land acquisition programs in the entire national park system. But the story at the local level might be told differently.

"Under the Gun"

Relocation and federal protection of the AT often sparked virulent local resentment. Although small, local hiking clubs supported the trail, members of the general public often resisted the idea of the federal government taking over private land in their town and did not feel their local concerns were being respected or even heard.

"It was like we were a highway coming through," says Hennessy. "The thing that was missing was that we never took the time to ask, 'what does this section of trail *mean* to Sheffield, Massachusetts or to Hot Springs, North Carolina?'" Hennessy notes that there were public hearings, "but they weren't enough. They aren't the venue to have that conversation."[19]

Longtime ATC executive director David Startzell was active in AT land acquisition in the 1980s.[20] Recalling "countless" public hearings, Startzell notes that too often, public hearings are "not conversational; they're confrontational." Startzell favors smaller focus groups representing different points of view. "But the trouble is," he says, "you need an understanding of the community to begin with. And we didn't have that necessarily." The three-year deadline was looming, and the National Park Service was working on land acquisition in as many as nine or ten states at a time. "We all felt like we were under the gun," Startzell recalls.

Citizens pushed back. The biggest controversies were in communities where the AT was being relocated. In public meetings, one resident compared the federal land acquisition program to Civil War troops marching through their community. Startzell recalls another hearing participant testifying, "The National Park Service is like the Mafia. They grab you by the balls and they squeeze and they squeeze."

One afternoon after negotiations with a farmer on land that would be added to the AT in Viginia, park manager Pamela Underhill drove away from the farm in a federal vehicle, only to have the tires come flying off the car. It was clear that someone had deliberately loosened the lug nuts on the wheels. Underhill was nearly killed.

Lack of engagement with local citizens' interests had additional spillover effects. In some areas, local resentment poisoned hikers' experience. AT trail-head signs were vandalized. Hikers' cars were broken into and tires slashed. And longtime hikers have all heard frightening stories of being harassed by local residents—including one often-circulated horror story of fishhooks being hung across the trail at eye level.

Limited communication only added to misunderstandings. Recent decades have seen an increase in thru-hikers—the name for those making the challenging end-to-end AT trek, usually taking five to seven months. Thru-hikers bring back stories of wilderness trekking, personal achievement, and new friendships, but local residents can be understandably wary. The hikers often emerge from the woods wild-haired, unshaven, wearing huge backpacks and smelling like unwashed socks. Says Hennessy, "People think they are vagabonds." Recalling a controversial AT relocation in suburban New Jersey, Hennessy notes that some neighbors "didn't want these people in their backyards—they were afraid their kids would be kidnapped."

A final wake-up call about the need for community engagement came with the results of a natural and cultural resource inventory of the new land acquired for the AT. The Park Service was astounded by what they discovered. Some 360 plant or animal species listed at the state level as rare, threatened, or endangered live along the AT, along with another nine federally listed species and more than eighty species that are globally rare. Also on AT land is South Mountain, Maryland, the site of a turning point in the Civil War, and Brown Mountain Creek, Virginia, home to the first freed black community in the United States, and the list goes on. The land that had been acquired simply as a buffer for the AT was in fact a necklace of cultural and ecological jewels.

"The local value and local stories became clear to us," says Hennessy. A managerial culture shift was needed, with more focus on the local. It was once again time for MacKaye's giant to look closely at the communities and individuals who resided along the trail.

In the last decade, Appalachian Trail organizers have taken a more comprehensive look at the relationship between the AT and the communities it passes through. Three new programs—in community development, youth involvement, and citizen-based scientific research—are all designed to remind community members that the AT is their own. The new AT programming is a promising example of how sides once pitted against each other in the advocacy stage can come together and move forward with sincere cooperation. It's a study in the creative application of slow democracy.

Trail Communities: (Re)connecting Place with Power

Unicoi County in eastern Tennessee is practically synonymous with the Appalachian Mountains. Until recently, however, there was little positive connection between Unicoi residents and the AT itself.

About half of Unicoi County was already in public ownership when, in recent years, the huge Rocky Fork land protection project succeeded in acquiring and protecting an additional 9,600 acres, partly for use by the AT. The project was divisive and political. Traditional extractive land uses such as mining and timber were in decline, and now the federally protected land would be unavailable for development as gated communities, golf courses, or industrial parks. Residents worried about how they would feed their families.

"People felt like, 'The government took my land,'" says Julie Judkins, community program manager at the Appalachian Trail Conservancy (ATC). "And let's face it, they're right."[21]

The Unicoi-AT relationship has begun to improve, however, in part thanks to the first prong of the ATC's new approach, the Appalachian Trail Community program.

Residents of any town or county along the AT can apply to be a part of the program. Designated towns receive a host of benefits, including support for sustainable economic development initiatives. The initiatives are designed to help trail communities take advantage of the economic opportunities provided by the AT, which draws hikers, tourists, and other recreationists from all over the country. The program provides towns with training and facilitates information exchange with other trail communities, so that each can see what others are doing. The program also provides free training for teachers in its partner communities, with tools to inspire schools to make full use of the AT as an educational resource.

The Appalachian Trail Community process invites towns to create a diverse advisory committee of hikers and people from local government, business, tourism, and education. Towns are invited to host an annual celebration or other trail-related project, to launch a trail-based education program with the schools, and to protect the AT in local land use plans and ordinances. Indeed, the application process serves as de facto community organizing, helping each town determine its own AT-related goals and create inclusive local teams to achieve them.

Although hiking groups, forest managers, and other community partners can initiate the partnership process, Judkins notes that "a lot of applications come from within the town, which we consider a great success. Officials come and go. The people in the community are the ones who tell the story." Communities are finding that the partnerships they're creating improve communication among citizens and participating organizations such as town government, businesses, the U.S. Forest Service, and the National Park Service. The communication builds local capacity for communities and land managers to find creative solutions to land issues.

In the case of Unicoi County, when the community decided it would focus on sustainable economic development, the ATC and other partners sent a team of area residents to a weeklong workshop on balancing nature and commerce. There, government officials, business leaders, and community members who had most recently seen each other from opposite sides of contentious public hearings came together to find common ground. At the workshop, participants heard from other regions that had successfully marketed themselves as recreation destinations. Trainings on marketing, bed-and-breakfast networks, and other techniques highlighted both the natural resource and economic assets of Unicoi County. Ralph Knoll of the Conservation Fund was an event cosponsor. He recalls, "After the workshop, was everyone totally on board? No." But more importantly, he says, they came to see each other as partners rather than adversaries.[22]

The Appalachian Trail Community program is still in its early years, but the robust response indicates that it is a match with local interests. Some twenty-seven communities are already involved, and if participants' enthusiasm is any indication, more towns will be coming on board regularly.

"We're trying to adapt to unique and diverse community needs," says Judkins, "It's just unfortunate we didn't do it sooner."

A Trail to Every Classroom

The ATC and the National Park Service are also helping schools turn the AT into an educational resource. The next generation of stewards is being fostered through the Trail to Every Classroom (TTEC) professional development program for teachers of kindergarten through grade 12. More than just a field-trip destination, the AT is used across the curriculum to link science, math, and social studies to local trails and forests. One of the TTEC schools is in rural Blairsville, Georgia, located in a county with thirty-five miles of Appalachian Trail.

"All up and down southern Appalachia, you'll find kids who don't have a sense of what a great resource they live near," says Blairsville middle school principal Donnie Kelley. Kelley grew up in rural Appalachia, and he notes that some of the youth in this area spend time outdoors fishing, hunting, or riding ATVs, but he is concerned that many young people have little sense of responsibility for the natural world.[23] And this region has seen troubling cases of poaching and even arson on public forestlands.

Kelley adds that some area residents are less than "hiker friendly." In an area where residents had already experienced local disruption caused by the Tennessee Valley Authority and other federal programs, Kelley feels that residents may not feel animosity toward the Appalachian Trail per se, but they mistrust any "outside" entities that change their access to land for traditional uses. He is confident that by building people's understanding of the AT resource, more area residents will appreciate that the public resources are theirs to protect.

At Kelley's school, interest in the AT has caught on: the physical science teacher brings students to the AT for hands-on studies, for instance, and the art teacher has used it as a focus of a student art show. And naturally, the school's hiking club will be using the trail for work projects.

By its seventh year, TTEC had reached an estimated 275 teachers and, by extension, some twenty thousand students. Not only has such place-based education been proven to improve test scores, but teachers report that it awakens students' curiosity, enthusiasm, and sense of personal potential to contribute to their community.[24] The AT passes through some 165 school districts—that's a lot of potential place-based education.

MEGA-Transect: Hands-On Citizen Science

The third prong of the ATC and National Park Service's effort to engage the public in co-managing the trail's natural resources, the MEGA-Transect Project, invites hikers to monitor the health of the high-elevation AT corridor. "Transect" is a scientific term describing measurements taken along a line. The AT—a line from Georgia to Maine—offers a wealth of information.

The National Park Service and other scientific partners have developed monitoring protocols for volunteer citizen-scientists to collect data on climate change and rare species. Volunteers also work on heritage-species restoration projects, like that for the American chestnut, among other projects. In the end, the project helps deepen citizens' connection to the AT, and, since much of the AT is in higher altitudes and more fragile areas, where the effects of climate change can be most obvious, the information they collect about the health of plants and air and water quality can serve as a sort of early warning system for the Eastern seaboard and its 120 million inhabitants. In addition, the AT is oriented along the north-south line on which scientists predict species will migrate as they respond to climate change, which makes the MEGA-Transect data even more relevant.

David Startzell notes that reading about bird migrations or air quality is one thing, but "we think it's another thing when people learn about that first-hand by actually helping to collect that information." The MEGA-Transect Project inspires people to recognize the power they can have in environmental protection. "Part of our hope is that as people become more aware of trends affecting those lands, they'll be motivated to take action," Startzell said, "whether that means switching to a hybrid car or just conducting their own way of life in a little more energy efficient manner, or . . . advocating for more open space."[25]

Expanding the Base, Distributing the Power

From an outside perspective, AT supporters' commitment to broadening citizen support could be seen as self-serving, and to an extent that is correct. Expanding interest from an aging core of largely upper-class outdoors enthusiasts to include educators, businesses, families, and multicultural interests is in keeping with a larger question that environmental groups everywhere are grappling with: how to remain relevant in a sea of demographic changes.

In the past, environmental successes have been achieved primarily through transactional power: purchasing land, strengthening laws, and building environmental institutions. However, many people now see the conservation movement as an entrenched, elite power structure that does not invite diversity or new ideas.[26] As trainers at the Center for Whole Communities point out, new environmental leadership styles must focus more on inclusion and building understanding across cultures.[27]

The new AT programs rank inclusion and communication priorities high, but from a democratic perspective, they go one step further. Each program expands on the underlying AT management philosophy: empowering local citizens to take charge of their section of the trail.

Appalachian Trail management is a balance. On the one hand, the overarching goal of trail protection—fought for by advocates and passed by Congress—is nonnegotiable. On the other hand, supporters are committed to finding the best ways to pursue these conservation goals with local people and local decision making.

Pamela Underhill, the National Park Service's park manager for the entire AT, has worked on the trail for thirty-three years. She recalls that when federal land protection moneys were allocated, "I was naive enough to believe that we were protecting the trail for all time. It only dawned on me slowly that we were only putting a marker in the sand—that the true long-term protection of the trail depended on communities valuing it."[28]

Since the AT's inception, handshakes had informally bound together the ATC, local volunteers, government, and landowners. The partnership became more formal in 1984, after the federal government had invested millions of dollars in corridor protection, when the National Park Service and the ATC signed an agreement entrusting the ATC with the management of the trail. Startzell recalls that when the ATC began formal collaborations with federal agencies, one legislator warned him ominously, "Now that you've invited the feds in, they may well take over." Startzell now notes happily, however, that local engagement is alive and well.[29]

The Appalachian Trail cooperative management agreement is one-of-a-kind—unique in the history of American public lands. The opposite of a power grab, it is a power give. Here, a vast and valuable national resource is managed primarily by a nonprofit membership organization, with community volunteers making most of the decisions and doing most of the work. Citizens' efforts on the AT are inclusive, deliberative, and to a remarkable degree empowered.

While the National Park Service retains control over certain trail management decisions—for instance, regarding additional land acquisition and law enforcement—most policies and procedures are delegated to the ATC. The ATC creates trail design and maintenance standards and in turn empowers its thirty-one local trail clubs to create management plans ensuring their sections of the trail and surrounding lands are cared for. Each club creates its own governance structure and has considerable autonomy. Some 6,200 active local volunteers contribute two hundred thousand hours annually to maintain the trail. The labor is donated and draws on those who know their local places best.

Hawk Metheny, the ATC's New England regional director, began as a trail volunteer and in twenty-two years has worked at every level of trail management. He describes AT management as a three-legged stool: the ATC, the government agency relevant to the local parcel (such as the national or state park or forest service), and the local volunteer trail club. According to Metheny, "It really comes down to relationships . . . so it's inclusive almost to a fault." Local power is important, he notes: "It's really the fuel that makes it all work."[30]

Body, Heart, and Soul

Beginning with Benton MacKaye's dream of a skyline utopia, the Appalachian Trail evolved into a beloved, boots-on-the-ground footpath. But with AT advocates focused by necessity on trail protection, there was little energy left for the community-to-community connections MacKaye dreamed of. No relationship can suffer neglect forever; something had to change.

If it was going to last, the Appalachian Trail was probably destined to be governed by slow democracy. It began as, and has always remained, a partnership—a complex, sometimes uneasy, but ultimately successful collaboration necessitated by the range of parties involved.

Startzell is quick to note that in some cases, new local support for conservation has been as much a factor of a decline in the logging and mining economy as it has of the ATC's partnership efforts. Even if they had used a more collaborative stance in the '70s and '80s, trying to team with communities on trail protection, they might not have been as well received as such efforts have been in today's economy. But ultimately—whether undertaken earlier or later—slow, interdependent partnerships are integral to the maintenance of the trail.

"We simply can't buy everything that we want to have influence over," says Startzell. Future AT conservation efforts, he says, "will involve multiple partners and multiple sources of funds, but we'll do it in a community-based way. Yes, there is a real benefit to community connection."[31]

And AT management has an accent on "slow." While the AT and its surrounding buffer lands have an obvious role as a home for songbirds and a haven for stressed-out urbanites, the lands also offer more subtle values. Scientists call them "ecosystem services": ecological functions critical to fresh water cycles, air quality, soil fertility, and species diversity, as well as to mitigating noise and thermal pollution. These services are invisible, and their payback time is long; in the timeline of the natural world, these processes are the embodiment of slow.

Likewise, thousands of acres of the AT buffer lands serve as richly productive agricultural property, leased to farm vegetable crops, cattle, chickens, and the like, as well as for syrup production from over a thousand maple sugar taps. As Woody Tasch made eminently clear in his book *Slow Money*, investors in sustainable agriculture and soil fertility endeavors need patience measurable not by individuals, but by generations. Just as the AT protects long-term ecosystem services, its protection of agricultural land embodies the "slow" ethic.

Meanwhile, experiencing the Appalachian Trail itself is an object lesson in leisurely pacing. Toward the end of Benton MacKaye's long life, when he was frequently consulted as something of a sage, MacKaye expressed dismay with some AT hikers' interest in setting speed and distance records. "I hope the AT will never become a race track," he wrote. "But if so, I for one would vote to give the prize to the *slowest* traveler."[32]

In the trail's early decades, AT builders focused on the "body" of the trail—the land and natural resources that make up the physical trail experience. But this focus on the body needed corresponding attention to the spirit. The ATC emphasis in the twenty-first century is shifting to the heart and soul of the Appalachian Trail—the "heart" being the many thousands of walkers and hikers who use the trail, and the "soul" being the volunteers who maintain local sections.[33] Part of that shift means working directly with the communities through which the trail passes, inviting citizens to view their relationship to the trail as it truly is: one of democratic co-ownership. Today, like the proverbial blind men describing different parts of the elephant, individuals experience the trail as a reflection of their personal values: a physical challenge, a natural immersion experience, a chain that connects communities, a historical treasure.

Democratically speaking, in many ways the Appalachian Trail story has not followed a linear path but has traveled full circle. Linking the trail to towns' civic traditions and citizens' sense of place is a natural extension of the AT's original, Benton MacKaye–inspired vision.

Has MacKaye's vision been manifested—a vast mountaintop refuge where "cooperation replaces antagonism, trust replaces suspicion, emulation replaces competition"?[34] Not quite. But as a sturdy, hand-hewn chain that links collaborative, people-powered communities, it's a strong start.

CLOSING THOUGHTS:
THE ECOLOGY OF SLOW DEMOCRACY

When two different ecosystems connect, surprising things can happen Ecologists call such meetings "ecotones": the extraordinarily diverse, productive zones where unlike systems meet. Those brushy edges where field and forest meet are the best places to find songbirds. And where the water meets the land, we find wetlands, the breeding grounds and nurseries for an enormous variety of land and marine animals.

In communities where diverse citizens are empowered to make connections and make change, amazing things emerge. The local food and local economy are linked by farmers' markets, CSAs, and local restaurateurs. Educators, parents, and taxpayers find that they can act on common goals. Environmentalists working with loggers discover that their land protection goals can be met with collaborative strategies.

Living in these places of connection means doing things differently. When we open up a deliberative process or challenge traditional decision-making structures, we are often warned that we're "getting into the weeds." Staying on the efficient, well-trodden route has its advantages, but as ecologists know, exploring "the weeds" can open new possibilities.

Environmental scholar John Elder has noted that these "edge" places are exceptionally rich, with more species and denser populations than either of the ecosystems surrounding them; but also, since their boundaries are continually moving, ecotones can be dicey places to inhabit.[1] We who make our homes in the ecotones of communities need to be open and alert, ready to say "yes" to fresh ideas, as well as to loosen our grasp on old tools that may not suit the changing environment.

We are not utopians. We're aware that there are some issues on which we will not agree, and some perspectives about which we can never say "yes." But we agree with Parker J. Palmer in his practical assessment in *Healing the Heart of Democracy*:

> I am not chasing the fantasy that some day we will "all get along."
> Given human nature and the nature of politics, there will always be
> people with whom dialogue is impossible—and on some days I am

one of them. Suppose that those who can never be reached comprise 15 or 20 percent of both the right and the left, roughly the proportion of my own extended family with whom I cannot talk politics! That leaves 60 to 70 percent of us who *can* learn to talk across our differences; in a democracy, that is more than enough to save the day.[2]

In Vermont, the House Natural Resources and Energy Committee is working on a proposal to increase significantly the generation of renewable electricity over the next fifteen years. The committee invited climate change expert Bill McKibben to testify. Well known as the author of *The End of Nature*, which sounded the alarm about climate change, McKibben is founder of the activist group 350.org.

McKibben told legislators that the consequences of climate change, including drought, flood, and other natural disasters, have exceeded scientists' expectations and described a dire scenario if we don't take immediate action. Although action on a national, and ideally global, scale is clearly necessary, McKibben made the case that action at the local level was also part of the climate change solution.

"Vermont obviously by itself cannot make this happen," he told lawmakers. "By the same token, that argument is true of every single jurisdiction considering this stuff as well. If everyone takes that excuse, then nothing will happen. If some places are wise enough to take a leadership position, not only will they be setting themselves up more wisely for the century now dawning, they'll also at least be running the possibility of providing the example to others."

McKibben noted that even on issues of global importance, small-scale action has advantages. "Thank heavens that at least in Vermont the discussion can go on with some kind of level playing field, where the fossil fuel industry doesn't so dominate every discussion that it doesn't get off the ground. If there's any justification for small states and citizen government, this is one of those moments when we really need them to rise to the fore."[3]

Slow democracy creates a nourishing environment in which connections can emerge—connections that, in our drive for efficiency, we might have skimmed over in the past. Starting with a cautious "yes"—mingling with "others," perhaps wary, but at least curious and open—can bring forth surprising connections. With slow democracy, we enter that promising edge-place of creative change. The discoveries of slow democracy may be our last, best chance for the future.

We can't recommend one perfect tool, technique, or "best recipe" for slow democracy. There isn't one, any more than there is one best recipe for bread. Every community is unique, and local ingredients differ. However, we can offer some general guidelines and encourage you to explore on your own. Here are twenty reminders that can help make slow democracy work in your community.[1]

1. **Start with the assumption that local government is a "we," not a "they."** The root word of democracy, *demos*, means "the people." Your local government is yours to support, assist, or, if necessary, repair. We're all in this together.

2. **Avoid "drive-through" democracy.** An inclusive, deliberative process takes time to prepare and to carry out—as it should, if it wields power. If you're a leader, leave time for preparation and outreach. If you're a citizen, expect well-run democratic processes to take time.

3. **Make strange bedfellows.** The more inclusive and diverse your process, the more durable the decisions will be. Keeping in mind the lessons of cultural cognition (see chapter 5), remember to frame for inclusion and consider how you'll meet the goals of various cultural worldviews. Some key reminders:
   - Include expertise and sound information.
   - Show how your process will end in clarified choices or even consensus.
   - Allow and honor dissent, and if necessary create a way for people to participate anonymously (for instance, via surveys and some online methods).
   - Celebrate community.

   Once you've done that, look around and ask yourself: Who's not here, and how can we welcome them in?

4. **Involvement doesn't begin with the event.** In fact, involvement creates the event. Ideally, people from all interest areas in the community will be involved in every aspect of democratic engagement, from process design and recruiting for events to researching information, making decisions, and implementing of ideas. (See chapter 7.)

5. **Define your purpose, then design your process.** Identify and clearly define goals (preferably with a diverse group) before engaging the public in broad-based deliberation. Is this a process of exploration? Conflict transformation? Decision making? Or collaborative action? Choose a process to meet your deliberative goals.[2] (See chapter 9.)

6. **Match the technique to the goals.** Don't make the mistake of becoming enamored with a particular process, then trying to use it to meet goals it was not designed for. Different techniques work for different goals; a good facilitator can help you make the right match. (See chapter 9.)

7. **If you already know the answer, don't ask the question.** In other words: please don't enlist participation for participation's sake. Citizens should be included early enough in decision making for them to be able to generate new options. (See chapter 10.)

8. **Some things take a professional.** A good facilitator will work with you to define your goals and create a meeting plan to meet those goals. He or she will also have the skills to ensure that no one dominates the meeting and all views are heard. Facilitation skills are particularly important if the gathering will be especially large or divisive. (See chapter 9.)

9. **Develop local abilities.** In many cases, a facilitator will work with you to train a team of local people to facilitate small-group discussions, so that you have strengthened your community's capacity to have more, similar events later. This is what happened in Portsmouth, New Hampshire (see chapter 4), and many other deliberative community events.

10. **Find (or be) a neutral convenor.** The convenor of a slow democracy process may—or may not—be the local government itself. If there isn't sufficient trust, a multiperson steering committee with representatives from the different community sectors or factions can be a great way to go. (See chapter 7.)

11. **Choose rules and then follow them.** Take your pick—there are many options, from parliamentary procedure to consensus and beyond— but choose a decision-making process and then abide by it. One of the most typical downfalls of community organizations is the belief that because they are founded on common interest, they can operate like a friendship. Don't underestimate the value of accountability and record keeping if you want to *stay* friendly. (See chapter 9.)

12. **Use your power gauge.** Who makes the decision? Make sure you, and everyone involved, is clear about the process and their role in it. (See chapter 10.)

13. **Show the road map of decision making at every meeting.** Where are we now, and where is this meeting in the process? This will help participants pace themselves and understand where involvement is most critical. (See chapter 9.)

14. **Tell the story of power and change.** Provide open access to information involved in the process—minutes, lists of attendees, informational materials. But don't just assume that everyone will follow the issue or the process. Keep people posted, either individually or in public communication, and specifically show how public participation made a difference in decisions and outcomes. It will all add up to making the process transparent, trustworthy, and empowering. (See chapter 9.)

15. **Open up and let go.** Inclusive engagement means giving new participants real responsibilities and sharing power. Otherwise, communities wind up suffering from "STP" syndrome—the Same Ten People doing everything, because new participants did not feel included. (See chapter 10.)

16. **Democracy is a long-term relationship.** With every decision, consider the impact that the decision-making process will have on citizen confidence, once the issue of the day has come and gone. Work to create a diverse coalition made up of people who are as dedicated to the democratic process as they are to any one issue—a coalition that can continue to promote democratic engagement in your community.

17. **Make connections.** Productively link the outcomes of your efforts to others' efforts. (See chapter 4.)

18. **Come full circle.** Leave time for evaluation. Both among participants and in the broader community, ask how the process is going and how you can do better. Give yourself a chance to learn from your mistakes. (See chapter 9.)

19. **Require a democratic impact statement.** (See chapter 10.) Okay, there is no such form, but perhaps there should be. Just as we consider the environmental and economic impacts of all new policies, we should consider their long-term effects on inclusive, deliberative, empowered democracy.

20. **Celebrate your successes, and celebrate your community.** After all, as we learned from environmental educators, you have to love a thing before you will work to save it (see chapter 6). Take the time to appreciate your community and its decision making. It may be slow, but it's worth it.

The number of organizations and publications dealing with local, deliberative democracy is growing every day. For starters, we offer a small sampling here.

Organizations

National Coalition for Dialogue and Deliberation

NCDD represents dialogue and deliberation practitioners and scholars from a wide variety of fields. NCDD hosts conferences, creates educational materials, and facilitates online and in-person professional networking. NCDD's online resource center offers over 2,600 resources for dialogue, deliberation, and public engagement. Here you can find descriptions and links to books, articles, case studies, evaluation tools, videos, organizations, and foundations. www.ncdd.org

Canadian Community for Dialogue and Deliberation

C2D2 is a Canadian organization of individuals and organizations dedicated to creating vibrant communities, businesses, governments, nonprofits, and learning institutions through dialogue, deliberation, collaborative action, and decision-making processes. www.C2D2.ca

Deliberative Democracy Consortium

A network of practitioners and researchers of deliberative democracy that has developed new tools, assembled new networks, and assisted federal agencies. Listserv offers ongoing updates on the dialogue and deliberation field. Together with IAP2 (below), it publishes the Journal of Public Deliberation. www.deliberative-democracy.net

International Association for Public Participation

IAP2 is a networking, research, and advocacy organization. Among other things, IAP2 offers a certificate training course in public participation, and together with the Deliberative Democracy Consortium (above), it publishes the Journal of Public Deliberation. www.IAP2.org

National League of Cities

NLC is dedicated to helping city leaders build better communities. In addition to its advocacy and programs, it offers a variety of leadership and community-engagement-related studies, publications, and other resources. www.nlc.org

League of Women Voters

LWV is a nonpartisan political organization that encourages the informed and active participation of citizens in government, works to increase understanding of major public policy issues, and influences public policy through education and advocacy. LWV offers a wealth of resources for local LWV chapters to use in their consensus or concurrence processes, through which they research and take positions on issues. www.lwv.org

Everyday Democracy

The goal of Everyday Democracy's programs and services is to help create communities that work better for everyone because all voices are included in public problem solving, and to link that work to creating a stronger democracy. Creator of the Study Circles dialogue and deliberation process, Everyday Democracy offers community assistance, training, and a variety of tools and techniques. Find resources at www.everyday-democracy.org.

Kettering Foundation

Kettering is a nonprofit foundation focusing on what it takes to make democracy work as it should. It does not make grants but engages in joint research. It also produces issue books and videos for the National Issues Forum deliberations. Look for the group's research findings (books, research papers, videos) as well as its three periodicals (Connections, Higher Education Exchange, and Kettering Review) on its website. www.kettering.org

Orton Family Foundation

The Orton Family Foundation helps small cities and towns, primarily in the Northeast and the Rocky Mountain West, harness the inherent ability of citizens to imagine and achieve a better future for themselves and their communities. Through its Heart and Soul Community Planning process, the Foundation promotes inclusive, proactive decision making and land use planning by offering guidance, tools, research, capital, and other support to selected communities. Implementation guides and other tools are available at www.orton.org.

Davenport Institute for Public Engagement and Civic Leadership

The Davenport Institute is housed within Pepperdine University's School of Public Policy, with the purpose of promoting citizen participation in California governance. Case studies and technological innovations are featured on the institute's civic engagement blog at http://publicpolicy.pepperdine.edu /davenport-institute/incommon/index.php.

Publications

For a comprehensive list of engagement methods, see Peggy Holman, Tom Devane, and Steven Cady, *The Change Handbook: The Definitive Resource on Today's Best Methods for Engaging Whole Systems* (San Francisco: Berrett-Koehler Publishers, 2007).

For a comprehensive survey of the field of deliberative democracy, see John Gastil and Peter Levine, eds., *The Deliberative Democracy Handbook* (San Francisco: Jossey-Bass, 2005).

For a valuable assessment of online engagement tools and the goals they are best suited for, see Matt Leighninger, "Using Online Tools to Engage—and Be Engaged by—the Public," from the IBM Center for the Business of Government at http://www.businessofgovernment.org/report /using-online-tools-engage-public.

Recommended facilitation guides include:

Sam Kaner, *Facilitator's Guide to Participatory Decision-Making* (Gabriola Island, B.C.: New Society Publishers, 1998)

Sandy Schuman, *IAF Handbook of Group Facilitation: Best Practices from the Leading Organization in Facilitation* (San Francisco: Jossey-Bass, 2005)

Roger Schwartz, *The Skilled Facilitator: A Comprehensive Resource for Consultants, Facilitators, Managers, Trainers, and Coaches*, 2nd ed., (San Francisco: Jossey-Bass, 2002)

acknowledgments

Many colleagues, friends, and even complete strangers answered our call for help in pulling together this book.

The real story of slow democracy is told by the many community members who are engaged in local decision making; we thank them for their dedication to community, and for sharing their experiences with us.

We would like especially to acknowledge our research assistants. The inimitable Sharon Dinitz was part of the process almost from the beginning, brainstorming, finding case studies, researching, fact checking, and making incisive suggestions on the text. She was a source of inspiration throughout. Monarch Fite gamely ventured on a kind of scholarly heroine's journey, taking on impossible research questions and returning with all kinds of fascinating and relevant sources; her curiosity and sense of possibility were invaluable assets.

We cannot thank enough the library staff at Union Institute and University: Tess Zimmerman, for her patience and good humor with our many interlibrary loan requests; Susan Whitehead, for her research strategies and for tracking down hard-to-find sources; and Lynda Howells, for answering those all-too-frequent calls for technical help.

For ongoing encouragement, sage counsel, and a bracing perspective, we thank Frank Bryan.

For their insights and guidance, our deep appreciation goes to John Gastil, Matt Leighninger, and Martha McCoy. Their kind cooperation does not necessarily indicate any endorsement on their part of the view put forward by the authors.

For terrific ideas and networking, thanks to Sandy Heierbacher and the members of the National Coalition for Dialogue and Deliberation Listserv, including Elizabeth Kennedy-Wong, Jennifer Hurley, and Tim Bonnemann.

For valuable case study ideas, thanks to the Robert and Patricia Switzer Foundation and members of the Switzer Fellowship Network, including Lisa J. Bunin, Chris Greacen, Betsy Herbert, Hugh Hogan, John Hultgren, Marcy Lyman, Helena Meryman, Susan Ornelas, Steve Parry, Kristen Pratt, Roger Smith, Dipti Vaghela, and David Wiley.

Our appreciation also goes to the Middlesex (Vermont) School Board, Selectboard, and Solutions Committee for their hard work, creativity, and willingness to engage with citizens.

Thanks to editor Joni Praded for her sound advice, and to the other skilled professionals at Chelsea Green including Bill Bokermann, Pati Stone, and Shay Totten and his team Jillian Leclerc, Jenna Stewart, and Lorenne Gavish.

Well after this book got under way, we came across a chapter called "A Call for Slow Democracy" in Andrea Batista Schlesinger's *The Death of "Why?" The Decline of Questioning and the Future of Democracy* (San Francisco: Berrett-Kohler, 2009). In it, Schlesinger decries "fast politics" and notes, "We can begin to define transparency as openness rather than immediacy. We can demand that we build in time for questions" (209). We were delighted to discover a kindred spirit.

Woden would like to thank:

Ann Armbrecht, for her unflinching clarity, which keeps me honest.

Ben Williams, for the hallway conversations, inspiration, and offers of help that I should have taken you up on.

Brian Webb, Kris Wells, and Debra Denison, for making me laugh and for tolerating the groans and sighs from my office.

Tasha Forest, for her flexibility, sense of humor, and general delightfulness.

Mary and Peter Teachout, for being such generous parents and inspired grandparents.

Alyssa, Waylon, Jed, Celia, Angus, Garth, and Lise, for bringing me so much joy.

And Mark, for everything.

Susan offers these thanks:

For thoughtful reading and encouragement, Susan Palmer, Kathleen Hentcy, and Tim Traver. For skilled attention to detail, Linda Belt-Burnier. For professional inspiration, Kelly Young, Susan McCormack, Deena Frankel, Sharon Behar, Lisa Bedinger, Heidi Klein, and the others in the On The Rise public engagement group. Also, thanks to the courageous Sorsha Anderson and Margaret Maclean, and the magnifique Manon Abud.

Like so many of the finest examples of citizen engagement on the planet, our Appalachian Trail example was inspired by the remarkable facilitator and place-based educator Delia Clark. Thank you, Delia, for being such a great colleague, sister, and soulmate.

Mark Bushnell, talented editor, journalistic sleuth, honest critic, listening ear, and wiseacre, you're the best friend and husband I could ever wish for.

Harrison Onward Clark Bushnell, don't worry, I won't take this opportunity to lay the burden of making slow democracy a reality on you and your generation. I'll just say that your positive spirit and sense of justice make my heart sing. And thank you for wishing we'd just be *done* writing this book; your inspiration kept me going.

notes

Introduction

1. Marilyn Alva, "World's Largest McDonald's Opens to Big Crowds in Rome; Some Call New 425-Seat Unit the 'Death of Italian Cuisine,'" *Nation's Restaurant News*, May 5, 1986, http://findarticles.com/p/articles/mi_m3190/is_v20/ai_4234025/?tag=content;col1.
2. From the Slow Food International Manifesto, endorsed by representatives from fifteen countries in November 1989, at http://www.slowfood.org.uk/Cms/Page/history.
3. Pam Shoberg, organizer of Slow Food Port Susan in Stanwood, Oregon, as quoted in Gale Fiege, "Stanwood Nonprofit Spreads Word on Merits of Local Food," *HeraldNet*, September 24, 2010, at http://www.heraldnet.com/article/20100924/NEWS01/709249893/-1/rss02.
4. This statistic refers to a *USA Today*/Gallup poll of 1,021 adults taken October 21–24, 2010, with an overwhelming 89% of respondents saying that it was important to them to be involved in their communities. The results cut across regions as well as socioeconomic lines such as gender and education. Chris Hoene, director of the Center for Research and Innovation at the National League of Cities, was quoted in the accompanying news story: "Think about the national debates that are happening. . . . On the one hand, there's discussion about anti-government. On the other side, there is this kind of underlying populism out there, people wanting to be more engaged in what government is doing or not doing." From Haya El Nasser, "Community Involvement Important across Demographic Lines," *USA Today*, December 8, 2010, http://content.usatoday.com/news/americawants/story/2010/12/Community-involvement-important-across-demographic-lines/41598136.
5. In many cases, there is a further element: the way that power is actually enforced. In the Civil Rights–era South, for example, enforcement of voter registration laws varied widely according to race. Town clerks would often wave new white voters into the booth while demanding that African-Americans write long and detailed essays on the Constitution.
6. Benjamin R. Barber, *Strong Democracy: Participatory Politics for a New Age* (Berkeley: University of California Press, 1984).
7. For more on slow money principles, visit the website of the Slow Money Alliance at http://www.slowmoney.org/principles.
8. Joseph Ellis, *American Creation: Triumphs and Tragedies in the Founding of the Republic* (New York: Knopf, 2007), 123. Emphasis added.

Chapter 1: "Town Halls" from Hell, and Other Stories

1. "Health Care Town Halls Turn Violent in Tampa and St. Louis," Fox News, August 7, 2009, http://www.foxnews.com/politics/2009/08/07/health-care-town-halls-turn-violent-tampa-st-louis/.
2. "Health Care Town Hall Turns Nasty," The Denver Channel, August 12, 2009, http://www.thedenverchannel.com/news/20380007/detail.html.
3. "Health Care Reform Sparks Meeting Mayhem," WTSP.com (Tampa, Fla.), August 7, 2009 http://www.wtsp.com/news/local/story.aspx?storyid=111086&catid=8.
4. Chris Cillizza, "Congress' Approval Problem in One Chart," *Washington Post*, November 15, 2011, http://www.washingtonpost.com/blogs/the-fix/post/congress-approval-problem-in-one-chart/2011/11/15/gIQAkHmtON_blog.html.
5. Jeff Zeleny and Meghan Thee-Brenan, "New Poll Finds a Deep Distrust of Government," *New York Times*, October 25, 2011, http://www.nytimes.com/2011/10/26/us/politics/poll-finds-anxiety-on-the-economy-fuels-volatility-in-the-2012-race.html?_r=1.
6. Pew Research Center for the People and the Press, "Distrust, Discontent, Anger and Partisan Rancor: The People and Their Government," April 18, 2010, 2, http://pewresearch.org/pubs/1569/trust-in-government-distrust-discontent-anger partisan-7.
7. Ibid., 4.
8. Ibid., 7.

9. Ibid., 3.
10. Ibid, 50.
11. Ibid.
12. Ibid, 32.
13. Claudia H. Deutsch, "Poll Shows Americans Distrust Corporations," *New York Times*, December 10, 2005.
14. Pew Research Center, "Distrust, Discontent," 50.
15. Jo Waters, quoted in Zeleny and Thee-Brenan, "New Poll."
16. See Steven J. Rosenstone and John Mark Hansen, *Mobilization, Participation, and Democracy in America* (New York: Macmillan Publishing Company, 1993).
17. Guy Trebay, "Uprooted: The City Yanks More Gardens Out of Harlem," *Village Voice*, November 17, 1998, http://www.villagevoice.com/1998-11-17/news/uprooted/.
18. Jennifer Tierney, "Bulldozing the Grassroots Gardeners: Arcadia," *Financial Times*, August 15, 1998, http://faculty.virginia.edu/ejus/NYaug15.htm.
19. Trebay, "Uprooted."
20. Ibid.
21. Tierney, "Bulldozing."
22. Jesse McKinley, "Browning of Hope for Village Gardens," *New York Times*, October 19, 1997, http://www.nytimes.com/1997/10/19/nyregion/neighborhood-report-lower-east-side-browning-of-hope-for-village-gardens.html.
23. Monica Polanco, "'No Gardens, No Peas,' Cry Protestors in Park," *Daily News*, April 11, 1999, http://faculty.virginia.edu/ejus/nogardens.htm.
24. Dan Barry, "Sudden Deal Saves Gardens Set for Auction," *New York Times*, May 13, 1999, http://www.nytimes.com/1999/05/13/nyregion/sudden-deal-saves-gardens-set-for-auction.html?pagewanted=all&src=pm.
25. Tierney, "Bulldozing."
26. Barry, "Sudden Deal."
27. Terry Drach, quoted in Trebay, "Uprooted."
28. Manuel Couret Branco, "Economics against Democracy," *Review of Radical Political Economics*, August 15, 2011, http://rrp.sagepub.com/content/early/2011/08/24/0486613411418051.
29. William Mathis, "Mathis: Beware of Economists Bearing Education Reforms," VTDigger.org, May 29, 2011, http://vtdigger.org/2011/05/29/mathis-beware-of-economists-bearing-education-reforms/.
30. Paul Krugman, "How Did Economists Get It So Wrong?" *New York Times*, September 2, 2009, http://www.nytimes.com/2009/09/06/magazine/06Economic-t.html?pagewanted=all.
31. Three classic studies are W. Lloyd Warner and Paul S. Lunt, *The Social Life of a Modern Community* (New Haven, Conn.: Yale University Press, 1941); Arthur J. Vidich and Joseph Bensan, *Small Town in Mass Society* (Princeton, N.J.): Princeton University Press, 1958); and Alan Peshkin, *Growing Up American* (Chicago: University of Chicago Press, 1978). More recently, a number of studies have shown the centrality of schools to community in the context of consolidation. See especially M. T. Bryant and M. L. Grady, "Community Factors Threatening Rural School District Stability," *Research in Rural Education* 6:3 (1990): 21–26; Alan DeYoung, *The Life and Death of a Rural American High School: Farewell Little Kanawha* (New York: Garland, 1995); T. A. Lyson, "What Does a School Mean to a Community? Assessing the Social and Economic Benefits of Schools to Rural Villages in New York," Department of Rural Sociology, Cornell University, Ithaca, New York (2002); and Randall S. Sell, F. Larry Leistritz, and JoAnn M. Thompson, "Socio-economic Impact of School Consolidation on Host and Vacated Communities (Agricultural Economics Report no. 347), Fargo, North Dakota, Agricultural Experiment Station.1996 One study stands as an exception to this claim, but its methodology has been criticized: Donald E. Voth and Diana M. Danforth, "Effect of Schools upon Small Community Growth and Decline." *The Rural Sociologist* 1, no. 6 (1981): 364–69.
32. M. T. Bryant and M. L. Grady, "Community Factors Threatening Rural School District Stability," *Research in Rural Education* 6, no. 3 (1990): 21–26.
33. John Dewey, "My Pedagogic Creed," *School Journal* 54 (January 1897): 77–80.
34. See Karen Tracy, *Challenges of Ordinary Democracy: A Case Study in Deliberation and Dissent* (University Park: Pennsylvania State University Press, 2010).

35. See D. H. Purdy, "An Economical, Thorough, and Efficient School System. The West Virginia School Building Authority 'Economy of Scale' Numbers," *Journal of Research in Rural Education* 13, no. 3 (1997): 170–82.

36. Robert Byers, "Saving the School: Webster Community Unites to Keep Its Elementary Open," *Charleston Gazette*, July 31, 1995, Beth Spence, "If This Is Democracy, Then I Missed the Bus: The Story of Small Schools Advocates Who Were Blocked from Participating in Facilities Planning in West Virginia," May 2002, 14, http://challengewv.org/wp-content/uploads/publications/if _this_is_democracy.pdf.

37. Spence, "If This Is Democracy," 2, 11.

38. Ibid., 11.

39. Ibid., 3.

40. Ibid., 12.

41. Ibid.

42. Ibid., 1–13.

43. Ibid., 11.

44. Ibid., 12.

45. Ibid., 4.

46. Ibid., 5.

47. Ibid.

48. Eric Eyre and Scott Finn, "Counting Bolts: Tommy's Long Ride," part of the series *Closing Costs: School Consolidation in West Virginia*, by the *Charleston Gazette*, August 25, 2002.

49. Linda Martin, telephone interview with Woden Teachout, March 12, 2012; Purdy, "An Economical, Thorough, and Efficient School System," 180.

50. Purdy, "An Economical, Thorough, and Efficient School System," 180.

51. Linda Martin, telephone interview with Woden Teachout, March 12, 2012.

Chapter 2: The Rise of Experts and Decline of Local Decision Making

1. Alexis de Tocqueville, *Democracy in America*, trans. Henry Reeve (New York: Vintage Books, 1955), vol. 1, 259.

2. Ibid., 260.

3. Mary P. Ryan, *Civic Wars: Democracy and Public Life in the American City during the Nineteenth Century* (Berkeley: University of California Press, 1998), 96.

4. *The Democrat*, September 5th, 1836, quoted in Fitzwilliam Birdsall, *The History of the Loco-foco, or Equal Rights Party* (New York: Clement and Packard, 1842), available at http://www.archive .org/stream/historyoflocofoc00byrduoft/historyoflocofoc00byrduoft_djvu.txt.

5. Ryan, *Civic Wars*, 110.

6. Tocqueville, *Democracy in America*, 260.

7. Ibid., 63.

8. Michael Pollan, "Unhappy Meals," *The New York Times Magazine*, January 28, 2007. http:// michaelpollan.com/articles-archive/unhappy-meals/.

9. Frederick Taylor, "Scientific Management," *American Magazine* 71 (1911), 577, http://books .google.com/books?id=l3EXAQAAIAAJ&printsec=frontcover#v=onepage&q&f=false.

10. Quoted in Peter Levine, *The Future of Democracy: Developing the Next Generation of American Citizens* (Hanover, N.H.: University Press of New England, 2007), 115.

11. For an insightful history of public deliberation in the United States, see John Gastil and William Keith, "A Nation That (Sometimes) Likes to Talk," in *The Deliberative Democracy Handbook: Strategies for Effective Civic Engagement in the 21st Century*, ed. John Gastil and Peter Levine (San Francisco: Jossey-Bass, 2005), 13.

12. John Keefe, "Are There Too Many State & Local Government Workers?" CBS News, March 27, 2011, http://www.cbsnews.com/8301-505123_162-36743278/are-there-too-many-state-38-local -government-workers63/.

13. The verdict was later overturned on a technicality.

14. H. L. Mencken, "The Scopes Trial: Darrow's Eloquent Appeal Wasted on Ears That Heed Only Bryan," in *The Impossible H. L. Mencken: A Selection of His Best Newspaper Stories*, ed. Marion Elizabeth Rodgers (New York: Doubleday, 1991), 585.

15. MIT landscape professor Anne Whiston Spirn described her conversation with a local teacher, who told her that students called their neighborhood "The Bottom." "So they already know it is in a floodplain?" Spirn asked. "No, they mean it's at the bottom," said the teacher. Anne Whiston Spirn, "Restoring Mill Creek: Landscape Literacy, Environmental Justice and City Planning and Design," *Landscape Research* 30 (2005): 403.

16. Ibid., 400.

17. Ibid.

18. Irene Erika Ayad, "Louis I. Kahn and Neighborhood Design: The "Mill Creek Redevelopment Area Plan," 1951–54 (Ph.D. diss, Cornell University, 1995), 258–59.

19. Catherine Bauer, *"Clients for Housing:* The Low-Income Tenant—Does He Want Supertenements?" *Progressive Architecture* (May 1952): 61; Ayad, "Louis I. Khan and Neighborhood Design," 203.

20. Bauer, "Clients for Housing," 61.

21. John F. Bauman, *Public Housing, Race and Renewal* (Philadelphia: Temple University Press, 1987), 107.

22. Ayad, "Louis I. Khan and Neighborhood Design," 74.

23. Kahn, quoted in Ayad, "Louis I. Khan and Neighborhood Design," 247.

24. Bauman, *Public Housing,* 150

25. Ayad, "Louis I. Khan and Neighborhood Design," 227.

26. Lisa Levenstein, *Movement without Marches: African American Women and the Politics of Poverty in Postwar Philadelphia* (Chapel Hill: University of North Carolina Press, 2009), 94.

27. Frances Krause, quoted in Lisa Levenstein, "The Gendered Roots of Modern Urban Poverty: Poor Women and Public Institutions in Post–World War II Philadelphia," (Ph.D. diss., University of Wisconsin–Madison, 2002), 156.

28. Levenstein, *Movement without Marches,* 98.

29. Ibid., 62.

30. Bauer, "Clients for Housing," 61

31. L. E. White, "Community or Chaos: Housing Estates and Their Social Problems," National Council of Social Services in London (1950), quoted in Bauer, "Clients for Housing," 63.

32. Levenstein, *Movement without Marches,* 110, 167.

33. Ibid., 107–8.

34. Ibid., 114.

35. Levenstein, "Gendered Roots," 162.

36. Ibid., 163.

37. Levenstein, *Movement without Marches,* 114.

38. It is interesting that Kahn was a firm believer in soliciting community input in planning, but he does not seem to have followed that process in designing the Mill Creek Apartments.

39. Lisa Chamberlain, "In Minneapolis, a Block Transformed," *New York Times,* December 16, 2007, http://www.nytimes.com/2007/12/16/realestate/16nati.html?_r=1&pagewanted=print; "Turning a Corner," *Affordable Housing Finance Magazine,* May 2008, http://www.aeonmn.org /turning_a_corner.aspx.

40. Brian DeVore, "Hope for a Healthy Food System," Minnesota Environmental Partnership, September 15, 2011, http://www.mepartnership.org/hope-for-a-healthy-food-system/.

41. "Turning a Corner."

42. Enterprise Green Communities, "The Success of Charrettes: Evidence in Practice for Engaging in an Integrative Design Process," Enterprise Community Partners, 2011, http://www .practitionerresources.org/cache/documents/675/67598.pdf, 16–17.

43. "Turning a Corner."

44. Levenstein, "Gendered Roots," 167.

45. Devore, "Hope for a Healthy Food System"; "Growing Healthy Food: Spring Opportunities," Hope Community, http://www.hope-community.org/node/210.

Chapter 3: Communities Taking Action in a Big World

1. Rosalyn Frontiera, telephone conversation with Woden Teachout, October 23, 2011.

2. The so-called Perfect Storm struck Gloucester in October 1991. Remnants of Hurricane Gale combined with an Atlantic storm to claim the lives of six fisherman and cause more than $35

million in damages. The Perfect Storm became the name of a book and later a movie chronicling these events.

3. "Gloucester-Babson Water Treatment Plant," YouTube video, 5:26, uploaded by SaveCapeAnn on December 20, 2009, http://www.youtube.com/watch?v=gpW4g6-Qiyk&feature=related.

4. "Projects and Key Figures," Suez Environnement, http://www.suez-environnement.com /water/projects-key-figures/.

5. Betsy Herbert, telephone conversation with Woden Teachout, November 4, 2011.

6. Ibid.

7. Food and Water Watch Fact Sheet, "Selling Out Consumers: How Water Prices Increased after 10 of the Largest Water System Sales," http://www.foodandwaterwatch.org/factsheet/selling -out-consumers.

8. Amy Merrick, "Cash Flows in Water Deals: Cities Seek New Funding Streams with Plans to Privatize Municipal Systems," Wall Street Journal, August 12, 2010, http://online.wsj.com/article /SB10001424052748704216804575423633799731128.html.

9. Douglas Jehl, "As Cities Move to Privatize Water, Atlanta Steps Back," New York Times, February 10, 2003, http://www.nytimes.com/2003/02/10/us/as-cities-move-to-privatize-water-atlanta -steps-back.html?pagewanted=all&src=pm.

10. Ray Smith, "Water Woes: United Water Says Main Breaks Not Out of Ordinary; City Working on Master Plan," Hudson Reporter, March 6, 2011, http://www.hudsonreporter.com/view/full _stories_home/12183672/article-Water-woes-United-Water-says-main-breaks-not-out-of -ordinary--city-working-on-master-plan-?; Ray Smith, "What's in Your Water: Breaking Down Hoboken's Water Quality Report," Hudson Reporter, September 12, 2010, http://www.hudsonreporter .com/view/full_stories_home/9482755/article-What%E2%80%99s-in-your-water---Breaking -down-Hoboken%E2%80%99s-water-quality-report-?instance=hoboken_story_left_column.

11. There are exceptions, usually international: water privatization advocates point to successes in Manila, in the Philippines, and in a number of cities in Colombia as examples.

12. Rosalyn Frontiera, conversation with Woden Teachout, October 23, 2011.

13. Gloucester Public Water Systems Ordinance, whodecides.net/uploads/Oridnance_Amended _with_Council_9-10.doc.

14. Rosalyn Frontiera, conversation with Woden Teachout, March 1, 2012.

15. Rosalyn Frontiera, conversation with Woden Teachout, October 23, 2011.

16. Pew Research Center for the People and the Press, "Distrust, Discontent, Anger and Partisan Rancor: The People and Their Government," April 18, 2010, 8, http://pewresearch.org /pubs/1569/trust-in-government-distrust-discontent-anger-partisan-rancor.

17. Pew Research Center for the People and the Press, "Fewer Want Spending to Grow, but Most Cuts Remain Unpopular," February 10, 2011, 23, http://www.people-press.org/2011/02/10 /section-4-dealing-with-state-budget-problems/.

18. Ibid.

19. Ibid.

20. Bob St. Peter, quoted in Rebecca Wilce, "Local Food Ordinances from Maine to California," PRWatch, October 10, 2011, http://www.prwatch.org/news/2011/10/11034/local-food -ordinances-maine-california.

21. Ibid.

22. Ibid.

23. The Town of Blue Hill, "Local Food and Community Self-Governance Ordinance of 2011," April 1, 2011, http://www.bluehillme.govoffice2.com/vertical/sites/%7BCFAC2362-D24C-41E6-9CF0 -9A8A1EEDCE21%7D/uploads/%7BA4EF50AD-225B-4FC7-9D63-D2C70DED404A%7D.PDF.

24. Rebecca Wilce, "We Are Farmer Brown," PRWatch, December 9, 2011, http://www.prwatch. org/news/2011/11/11147/we-are-farmer-brown.

25. Nathan Rice, "Boulder, Colo., Votes for Energy Independence—from Its Corporate Utility," High Country News, December 26, 2011, http://www.hcn.org/issues/43.22/ boulder-colo-votes-for-energy-independence-from-its-corporate-utility.

26. "Electric Utility," City of Winter Park, Florida, http://www.cityofwinterpark.org/Pages /Departments/Electric_Utility.aspx; Laura Snider, "Boulder's Municipal Utility Follows

Few Forerunners," *Daily Camera*, November 5, 2011, http://www.dailycamera.com/energy/ci_19270136.

27. Steve Pomerance, "A Municipal Electric Utility for the 21st Century," *Denver Post*, October 16, 2011, http://www.denverpost.com/opinion/ci_19108814.

28. Rice, "Boulder, Colo."

29. Snider, "Boulder's Municipal Utility."

30. Rice, "Boulder, Colo."

31. Els Cooperrider, "Leading the Fight against Genetically Modified Organisms," in Thais Mazur, *Warrior Mothers: Stories to Awaken the Flames of the Heart* (Scotts Valley, Calif.: Rising Star Press, 2004), 86.

32. "Mendocino Renegade," interview of Els Cooperrider by Peak Moment Television, YouTube video, 27:55, uploaded by Peak Moment on January 19, 2008, http://www.youtube.com/watch?v=pVcexGJGNs4.

33. Kenda Swartz Pepper, "GMOs—Banning Together: What to Do about GMO Foods," blog entry posted on behalf of the Society for a G.E. Free B.C., February 8, 2010, http://gefreebc.wordpress.com/2010/02/24/what-to-do-about-gmo-foods.

34. Melissa Moore, "Measure H Makes Mendocino the First County to Ban GM Crops in the Country," press release, March 3, 2004, http://www.foodfirst.org/en/node/287.

35. Britt Bailey, "What Is Mendocino's Measure H & What Does It Have to Do with Food Democracy?" Environmental Commons, http://environmentalcommons.org/measure-h.html.

36. "Food Fights in California," PowerPoint presentation by UCbiotech.org, http://ucbiotech.org/resources/presentations/new_talks/Monterey_March_08/Monterey_Part2_Food_Fights.pdf.

37. Quoted in Britt Bailey, "Consigning Citizens to Mere Spectators: How Preemptive Seed Legislation Is Destroying Democracy," *Rural Vermont Farm Policy Network News* 29 (April 2005): 1, http://environmentalcommons.org/VT-farm-policy-news.pdf.

38. "Food Fights in California."

39. Jeffrey Kaplan, "Consent of the Governed: The Reign of Corporations and the Fight for Democracy," *Orion Magazine*, November/December 2003, http://www.orionmagazine.org/index.php/articles/article/132/.

40. Ibid.

41. Adam D. Sacks, "Rights Fight: Local Democracy vs. Factory Farms in Pennsylvania," *Backgrounder* 10 (Winter/Spring 2005): 1, http://www.foodfirst.org/fr/backgrounders/rights_fight.

42. "Defending the Family Farm: Program Protects Communities from Agribusiness Bullies," an interview with Thomas Linzey, *Acres USA* 33, no. 5 (May 23, 2003): 3, http://www.acresusa.com/toolbox/reprints/LinzeyInterview_May03.pdf.

43. Ibid., 3.

44. Kaplan, "Consent of the Governed."

45. "Pa. Beginning to Worry about Sludge Dumping Environment," *Baltimore Sun*, September 14, 1997, http://articles.baltimoresun.com/1997-09-14/news/1997257117_1_new-jersey-new-york-york-city.

46. "Biosolids: Targeted National Sewage Sludge Survey Report—Overview," U.S. Environmental Protection Agency, January 2009, http://water.epa.gov/scitech/wastetech/biosolids/tnsss-overview.cfm.

47. Ruth Caplan, "Rural Communities Act to End Corporate Domination," Justice Rising, http://www.thealliancefordemocracy.org/pdf/AfDJR3109.pdf.

48. Kaplan, "Consent of the Governed."

49. "Defending the Family Farm," 3.

50. Ibid., 1.

51. Thomas Linzey, "Frequently Asked Questions: Southampton Anti-Corporate Farming Ordinance," Community Environmental Legal Defense Fund, http://www.celdf.org/article.php?id=761.

52. Chris Morrison, quoted in "Tamaqua Borough, Schuylkill County, Pennsylvania," Community Environmental Legal Defense Fund website, http://www.celdf.org/section.php?id=198.

53. "Issues," Community Environmental Legal Defense Fund, http://www.celdf.org/section.php?id=28.

54. Doug Pibel, "Communities Take Power," *Yes!*, July 29, 2007, http://www.yesmagazine.org/issues/stand-up-to-corporate-power/communities-take-power.

55. "Mahanoy Township, Pennsylvania, Bans Corporate Sludge Dumping," Environmental Research Foundation, February 28, 2008, http://www.rachel.org/?q=es/node/6687.

56. Interview with Victor Crawford, *Journal of the American Medical Association* 273, no. 3 (July 19, 1995): 199–202.

57. Mark Kuhn, quoted in Bailey, "Consigning Citizens to Mere Spectators." This quotation is not in the original *Rural Vermont Farm Policy Network News* newsletter but is in the online version at Environmental Commons: http://environmentalcommons.org/preemption-undemocratic.html.

58. Quoted in Moore, "Measure H Makes Mendocino."

59. Bailey, "What Is Mendocino's Measure H."

Chapter 4: The Time Is Right

1. Jared Duval, *Next Generation Democracy: What the Open-Source Revolution Means for Power, Politics, and Change* (New York: Bloomsbury, 2010).

2. Eric Raymond, *The Cathedral and the Bazaar* (Sebastopol, Calif.: O'Reilly & Associates, Inc., 1999), 2. As quoted in Duval, *Next Generation Democracy*, 70.

3. Author Don Tapscott comes to similar conclusions in his research on people born between 1978 and 1994, noting "as the Net Generation grows in influence, the trend will be toward networks, not hierarchies, toward open collaboration rather than command, toward consensus rather than arbitrary rule, and toward enablement rather than control." Don Tapscott, *Grown Up Digital* (New York: McGraw-Hill, 2009), 308.

4. Valdis Krebs and June Holley, "Building Smart Communities through Network Weaving," http://www.orgnet.com/BuildingNetworks.pdf.

5. For an exploration of this phenomenon, see Steven Johnson, *Emergence: The Connected Lives of Ants, Brains, Cities and Software* (New York: Scribner, 2001). Writing a decade before OWS, Johnson notes that early anti-World Trade Organization protests were less like an organization than a "swarm," and noted, "there can be power and intelligence in a swarm, and if you're trying to do battle against a distributed network like global capitalism, you're better off becoming a distributed network yourself" (225–226).

6. Diana Scearce, Gabriel Kasper, and Heather McLeod Grant, "Working Wikily," *Stanford Social Innovation Review*, Summer 2010.

7. Douglas Rushkoff, special commentator to CNN, October 5, 2011, http://www.cnn.com /2011/10/05/opinion/rushkoff-occupy-wall-street/index.html.

8. Rob Hopkins, *The Transition Companion: Making Your Community More Resilient in Uncertain Times* (White River Junction, Vt.: Chelsea Green Publishing, 2011).

9. Marvin Weisbord and Sandra Janoff, *Future Search: An Action Guide to Finding Common Ground in Organizations and Communities* (San Francisco: Berrett-Koehler Publishers, 1995), 2. Weisbord and Janoff are the creators of the groundbreaking Future Search process, a technique that allows diverse groups to identify shared values, goals, and action strategies. More information is available at www.futuresearch.net.

10. Tom Atlee, *The Tao of Democracy: Using Co-Intelligence to Create a World That Works for All* (Cranston, R.I.: The Writers' Collective, 2003), 271.

11. Matt Leighninger, *The Next Form of Democracy* (Nashville, Tenn.: Vanderbilt University Press, 2006), 226.

12. The Center for Information and Research on Civic Learning and Engagement, "Civic Health of the Nation: Election Energizing & Engaging Americans but Many Are Frustrated," press release from the National Conference on Citizenship, 2008, at www.civicyouth.org/PopUps/08_pr _civic_index.pdf.

13. Tina Nabatchi, John Gastil, Michael Weiksner, and Matt Leighninger, eds., *Democracy in Motion: Evaluating the Practice and Impact of Deliberative Civic Engagement* (New York: Oxford University Press, 2012).

14. James Noucas, "The Portsmouth Experience," in "Presentation to: Reinhard Mohn Evaluation Team, 'Vitalizing Democracy' in Portsmouth, New Hampshire," (City of Portsmouth and Portsmouth Listens, Portsmouth, New Hampshire, 2010), 4.

15. John Bohenko, telephone interview with Susan Clark, December 30, 2011.

16. Noucas, "The Portsmouth Experience," 4.
17. The Study Circles Resource Center, renamed Everyday Democracy, was founded in 1989 by Paul Aicher and is used to address a wide variety of local issues. More information on study circles is available at www.everyday-democracy.org.
18. James Noucas, telephone interview with Susan Clark, November 18, 2011.
19. Noucas, "The Portsmouth Experience," 5.
20. Ibid.
21. James Noucas, personal communication to Susan Clark, November 16, 2011.
22. City of Portsmouth and Portsmouth Listens, "Presentation," 3.
23. Patrick L. Scully and Martha L. McCoy, "Study Circles: Local Deliberation as the Cornerstone of Deliberative Democracy," in *The Deliberative Democracy Handbook*, ed. John Gastil and Peter Levine (San Francisco: Jossey-Bass, 2005), 208.
24. The Study Circles Resource Center (now Everyday Democracy) reported that in 2005, about 60% of all of the study circles programs they had tracked addressed issues of race. The second most common issue was K–12 education reform (20%); other common issues included community-police relations, growth and planning, neighborhood revitalization, and immigration.
25. City of Portsmouth, "City of Portsmouth New Hampshire Master Plan," March 2005, at http://www.cityofportsmouth.com/masterplan/index.html.
26. World Café is a methodology for hosting a large number of people in small-group dialogues, inviting exploration of diverse perspectives. Focusing on common questions, participants rotate among tables to exchange discoveries and make connections. More information is available at www.theworldcafe.com.
27. As quoted in City of Portsmouth and Portsmouth Listens, "Presentation," 14.
28. Elena Fagotto and Archon Fung, *Sustaining Public Engagement: Embedded Deliberation in Local Communities* (Everyday Democracy and the Kettering Foundation, 2009).
29. Fagotto and Fung, *Sustaining Public Engagement*, 25.
30. Chris Dwyer, telephone interview with Susan Clark, January 17, 2012.
31. John Bohenko, telephone interview with Susan Clark, December 30, 2011.
32. James S. Fishkin, Baogang He, Robert C. Luskin, and Alice Siu, "Deliberative Democracy in an Unlikely Place: Deliberative Polling in China," *British Journal of Political Science* 40 (2010), doi:10.1017/S0007123409990330.
33. See the resource list in appendix B for a list of dialogue and deliberation networks.
34. For more information, see www.publicconversations.org.
35. For more information, see www.theworldcafe.com.
36. For more information, see www.nifi.org.
37. For more information, see www.futuresearch.net.
38. For more information, see www.charretteinstitute.org.
39. For more information, see www.AmericaSpeaks.org.
40. For more information, see www.jefferson-center.org.
41. The Center for Deliberative Democracy, housed in the Department of Communication at Stanford University, is devoted to research about democracy and public opinion obtained through Deliberative Polling. For more information, see http://cdd.stanford.edu/.
42. Peggy Holman, Tom Devane, and Steven Cady, *The Change Handbook: The Definitive Resource on Today's Best Methods for Engaging Whole Systems* (San Francisco: Berrett-Koehler, 2007).
43. For a list of business, nonprofit, and academic organizations and foundations involved in deliberative civic engagement, see Nabatchi et al., *Democracy in Motion*, chapter 2.

Chapter 5: Cultural Cognition and Slow Democracy

1. Cultural cognition builds on the work of political scientist Aaron Wildavsky and anthropologist Mary Douglas. For more background on the theoretical roots of cultural cognition, see John Gastil, Donald Braman, Dan M. Kahan, and Paul Slovic, "The 'Wildavsky Heuristic': The Cultural Orientation of Mass Public Opinion," Yale Law School Public Law and Legal Theory research paper no. 107, Yale Law School, New Haven, Conn., 2005.

2. ScienceDaily, "Emory Study Lights Up the Political Brain," at http://www.sciencedaily.com /releases/2006/01/060131092225.htm. Drew Westen and his colleagues' study was published in the *Journal of Cognitive Neuroscience* 18, no. 11 (2006): 1947–58.

3. Our description of the pathway to public opinion is based on the work of cultural cognition researchers, who drew from a variety of research in the fields of psychology, communications, and political science. See John Gastil, Justin Reedy, Donald Braman, and Dan M. Kahan, "Deliberation across the Cultural Divide: Assessing the Potential for Reconciling Conflicting Cultural Orientations to Reproductive Technology," *George Washington Law Review* 76, no. 6 (2008): 1778–81.

4. Pew Research Center for the People and the Press, "Key News Audiences Now Blend Online and Traditional Sources," August 17, 2008, http://www.people-press.org/2008/08/17/key-news -audiences-now-blend-online-and-traditional-sources/.

5. Pariser calls on web builders not only to make the system more transparent, so that users can control what gets through, but also to encode the algorithms with a civic sense so that we will be more likely to be introduced to new ideas and perspectives. See Eli Pariser, *The Filter Bubble: What the Internet Is Hiding from You* (New York: Penguin Press, 2011).

6. For an interesting discussion, see Diana C. Mutz, *Hearing the Other Side: Deliberative versus Participatory Democracy* (New York: Cambridge University Press, 2006).

7. Dan Kahan, "Fixing the Communications Failure," *Nature* 463 (2010), http://www.nature.com /nature/journal/v463/n7279/full/463296a.html.

8. The idea of "rapid cognition," the wisdom we bring to first impressions, was popularized by Malcolm Gladwell, *Blink: The Power of Thinking without Thinking* (New York: Little, Brown and Company, 2005).

9. John Gastil, Dan M. Kahan, and Donald Braman, "The Good News about the Culture Wars," *Boston Review*, March/April 2006, www.bostonreview.net/BR31.2/gastilkahanbraman.php.

10. Damariscotta's Heart and Soul planning process was a collaboration of the town government, Friends of Midcoast Maine, and the Orton Family Foundation, with funding or staff support from all three organizations.

11. Ariana McBride, "From Big Boxes to Building Community: Damariscotta Maine Creates a Values Based Vision," press release from the Orton Family Foundation, http://www.orton.org /news/release/from_bigboxes_to_building_community.

12. The Cultural Cognition Project at Yale Law School, "First National Risk & Culture Study," http://www.culturalcognition.net/projects/first-national-risk-culture-study.html.

13. This study was conducted over a nine-month period between December 2006 and September 2007. Findings are available at http://www.culturalcognition.net/projects/second-national-risk -culture-study.html.

14. John Gastil et al., "Deliberation across the Cultural Divide."

15. Ibid., fig.3.

16. Gekko, exemplifying the character's hierarchical individualism, goes on, "Greed, for lack of a better word, is good. Greed is right, greed works. Greed clarifies, cuts through, and captures the essence of the evolutionary spirit. Greed, in all of its forms; greed for life, for money, for love, knowledge has marked the upward surge of mankind." For the full text, see http://www.imdb .com/title/tt0094291/quotes.

17. Gastil et al., "Deliberation across the Cultural Divide," 1788.

18. Dan M. Kahan, Donald Braman, Paul Slovic, John Gastil, and Geoffrey Cohen, "The Second National Risk and Culture Study: Making Sense of—and Making Progress in—the American Culture War of Fact," Cultural Cognition Project at Yale Law School, http://www.cultural cognition.net/projects/second-national-risk-culture-study.html.

19. Frank Luntz has been credited with orchestrating Newt Gingrich's "Contract with America" campaign that helped Republicans regain Congress in 1994. The 2002 Luntz Research Companies memo is titled "Straight Talk 132." The environmental section is available through the Environmental Working Group at http://www.ewg.org/files/LuntzResearch_environment.pdf.

20. Carol Platt Liebau, "Obama Uses Euphemism to Obscure His Unpopular Agenda," Townhall. com, September 5, 2011, http://townhall.com/columnists/carolplattliebau/2011/09/05

/obama_uses_euphemism_to_obscure_his_unpopular_agenda. In fact, the phrase "revenue enhancement" to replace "tax increase" is actually popular with politicians of all stripes and can be traced back to the Reagan administration.

21. Gastil et al., "Deliberation across the Cultural Divide," 1792.

22. Ibid., 1787–88.

23. Caroline Lee and Francesca Polletta, "The 2009 Dialogue and Deliberation Practitioners Survey: What is the State of the Field?" Easton, Pa.: Lafayette College. http://sites.lafayette.edu/ddps/.

24. John Gastil, telephone interview with Susan Clark, December 12, 2011.

25. George Lakoff, *Don't Think of an Elephant! Know Your Values and Frame the Debate—The Essential Guide for Progressives* (White River Junction, Vt.: Chelsea Green Publishing, 2004).

26. James Noucas, personal communication to Susan Clark, November 16, 2011.

27. David L. Willcox, "The Story of the Randolph Community Forest: Building on Local Steward-ship," in *Community Forests: A Community Investment Strategy*, a report by the Community Forest Collaborative (August 2007), http://www.tpl.org/publications/books-reports/community-forest-report.html. The Community Forest Collaborative is a partnership of the Trust for Public Land, the Northern Forest Center, and the Quebec-Labrador Foundation/Atlantic Center for the Environment.

28. Details about Samsø's experience are drawn from Søren Hermansen, personal communications with Susan Clark, January 17, 2012, and from the Energy Development in Island Nations website at http://www.edinenergy.org/samso.html.

29. Elizabeth Kolbert, "The Island in the Wind," *New Yorker*, July 7, 2008, 68–77.

30. Henrik Lund and Sören Hermansen, "Denmark's Renewable Energy Strategy and the 'Energy Positive' Island," an address to the Institute of International and European Affairs, April 18, 2011, at http://www.iiea.com/events/denmarks-renewable-energy-strategy-and-the-energy-positive-island-lessons-for-ireland.

31. John Tagliabue, "From Turbines to Straw, Danish Self-Sufficiency," *New York Times*, September 29, 2009, http://www.nytimes.com/2009/09/30/world/europe/30samso.html.

32. Bryan Walsh, "Scientists and Innovators: Søren Hermansen," *Time*, September 24, 2008, http://www.time.com/time/specials/packages/article/0,28804,1841778_1841782_1841789,00.html.

Chapter 6: The Promise of Local

1. David Sobel *Beyond Ecophobia: Reclaiming the Heart in Nature Education* (Great Barrington, Mass: The Orion Society and the Myrin Institute, 1996).

2. Ibid., 9.

3. Richard Louv, *Last Child in the Woods: Saving Our Children from Nature-Deficit Disorder* (Chapel Hill, N.C.: Algonquin Books, 2005).

4. Ibid., 117.

5. Harold R. Hungerford and Trudi L. Volk, "Changing Learner Behavior through Environmental Education," *Journal of Environmental Education* 21, no. 3 (1990): 8–21. Hungerford and Volk's findings, which built on a comprehensive meta-analysis of environmental-education-related behavior research, featured seven major variables and six minor variables predicting environmental citizenship. The major variables included a prerequisite of environmental sensitivity (empathy toward the natural world), two "ownership" variables (understanding of and a personal investment in the issues), and four "empowerment" variables: perceived skill, knowledge of action strategies, belief in success, and intention to act.

6. Ibid., 145.

7. For a review of various uses of the term "democratic deficit," see Joseph Peters and Manon Abud, "E-Consultation: Enabling Democracy between Elections," with comments by Kathleen McNutt and Colin McKay, Institute for Research on Public Policy, *Choices* 15, no. 1 (2009). Peters and Abud note that the term is used in at least two ways: to describe the downturn in such civic indicators as voting, trusting in leaders, and engaging in political parties, and to indicate a "preference gap," that is, government's inability to fulfill citizens' wishes.

8. Parker J. Palmer, *Healing the Heart of Democracy: The Courage to Create a Politics Worthy of the Human Spirit* (San Francisco: Jossey-Bass, 2011), 6.

9. Ibid., 7.
10. United Nations World Commission on Environment and Development, *Our Common Future* (Oxford: Oxford University Press, 1987). This document is also often referred to as the "Brundt-land Report."

Chapter 7 Inclusion

1. Douglas Adams, *The Ultimate Hitchhiker's Guide to the Galaxy* (New York: Del Rey Books, 2005), 9.
2. Slow democracy focuses on building local communities, and as such, it emphasizes techniques that bring a critical mass of citizens together. Another, complementary branch of deliberative engagement focuses on gathering public input in order to advise public policy makers (using such techniques as Citizen Juries, Deliberative Polling, and America Speaks). With these techniques, a representative sample is the priority.
3. Martha L. McCoy and Patrick L. Scully, "Deliberative Dialogue to Expand Civic Engagement: What Kind of Talk Does Democracy Need?" *National Civic Review* 91, no. 2 (Summer 2002): 129.
4. *CAPS at Five: A Report on the Progress of Community Policing in Chicago* (Chicago: Chicago Police Department, 1998), 9. Available at https://portal.chicagopolice.org/i/cpd/clearpath/CAPSat5 .pdf. On CAPS generally, see Wesley G. Skogan, *Police and Community in Chicago: A Tale of Three Cities* (Oxford: Oxford University Press, 2006).
5. "Chicago Police and Community Reclaim a Neighborhood Park," Chicago Police Department, 1998, 1–3, http://www.popcenter.org/library/awards/goldstein/1997/97-08.pdf.
6. Ibid., 4–6.
7. Ibid., 9.
8. There remains a significant gap in satisfaction between whites, African-Americans, and Latinos, but overall rates have risen across racial groups. See Wesley G. Skogan and Lynn Steiner, "CAPS at Ten: Community Policing in Chicago, An Evaluation of Chicago's Alternative Policing Strategy," Chicago Community Policing Evaluation Consortium, January 2004, 41.
9. Wesley G. Skogan, Lynn Steiner, Jill DuBois, J. Erik Gudell, and Aimee Fagan, "Taking Stock: Community Policing in Chicago," National Institute of Justice, July 2002, 7, https://www.ncjrs .gov/pdffiles1/nij/189909.pdf.
10. Ibid., 28.
11. Delia Clark and Susan Clark, "Community Vision to Action Forums: An Organizers Guide to Participatory Planning," October 2003, www.confluenceassociates.org.
12. John P. Kretzmann and John L. McKnight, *Building Community from the Inside Out: A Path toward Finding and Mobilizing a Community's Assets* (Chicago: ACTA Publications, 1993), 347.
13. Jonathan F. Zaff, James Youniss, and Cynthia M. Gibson, "An Inequitable Invitation to Citizenship: Non-College-Bound Youth and Civic Engagement," Philanthropy for Active Civic Engagement (PACE), October 2009.
14. Lynn M. Sanders, "Against Deliberation," *Political Theory* 25 (1997): 369.
15. *Managing Marcellus* was written by Shannon Deep, http://hss.cmu.edu/pdd/polls/dt/MM _DT_%20Epilogue.pdf.
16. Barbara Ganley, "Re-Weaving the Community, Creating the Future Storytelling at the Heart and Soul of Healthy Communities," from the Orton Family Foundation at http://www.orton.org /sites/default/files/resource/1611/Storytelling_Whitepaper_hotlinked.pdf.
17. Larry Schooler, telephone interview with Susan Clark, January 27, 2012.
18. See Scott Bittle, Chris Haller, and Alison Kadlec, "Promising Practices in Online Engagement," at http://www.publicagenda.org/pages/promising-practices-in-online-engagement. See appendix for additional resources.
19. Joseph Peters and Manon Abud, "E-Consultation: Enabling Democracy between Elections," with comments by Kathleen McNutt and Colin McKay, Institute for Research on Public Policy, *Choices* 15, no. 1 (2009).
20. Aaron Smith, "Government Online. Part Two: Government Engagement Using Social Media and the Government Participatory Class," Pew Internet, April 27, 2010, http://pewinternet.org /Reports/2010/Government-Online/Part-Two.aspx.

Chapter 8: Dialogue and Building Understanding

1. For a more detailed description of dialogue, see Martha L. McCoy and Patrick L. Scully, "Deliberative Dialogue to Expand Civic Engagement: What Kind of Talk Does Democracy Need?" *National Civic Review* 91, no. 2 (Summer 2002): 129.

2. For more information see www.LivingRoomConversations.org. Organizers hope that others will adapt the model in their communities and feed back their results.

3. Living Room Conversations has affiliated with the Public Conversations Project, www.public conversations.org. They credit dialogue consultants from Changing the Game for pilot cocreation, and were inspired by initiatives including the Family Dinner Project, America Speaks, and Conversation Cafés.

4. Dan Pine, "The End of Rude: Did the Year of Civil Discourse Make It Easier to Talk about Israel?" jweekly.com, January 5, 2012, http://www.jweekly.com/article/full/63860/the-end-of-rude -did-the-year-of-civil-discourse-make-it-easier-to-talk-abou/.

5. This dialogue process was described by the participants themselves in Anne Fowler, Nicki Nichols Gamble, Frances X. Hogan, Melissa Kogut, Madeline McCommish, and Barbara Thorp, "Talking with the Enemy," *Boston Globe*, January 28, 2001, Focus section. For more on the Public Conversations Project, see www.publicconversations.org.

6. For a valuable discussion of community capital and sustainability, see Maureen Hart, *Guide to Sustainable Community Indicators* (North Andover, Mass.: Hart Environmental Data, 1999), http://www.sustainablemeasures.com/.

7. Robert D. Putnam, *Bowling Alone: The Collapse and Revival of American Community* (New York: Simon & Schuster, 2000).

8. Robert D. Putnam and Lewis M. Feldstein, *Better Together: Restoring the American Community* (New York: Simon and Schuster, 2003).

9. Sara M. Evans and Harry C. Boyte, *Free Spaces: The Sources of Democratic Change in America* (Chicago: University of Chicago Press, 1992).

10. Project for Public Spaces, "What Is Placemaking," http://www.pps.org/articles/what _is_placemaking.

11. Project for Public Spaces, "Eleven Principles for Creating Great Community Places," http:// www.pps.org/articles/11steps/.

12. Keith Hampton, Lauren Sessions Goulet, Lee Rainie, and Kristen Purcell, "Social Networking Sites and Our Lives," Pew Internet, June 16, 2011, http://www.pewinternet.org/Reports/2011/ Technology-and-social-networks.aspx.

13. Steven Clift, "Are You Ready to BeNeighbors.org—Using Online Forums to Boost Deep Dish Pizza Sales—and Engage People Less Likely to Participate Online," posting on the e-Democracy. org blog, February 16, 2012, http://blog.e-democracy.org/posts/1372.

14. Michael Wood-Lewis, interview with Susan Clark, October 13, 2011.

15. These quotes are drawn from the results of a survey conducted by a college student of Front Porch Forum subscribers in Burlington, Vermont. See "Front Porch Forum Survey Results," on Ghost of Midnight (blog), May 12, 2008, http://blog.frontporchforum.com/2008/05/12/ front-porch-forum-survey-results/.

16. E-democracy is working to connect the various neighborhood forum efforts; see http://e-democracy.org/locals.

17. Steven Clift, "We Need Bubble-Popping Bridges—Highlights from the Knight Foundation Media Learning Seminar," posting on the e-Democracy.org blog, February 22, 2012, http:// blog.e-democracy.org/posts/1380.

18. National Conference on Citizenship, "Civic Health and Unemployment: Can Engagement Strengthen the Economy?" issue brief, September 2011. This report was created in partnership with CIRCLE (the Center for Information and Research on Civic Learning and Engagement), Civic Enterprises, Saguaro Seminar, and the National Constitution Center. See these organizations for additional research on social capital and community.

19. Francis Fukuyama, *Trust: The Social Virtues and the Creation of Prosperity* (New York: Free Press, 1996). Referenced in National Conference on Citizenship, "Civic Health."

20. Knight Foundation and Gallup, "Knight Soul of the Community 2010: Why People Love Where They Live and Why It Matters: A National Perspective," 2010, http://www.soulofthecommunity.org/sites/default/files/SOTC_2010_Report_OVERALL_11-12-10_mh.pdf.

21. Within this quote, the National Conference on Citizenship report ("Civic Health"; see above) cites the following studies: Robert D. Putnam, "Community-Based Social Capital and Educational Performance," in *Making Good Citizens: Education and Civil Society*, ed. Diane Ravitch and Joseph P. Viterittri (New Haven, Conn.: Yale University Press, 2001), 58–95; and Jeffrey Berry, Kent Portney, and Ken Thomson, *The Rebirth of Urban Democracy* (Washington, D.C.: Brookings Institution Press, 1993).

Chapter 9: Deliberation

1. Daniel Kemmis, *Community and the Politics of Place* (Norman, Okla: University of Oklahoma Press, 1990), 53. Emphasis added.

2. Abby Williamson and Archon Fung. "Public Deliberation: Where We Are and Where Can We Go?" *National Civic Review,* Winter 2004: 3–14.

3. Ibid.

4. John Gastil, *Political Communication and Deliberation* (Thousand Oaks, Calif.: Sage Publications, 2008), 189.

5. D. A. Mazmanian and J. Nienaber, *Can Organizations Change? Environmental Protection, Citizen Participation, and the Army Corps of Engineers* (Washington, D.C.: Brookings Institution, March 1979). As quoted in Williamson and Fung, "Public Deliberation."

6. Frances Moore Lappé and Paul Martin DuBois, *The Quickening of America: Rebuilding Our Nation, Remaking Our Lives* (San Francisco: Jossey-Bass, 1994).

7. William Barnes and Bonnie Mann, *Making Local Democracy Work: Municipal Officials' Views about Public Engagement* (Washington, D.C.: National League of Cities Center for Research and Innovation, 2010).

8. Matt Leighninger, *The Next Form of Democracy* (Nashville, Tenn.: Vanderbilt University Press, 2006), 226.

9. Diana C. Mutz, *Hearing the Other Side: Deliberative versus Participatory Democracy* (New York: Cambridge University Press, 2006).

10. Benjamin Barber, *Strong Democracy: Participatory Politics for a New Age.* (Berkeley: University of California Press, 1984), 187–88.

11. See Sandy Heierbacher, "Dialogue and Deliberation," in Peggy Holman, Tom Devane, and Steven Cady, *The Change Handbook: The Definitive Resource on Today's Best Methods for Engaging Whole Systems* (San Francisco: Berrett-Koehler Publishers, 2007), 102–17.

12. For a comprehensive overview of the field and the value, as well as the limitations, of its current research, see Tina Nabatchi, John Gastil, Michael Weiksner, and Matt Leighninger, eds., *Democracy in Motion: Evaluating the Practice and Impact of Deliberative Civic Engagement* (New York: Oxford University Press, 2012).

13. Scholars in this still-young field are intent on improving the growing body of empirical research. Dialogue and deliberation are occurring in a wide variety of community settings, which makes them difficult to track, and researchers still need to design more consistent analytical categories in order to allow for comparison. For a critique of deliberation's "better citizen" claims, see Heather Pincock, "Does Deliberation Make Better Citizens?" in *Democracy in Motion*, ed. Tina Nabatchi et al.

14. Stanford professor James Fishkin has pioneered Deliberative Polling, a social science tool whereby a representative sample of citizens gathers to discuss issues. Participants have access to balanced informational materials and expert panels and deliberate in small groups about the trade-offs of various policies. Polling participants before and after the process makes it clear that participants have a more accurate understanding of issue-related facts after deliberation, and that it can change their attitudes on issues. For example, see Robert C. Luskin, James S. Fishkin, and Roger Jowell, "Considered Opinions: Deliberative Polling in Britain," *British Journal of Political Science* 32 (2002): 455–87.

15. John Gastil, Chiara Bacci, and Michael Dollinger, "Is Deliberation Neutral? Patterns of Attitude Change during 'The Deliberative Polls,'" *Journal of Public Deliberation* 6, no. 2, art. 3 (2010).

16. John Gastil, E. Pierre Deess, Philip J. Weiser, and Cindy Simmons, *The Jury and Democracy: How Jury Deliberation Promotes Civic Engagement and Political Participation* (New York: Oxford University Press, 2010). See also Renée A. Daugherty and Sue E. Williams, "Applications of Public Deliberation: Themes Emerging from Twelve Personal Experiences Emanating from National Issues Forums Training," *Journal of Public Deliberation* 3, no. 1, art. 10 (2007).

17. Will Friedman, Alison Kadlec, and Lara Birnback, "Transforming Public Life: A Decade of Citizenship Engagement in Bridgeport, CT," *Case Studies in Public Engagement* no. 1 (2007), by the Center for Advances in Public Engagement, part of Public Agenda.

18. See Bo Kinney, "Deliberation's Contribution to Community Capacity Building," in *Democracy in Motion*, ed. Tina Nabatchi et al..

19. Examples from Deliberative Polling, study circles, and other deliberative processes show that participants found common interests and built bonds.

20. Although focused on citizen participation rather than specifically on deliberation, one case study meta-analysis of one hundred research studies in twenty countries concluded that in most cases citizen participation produces positive effects in, among other things, strengthening responsive and accountable governments and developing inclusive and cohesive societies. In the minority of cases, negative effects of participation (such as cynicism) were generally caused by unfair and poorly run public processes. See John Gaventa and Gregory Barrett, "So What Difference Does It Make? Mapping the Outcomes of Citizen Engagement," working paper 347, University of Sussex Institute of Development Studies, Brighton, U.K., 2010.

21. Summarizing case studies of deliberative democracy from across the globe, researchers wrote, "When deliberation is well organized, participants *like* it. In fact, they find it deeply satisfying and significant." See Peter Levine, Archon Fung, and John Gastil, "Future Directions for Public Deliberation," in *The Deliberative Democracy Handbook: Strategies for Effective Civic Engagement in the 21st Century*, ed. John Gastil and Peter Levine (San Francisco: Jossey-Bass, 2005), 272.

22. "Students, Teachers, Staff Address Racial Barriers to the Achievement Gap," YouTube video, 5:06, posted by Everyday Democracy, April 1, 2010, http://www.everyday-democracy.org/en/Resource.149.aspx.

23. Ibid.

24. Krissah Thompson, "Montgomery Parents' 'Study Circles' Aim to Close the Gap on Student Achievement," *Washington Post*, November 9, 2010, http://www.washingtonpost.com/wp-dyn/content/article/2010/11/08/AR2010110807128.html.

25. John Landesman, "Report on the DFCP Study Circles Program, October 13, 2011," 3 (internal report, Everyday Democracy, East Hartford, Connecticut). Landesman is Program Coordinator for Montgomery County Public Schools, and for this report he queried area principals for their comments on the Study Circles program in the Montgomery County Public Schools' Department of Family and Community Partnerships.

26. Ibid., 2.

27. "Students, Teachers, Staff Address Racial Barriers."

28. Julie Wade, "Evaluation of the Montgomery County Public Schools Study Circles Program," Department of Shared Accountability, December 2007, 21–22, http://www.montgomeryschoolsmd.org/uploadedFiles/departments/studycircles/aboutus/Study_Circles_Final_Eval_Mar10.pdf.

29. "Montgomery County Public Schools Study Circles Program," YouTube video, 6:27, posted by Everyday Democracy, February 21, 2008, http://www.youtube.com/watch?v=K73vOx-pPo4.

30. John Landesman, "Report on the DFCP Study Circles Program," 4.

31. Thompson, "Montgomery Parents' 'Study Circles.'"

32. Wade, "Evaluation," 24.

33. Ibid., 12.

34. John Landesman, "Report on the DFCP Study Circles Program," 3.

35. Diane L. Morehouse, "Northwest Area Foundation Horizons Program 2002–2010: Final Evaluation Report," http://www.extension.uidaho.edu/horizons/reports/Horizons%20Final%20Report%202010%2082410.pdf.

36. Horizons also used the study circles approach for the initial "dialogue" phase.

37. Joyce Hoelting, "Horizons Program Mobilizes Communities to Address Rural Poverty," *Community Dividend*, April 2010, 6, http://www.minneapolisfed.org/pubs/cd/10-04/CommDiv_2010_04.pdf.

38. Ibid., 5.

39. Ibid., 4

40. Horizons impact brochure, 1. Brochure created by the Northwest Area Foundation, St. Paul, Minnesota [undated], www.nwaf.org.

41. The National Coalition on Dialogue and Deliberation offers the Engagement Streams Framework to help communities determine which type of process they are entering into and which tools might serve them best. See http://ncdd.org/rc/item/2142.

42. John Gastil, *Political Communication and Deliberation* (Thousand Oaks, Calif.: Sage Publications, 2008).

43. See the National Issues Forum's range of books at www.nifi.org and study circles issue guides at www.everyday-democracy.org. Depending on the topic your community is facing, these materials can be relevant and extremely useful. Even if the issues they cover don't match those you are facing in your community, these study guides are well worth examining as models for their thoughtful construction and inclusive, balanced approach.

44. As local decision-making processes increase in number, citizens may well fill this void. Deliberative theorist Tom Atlee envisions citizens creating an online "deliberapedia," an expanding, searchable wiki database of organized arguments on a wide variety of policy solutions to public issues. See Tom Atlee, *Empowering Public Wisdom* (Berkeley, Calif.: North Atlantic Books, Evolver Editions, in press).

45. James Noucas, "The Portsmouth Experience," in "Presentation to: Reinhard Mohn Evaluation Team, 'Vitalizing Democracy' in Portsmouth, New Hampshire" (City of Portsmouth and Portsmouth Listens, Portsmouth, New Hampshire, 2010),10.

46. Chris Dwyer, telephone conversation with Susan Clark, January 17, 2012.

47. Jane Mansbridge, *Beyond Adversary Democracy* (Chicago: University of Chicago Press, 1980), 3.

48. Ibid., 289.

49. Moderating or facilitating a group takes practice, and it is well worth taking a course or researching the skills needed before you try it. See the resource list in appendix B for suggested guides.

50. Katherine Cramer Walsh, *Talking about Race: Community Dialogues and the Politics of Disagreement* (Chicago: University of Chicago Press, 2007).

51. Friedman, Kadlec, and Birnback, "Transforming Public Life."

52. Francesca Polletta, *Freedom Is an Endless Meeting: Democracy in American Social Movements* (Chicago: University of Chicago Press, 2002).

53. See, for example, Lawrence E. Susskind and Jeffrey L. Cruikshank, *Breaking Robert's Rules: The New Way to Run Your Meeting, Build Consensus, and Get Results* (New York: Oxford University Press, 2006).

54. For more on dynamic facilitation, see www.tobe.net.

55. For additional reflections on this topic, see Tom Atlee and Rosa Zubizaretta, "Comparison of Robert's Rules of Order, Consensus Process and Dynamic Facilitation," at http://www.co-intelligence.org/I-comparisonRR-CC-DF.html.

56. John Gastil and Ned Crosby, "Voters Need More Reliable Information," *Seattle Post-Intelligencer*, November 5, 2003, http://www.seattlepi.com/local/opinion/article/Voters-need-more-reliable-information-1128957.php?searchpagefrom=1&searchdiff=96.

57. Cassie Strauss, "House Approves Creation of Citizen's Initiative Review," *Oregon Capitol News*, May 23, 2010, http://oregoncapitolnews.com/blog/2011/05/23/house-approves-creation-of-citizen's-initiative-review/.

58. Ibid.

59. William R. Potapchuk, Cindy Carlson, and Joan Kennedy, "Growing Governance Deliberatively: Lessons and Inspiration from Hampton, Virginia," in *The Deliberative Democracy Handbook: Strategies for Effective Civic Engagement in the 21st Century*, ed. John Gastil and Peter Levine (San Francisco: Jossey-Bass, 2005), 254–67.

Chapter 10: Power

1. The "Me, We, You" dial draws on the work of Victor H. Vroom of Yale University. See his model at http://www.lederne.dk/NR/rdonlyres/E8715858-DCEE-4355-88BB-B3E82FE7DA9B/0/18 VictorVroom2.pdf.

2. Sherry Arnstein, "A Ladder of Citizen Participation," *American Institute of Planners* (July 1969): 219.

3. International Association of Public Participation, spectrum of citizen participation tool, at www.iap2.org/associations/4748/files/spectrum.pdf.

4. Jennifer Hurley, personal communication with Susan Clark, September 27, 2011. For more information on Hurley's work, see http://www.hfadesign.com.

5. Elizabeth Kennedy-Wong to NCDD-discussion@lists.thataway.org, September 28, 2011, National Coalition for Dialogue and Deliberation Discussion List, http://ncdd.org/rc /item/2624.

6. The concept of a democratic impact statement is developed in Susan Clark and Frank Bryan, *All Those in Favor: Rediscovering the Secrets of Town Meeting and Community* (Montpelier, Vt.: Ravenmark, 2005), 81–83.

7. Daniel Kemmis and Matthew McKinney, *Collaboration and the Ecology of Democracy* (Dayton, Ohio: Kettering Foundation, 2011).

8. George Cameron Coggins, "Of Californicators, Quislings and Crazies: Some Perils of Devolved Collaboration," *Chronicle of Community* 2, no. 2 (Winter 1998): 30. As quoted in Kemmis and McKinney, *Collaboration*, 34.

9. Kemmis and McKinney, *Collaboration*, 18.

10. In its early years, the act was also supported by the Community Preservation Initiative, an innovative program focused on fostering participation in community land-use planning. For an overview and practical tool kit related to this work, see Elisabeth M. Hamin, Priscilla Geigis, and Linda Silka, eds., *Preserving and Enhancing Communities: A Guide for Citizens, Planners, and Policymakers* (Amherst: University of Massachusetts Press, 2007).

11. State of Massachusetts, "Community Preservation Act," at http://commpres.env.state.ma.us /content/cpa.asp; Community Preservation Coalition, "Community Preservation Act: An Over-view," at http://www.communitypreservation.org/content/cpa-overview; and Community Preservation Coalition, "CPA Trust Fund Distribution," http://www.communitypreservation .org/content/trustfund.

12. Community Preservation Coalition, "Community Preservation Act: An Overview."

13. Roger Smith, director of the New England Energy Program for the Clean Water Action/Clean Water Fund, in personal communication with Susan Clark, October 30, 2011.

14. The Chicago Department of Environment (DOE) didn't come up with the C3 idea on its own; in 2006, the DOE convened over a dozen municipal agencies and environmental organizations to determine the best way to make use of citizens' interest. Suzanne Malec-McKenna, the com-missioner at the time, had a background in grassroots activism. Based on this collaborative analysis, the local nonprofits were pleased to have the City coordinate the effort. What might have been a turf war is anything but; the nonprofits continue to serve as resource partners to the program and funnel volunteers to it.

15. Kristen Pratt, Chicago Conservation Corps project coordinator, in personal communication with Susan Clark, October 25, 2011.

16. Ibid.

17. World Bank, "Participatory Budgeting in Brazil," http://siteresources.worldbank.org/INTEM-POWERMENT/Resources/14657_Partic-Budg-Brazil-web.pdf.

18. Michael Levitin, "Participatory Budgeting Gains Steam in San Francisco," posted on the Shareable:Civicsystem blog, August 10, 2011, http://shareable.net/blog/participatory -budgeting-gains-steam-san-francisco.

Chapter 11: The Jury, Town Meeting, and Slow Democracy

1. Alexis de Tocqueville, *Democracy in America*, trans. Henry Reeve (New York: Vintage Books, 1955), vol. 1, 296.

2. Ibid., 63.

3. Traditional town meetings are used to varying degrees in Maine, New Hampshire, Vermont, Massachusetts, and Connecticut, but they are almost nonexistent in Rhode Island. See Joseph F. Zimmerman, *The New England Town Meeting: Democracy in Action* (Westport, Conn.: Praeger, 1999).

4. Switzerland is the other place on the globe that uses town meetings. Every Swiss community, from alpine villages to the metropolis of Zurich, along with two remaining cantons, are governed through a form of town meeting. Understanding that one size doesn't fit all, in most Swiss cantons once a town grows beyond a certain population it switches from a traditional floor meeting to a large local parliament (similar to a New England representative town meeting). By Swiss protocol, the voters at a town meeting are addressed as "the sovereign"—a powerful reminder that the ruler is not a king, president, or leader at a podium; the sovereign body is the citizens themselves.

5. Paul Gillies, e-mail message to Susan Clark, March 1, 2012.

6. Frank M. Bryan, *Real Democracy: The New England Town Meeting and How It Works* (Chicago: University of Chicago Press, 2004).

7. At the average town meeting, 20.5 percent of the electorate attended—usually higher for small towns, lower for larger towns. Based on Bryan's data, towns with a population of over five thousand need to weigh their attendance numbers and, if necessary, consider other means of governance, such as the representative town meeting. In Susan Clark and Frank Bryan, *All Those in Favor: Rediscovering the Secrets of Town Meeting and Community* (Montpelier, Vt.: Ravenmark, 2005), 40.

8. Clark and Bryan, *All Those in Favor*, 40.

9. In Vermont, most of the best-attended town meetings include some element of food—traditionally a potluck lunch for a daylong meeting. In Switzerland, the post-meeting gatherings often center around the wine or beer native to the region.

10. Rose Arce, "Does Class Size Matter?" posted on CNN's Schools of Thought blog, December 7, 2011, http://schoolsofthought.blogs.cnn.com/2011/12/07/does-class-size-matter-2/.

11. Jane Mansbridge, *Beyond Adversary Democracy* (New York: Basic Books, 1983).

12. Robert Putnam, *Bowling Alone: The Collapse and Revival of American Community* (New York: Simon and Schuster, 2000). See also Tom W. Rice and Alexander F. Sumberg, "Civic Culture and Government Performance in the American States," *Publius: The Journal of Federalism* 27 (Winter 1997).

13. Clark and Bryan, *All Those in Favor*, 31.

14. As quoted in Clark and Bryan, *All Those in Favor*, 76.

15. John Gastil, *Political Communication and Deliberation* (Thousand Oaks, Calif.: Sage Publications, 2008), 156.

16. John Gastil, E. Pierre Deess, Philip J. Weiser, and Cindy Simmons, *The Jury and Democracy: How Jury Deliberation Promotes Civic Engagement and Political Participation* (New York: Oxford University Press, 2010).

17. Gastil, *Political Communication*, 172.

18. For a thoughtful critique of the power dynamics of juries, see Lynn Sanders, "Against Deliberation," *Political Theory* 25 (1997).

19. Gastil et al., *The Jury and Democracy*, 106.

20. Some states have experimented with hybrid variations on the town meeting. In New Hampshire, some towns have instituted an official ballot referendum system known as SB 2, which features a deliberative session at which ballot items can be amended, followed by a ballot vote at a later date. Over forty towns in Massachusetts and a small number of towns in other states have moved to a representative town meeting, where voters elect a relatively large number of representatives to make town decisions but reserve the right to reverse representatives' actions via public referendum. For more information, see Zimmerman, *The New England Town Meeting*, 73–78 and 139–61.

21. Gastil et al., *The Jury and Democracy*, 169.

22. Ibid., 9.

Chapter 12: When Advocacy Meets Slow Democracy

1. Martin Luther King, *Where Do We Go from Here: Chaos or Community?* (New York: Harper and Row, 1967), 136.

2. Peter Levine and Rose Marie Nierras, "Activists' Views of Deliberation," *Journal of Public Deliberation* 3, no. 1, art. 4 (2007).

3. Ibid.

4. Ibid.

5. Joshua Cohen and Archon Fung, "Radical Democracy," *Swiss Journal of Political Science* 10, no. 4 (Winter 2004).

6. As quoted in Larry Anderson, *Benton MacKaye: Conservationist, Planner, and Creator of the Appalachian Trail* (Baltimore, Md.: John Hopkins University Press, 2002), 367. For those interested in MacKaye and his colleagues, the history of the AT, or the roots of American regional planning, Anderson's biography is an invaluable resource.

7. Ibid., 16.

8. Benton MacKaye, "An Appalachian Trail: A Project in Regional Planning," *Journal of the American Institute of Architects* 9 (October 1921): 327.

9. Ibid.

10. The Appalachian Trail Conference organization changed its name to the Appalachian Trail Conservancy in 2005.

11. As quoted in Anderson, *Benton MacKaye*, 152.

12. MacKaye remained interested in the Appalachian Trail until his death in 1975, but his attention largely shifted to his pioneering work in regional planning. He is also well known for his wilderness advocacy work, and he went on to cofound the Wilderness Society.

13. Robert Rubin, ed., "Trail Years: A History of the Appalachian Trail Conference," *Appalachian Trailway News*, 2000, 15.

14. Ibid.

15. Franklin Reed, district forester for District 7, encompassing the southern national forests, as quoted in Anderson, *Benton MacKaye*, 160.

16. Rita Hennessy, telephone interview with Susan Clark, September 8, 2011.

17. Don King, realty officer for the National Park Service, telephone interview with Susan Clark, February 6, 2012.

18. Rubin, "Trail Years," 57.

19. Rita Hennessy, telephone interview with Susan Clark, September 8, 2011.

20. David Startzell, telephone interview with Susan Clark, September 14, 2011. Startzell was executive director of the Appalachian Trail Conservancy at the time of our interview; he retired in 2011 after thirty-four years with the organization.

21. Julie Judkins, telephone interview with Susan Clark, June 13, 2011.

22. Ralph Knoll, telephone interview with Susan Clark, September 9, 2011.

23. Donnie Kelley, telephone interview with Susan Clark, September 2, 2011.

24. University of Colorado at Denver and Health Sciences Center, "Student Gains from Place-Based Education," fact sheet no. 2, December 2010, http://www.ucdenver.edu/academics/colleges/ArchitecturePlanning/discover/centers/CYE/Publications/Documents/CYE_FactSheet2_Place-Based%20Education_December%202010.pdf.

25. National Park Service, U.S. Department of the Interior, "AT to Launch 'MEGA-Transect' Project," *NPS Digest*, December 12, 2006, http://home.nps.gov/applications/digest/headline.cfm?type=Announcements&id=5036.

26. According to the Minority Environmental Leadership Development Initiative, among natural resource organizations, a mere 11% of staff members and 9% of board members are people of color. A full third of environmental institutions and 22% of environmental government agencies have no people of color on staff. As quoted in Helen Whybrow, "2042 Today: Cultivating Conservation Leaders of the Future," *Saving Land*, Land Trust Alliance, Fall 2011, 16.

27. It's not only a question of equity and justice; it's a matter of practical necessity. Aware that by 2042, people of color will comprise more than 50% of the U.S. population, environmental leaders such as the Center for Whole Communities, www.wholecommunities.org, are working to understand the patterns of power and privilege that have combined to exclude minorities—soon to be majorities—from their work.

28. Pamela Underhill, telephone interview with Susan Clark, May 4, 2012.

29. David Startzell, telephone interview with Susan Clark, September 14, 2011.
30. Hawk Metheny, telephone interview with Susan Clark, May 2, 2012.
31. David Startzell, telephone interview with Susan Clark, September 14, 2011.
32. Benton MacKaye, in a letter to Robert Wirth, June 7, 1966, quoted in Anderson, *Benton MacKaye*, 364.
33. Rubin, "Trail Years," 63.
34. MacKaye, "An Appalachian Trail," 329.

Epilogue: Closing Thoughts: The Ecology of Slow Democracy

1. John Elder, *Stories in the Land: A Place-Based Environmental Education Anthology*, Nature Literacy Series, no. 2 (Great Barrington, Mass.: The Orion Society, 1998). This is from his introduction to this booklet.
2. Parker J. Palmer, *Healing the Heart of Democracy: The Courage to Create a Politics Worthy of the Human Spirit* (San Francisco: Jossey-Bass, 2011), 17.
3. Carl Etnier, "McKibben: There's No Time to Wait on Climate Change," VTDigger.org, February 7, 2012, http://vtdigger.org/2012/02/07/mckibben-theres-no-time-to-wait-on-climate-change/?utm_source=rss&utm_medium=rss&utm_campaign=mckibben-theres-no-time-to-wait-on-climate-change&utm_source=VtDigger+Subscribers&utm_campaign=cf33efd54f-RSS_EMAIL_CAMPAIGN&utm_medium=email.

Appendix A

1. For a more detailed list of overarching principles, see the National Coalition for Dialogue and Deliberation "Core Principles for Public Engagement," http://ncdd.org/rc/item/3643.
2. A valuable tool for matching the correct tool to your process goals, the "Engagement Streams Framework" is available from the National Coalition for Dialogue and Deliberation at http://www.ncdd.org/files/NCDD2010_Engagement_Streams.pdf.

index

abortion, dialogue on, 133–35
active listening, 157
adversary democracy, 130, 155, 180
advisory committees, 165
advocacy, xviii–xix, xxvii, 56–57, 186–202. *See also* Appalachian Trail
Aeon, 35
agricultural issues
  factory-farm waste regulation, 51–53
  food-sovereignty laws, 45–48
  genetically engineered crops moratorium, 49–51, 55–56, 186
America Speaks, 80
Antioch New England Institute, 119
Apathy Is Boring, 124–25
Appalachian Trail, 188–202
  activist development of, 191–93
  Appalachian Trail Community, 195–97
  cooperative management agreement, 199–200
  MacKaye's vision for, 189–91
  MEGA-Transect Project, 198
  Trail to Every Classroom, 197–98
Arnstein, Sherry, 164–65
arts, inclusion process using, 122–25
Atlanta, 42
Atlee, Tom, 65
Austin, Texas, community engagement process, xxvi, 125–28
Austin Corps, 126
authority, ix, xi, 53, 82, 90, 96–97, 115, 163
Avery, Myron, 191–93

Bailey, Britt, 56
ballot initiatives, 160–61
Barber, Benjamin, 146–47
Barnstead, New Hampshire, 54
Belvidere, Vermont, 181
Ben Hewitt, xxiv
BeNeighbors.org, 138–39
Beyond Adversary Democracy, 155
Blades, Joan, 131
Blairsville, Georgia, 197–98
Blizzard, Roy, 14–16
Blue Hill, Maine, food sovereignty law, 45–48
Bohenko, John, 68, 77–78
Boulder, Colorado, municipal utility, 48–49, 186
Bowling Alone, 136

Boyte, Harry, 137
Branco, Manuel Couret, 9
Bridgeport, Connecticut, 157
Bryan, Frank, vii–xi, 178–79
budgeting
  participatory, xxvi, 79, 165, 171–72, 186
  Portsmouth Listen study circles, 75–77
bullying, 71–72

California
  genetically engineered crops moratorium, 49–51, 55–56, 186
  Public Utilities Commission, 41
California American Water, 41–42
Canadian Community for Dialogue and Deliberation, 209
Canadian creative arts programs, 124–25
candidate forums, 75
capital
  social, 135–37, 140, 180
  types of, 135–37
centralization, 9–11, 22–24, 109–10, 114, 173
  new technologies, effect of, 63
  public housing management, 33–35
  school consolidation, 13–19
Change Handbook, The, 80
charrette, 35–36, 88
Chicago
  Alternative Policing Strategy, xxvii, 67–70, 118–19
  Conservation Corps, 170–71
  participatory budgeting, xxvi, 172
churches, 136, 137
citizen control, 165
Citizen Juries, 80, 184
citizen-powered governance, 65–66
Citizens' Initiative Review, 160–61
CityWorks Academy, 126
civic engagement, xxiii, xxviii, 165
  Austin, Texas, community engagement process, xxvi, 125–28
  Davenport Institute for Public Engagement and Civic Leadership, 211
  deliberation and, 77–81, 147, 151
  economic strength and, 140–42
  Hampton, Virginia, Youth Civic Engagement initiative, 161–62
  public's skills for, 145–46
civic organizations, 121–22, 136

civil discourse, 1, 77, 132–33, 180. *See also* dialogue
Civil Rights movement, 28–29, 164
clarity, 97
Clift, Steven, 138, 140
climate change, 63–64, 92–93, 113, 131–32, 204
closure, 97
co-intelligence, 65
Cohen, Joshua, 188
collaboration, 165
  emergent, 62–65
  public land, 167–69
  self-governance, 63, 65
collectivism, 90–94, 97
common ground, finding, 88–89, 96, 147–48. *See also* deliberation; dialogue; inclusion
communications, 147, 207. *See also* information; Internet; study circles
  Appalachian Trail, 194, 199
  deliberative information, 153–54
  to empower citizens, xxviii, 195–200
  from government to citizens, 163, 164, 179, 182
  by political parties, 4
  World Café technique, 75, 80, 132
community, definition of, 113
community choice aggregation, 49
community engagement process, 125–28
Community Environmental Legal Defense Fund, 51, 53–54
community gardens, 7–9, 36
community organizations, 121–22, 136
community organizing, 44, 117, 140, 196
Community Preservation Act, Massachusetts, 169
community service, xxiii. *See also* civic engagement
community task forces, 127
complexity of problems, xxviii, 5, 26, 65, 102, 147, 166
  budgets, 76–77
  political opinions, 83–86
  storytelling and, 124
concentrated animal feedlot operations, 52
conformity, 96
Connecticut Clean Energy Finance and Investment Authority, 169
consensus, 96, 155, 159
conservatives, 92–93
consultation, 164–65
Cooperrider, Els, 49–50
corporations, government decision making and, 55

crime, approach to
  Chicago Alternative Policing Strategy, xxvii, 118–19
  gun control, 93–94
CropLife America, 50
crowd sourcing, 153
cultural cognition, 82–104
  common ground, finding, 88–89
  deliberation, effect of, 87–89, 99–102
  facts, response to, 82 83
  filtering, 85–86, 95
  framing for inclusion, 98–99, 101–2
  friends, selection of, 85, 131
  ideologues and, 88–89
  last message in/first out, 86
  political quadrants, 89–97
  selective listening, 84–85
  shortcuts, use of, 86–87
  source, consideration of, 84
  vouching, cultural, 99–102
Cultural Cognition Project, 82
culture wars, 94–99

Damariscotta, Maine, community building process, xxvii, 87–88
Davenport Institute for Public Engagement and Civic Leadership, 211
debate, 147
decentralization, 63
decision making, xxii–xxiii, xxvi, 6, 207. *See also* local decision making; power
  centralization and, 18–19, 109–10, 114
  corporations and, 55
  deliberative, 146–48, 155–60
  by executive, 130, 163–66
  identifying solutions, 156–57
  politically expedient, 111
  public hearings, timing of, 144–45
  unitary democracy, 155
Deep, Shannon, 123
Deess, E. Pierre, 182
deliberation, xxvi, 78–81, 88 89, 96–97, 143–62, 205. *See also* juries; study circles; town meetings
  advocacy and, 187–88
  analytic process, 152
  community values, identifying, 155–56
  Damariscotta, Maine, visioning process, 87–88
  decision making, 146–48, 155–60
  elements of, 151–53
  embedded, 76
  goals of, 152, 206
  Hampton, Virginia, Youth Civic

Engagement initiative, 161–62
Horizons antipoverty initiative, 150–51
information gathering, 153–54
Montgomery County schools, 148–50
Oregon Citizens' Initiative Review, 160–61
planning for, 152, 205–6
Portsmouth, New Hampshire,
    programs, 68–78
public hearings, 143–45
quality of meetings, 145–46, 183
size of group, xv, 179, 181
social process, 152
status of deliberators, 122
town meetings, 179–82
Deliberative Democracy Consortium, 65, 209
Deliberative Polling, 80
deliberative theater, 123
democracy
adversary, 130, 155, 180
facts and myths of, xxvii–xxix
local participation, effect of, 114–15
representative, viii–ix, 114–15
tyranny of majority and, 29
unitary, 155, 180
democratic impact statement, 167, 207
demonization of opposition, 111
Dewey, John, 12
dialogue, 68–81, 130–42
abortion, Public Conversations Project on,
    133–35
climate change, living room discussions
    on, 131–32
economic strength, role in, 140–42
Horizons antipoverty initiative, 150
Israel-Palestine issues, Year of Civil
    Discourse, 132–33
Montgomery County public schools, 148–50
online tools for place-based communities,
    138–40
public and free spaces, 137–38
social capital, strengthening, 135–37
difference, ability to make, 109, 111, 131
direct action, 170–71, 188
dissent, 96
diverse participation. See inclusion
divisiveness. See polarization
dominance of group members, 122
Duval, Jared, 61–62
Dwyer, Chris, 76–77, 154
dynamic facilitation, 159–60
Dynamic Planning process, 80

e-democracy.org, 80, 138–39
e-mail communications, 153. See also Internet

East Brunswick Township, Pennsylvania, 54
economy, strong community participation
    and, 140–42
education, 11–13. See also schools
efficiency, 18, 35, 37, 109–10
jury process and, 185
as value, 10–11, 24–25
egalitarianism, 90–96
Elder, John, 203
embedded deliberation, 76
emergence, 62–65, 79
energy independence, 99, 102, 131
energy policy, 113
clean-energy task forces, 169
sustainability, 102–4
Transition Town, 63–64
engagement. See civic engagement
environmental issues, 29. See also climate
    change; sustainability
Chicago Conservation Corps, 170–71
conservation movement, inclusion in, 199
ecosystem services, 201
education programs, 107–12, 197–98
natural resource preservation, 194–95, 198
public land collaborations, 167–69
sustainability, 74–75, 111–12
waste regulation, 51–53
equality, ix, 82, 91, 96, 186, 188
evaluation, 207
Evans, Sara, 137
Everyday Democracy, 79, 97, 117, 210
executive power, 130, 163–66
experts, xxviii, 25–27, 36–37, 96–97, 114
public housing planned by, 31–32, 34–37
at town meetings, 180

facilitator, use of, 122, 146–51, 206
guides, 211
solutions, identifying, 156–57
town meetings, 180
training, 157, 162, 206
facts, response to, 82–83
Family Farm Protection Ordinance, 53
fast democracy, 4–7, 37, 41. See also efficiency
federal government, 21, 109–10
agricultural regulations, 46
Appalachian Trail role, 192–94, 199–200
approval rating, 3–4, 45
Civil Rights movement, 28–29
issues appropriate to, 29–30
nuclear power, xviii
public land collaborations and, 167–69
size of, 26
Felton, California, 41–42

filtering, cognitive, 85–86, 95
focus groups, 193
Food and Water Watch, 42
fracking, 54, 123
Franklin-Portland Gateway, 35–36
free spaces, 137–38
freedom and unity, xxix–xxx
friends, selection of, 85, 131
Front Porch Forum, 139–40
Frontiera, Roz, 38–44, 57, 186
Fung, Archon, 188
Future Search, 80

Ganley, Barbara, 123–24
Gastil, John, 86–87, 92, 95–96, 152, 182–83, 185
genetically engineered crops moratorium,
    49–51, 55–56, 186
Georgia, 51
Gillies, Paul, 178
Giuliani, Rudolph, 8
Gloucester, Massachusetts, water supply,
    38–44, 186
government. See also federal government;
  local government; state government
  citizens' view of, 3–4, 45
  civic engagement, effect of, 141–42
  decision making (See decision making)
  public good and, 11
Grande, Oscar, 172
group activities, 136
group confidence and patience, 96
group dynamics, 122
gun ownership, 93–94

Hacker Valley, West Virginia, school
  system, 13–18
Hampton, Virginia, citizen engagement
  programs, 161–62
Healthy Democracy Oregon, 161
heartfelt connection, importance of,
  108, 110–11
Heierbacher, Sandy, 147
Hennessy, Rita, 192–95
Herbert, Betsy, 41–42
Hermansen, Søren, 103–4
hierarchism, 90–94, 96–97
Hiller, Marge, 157
Hoboken, New Jersey, 42
Holley, June, 62
home rule, 46–47
Hope Community, 35–36
Hopkins, Rob, 63–64
Horizons antipoverty initiative, 150–51
hot-button issues, 95

human rights, 29. See also Civil Rights
  movement
Hungerford, Harold, 109
Hurley, Jennifer, 165–66
hyper-local Internet forums, 138–40

Idaho, 167
ideologues, 88–89, 94–95
Illinois American Water, 42
inclusion, xxvi, 80–81, 87–89, 95–97, 116–29,
  205, 207
  Appalachian Trail, 196, 199
  arts, inclusion process using, 122–25
  asset mapping, 121
  Austin community engagement process,
    125–28
  Chicago Alternative Policing Strategy, 118–19
  creative process for, 122–25
  in deliberation goal setting, 152
  facilitator, use of, 122
  framing for, 98–99, 101–2
  group dynamics and dominance, 122
  Internet, use of, 127–29
  Portsmouth, New Hampshire, study
    circles, 68
  public spaces, 137
  recruiting participants, 117–18
  schools, role of, 12, 18, 101
  steering committee members, 120–21
  timing of, 166
  town meetings, 178–79
  Vision-to-Action Forum, 119–21
indecision, 96
individualism, 82, 90–94, 96–97
industrial farming, regulation of, 51–53
information. See also communications
  deliberative, 153–54
  facts, response to, 82–83
  sharing, 61–63
  source, response to, 84
interactive community forums, 127
International Association for Public
    Participation, 164, 209
Internet, 75, 80, 113
  deliberation tools, 153, 154, 157
  government use of, 127, 145
  inclusion, used for, 127–29
  place-based communities, 138–40
  selective listening and, 85
involvement, citizen. See civic engagement
Israel-Palestine issues, discourse on, 132–33
issue forums, 80

Jacobs, Jane, 137

Janoff, Sandra, 65
Jefferson County, Washington, 48
Judkins, Julie, 195–97
juries, 96, 165, 177, 182–85
justice, 186–87

Kahan, Dan, 85, 92–93
Kahn, Louis, 31–32, 34, 36, 37
Kalish, Rachel Eryn, 133
Kelley, Donnie, 197
Kemmis, Daniel, 143, 168–69
Kennedy-Wong, Elizabeth, 167
Kettering Foundation, 210
keywords, use of, 94–95, 98
King, Martin Luther, Jr., 187
Knoll, Ralph, 197
Koehn, Jonathan, 49
Kretzmann, John, 121
Krugman, Paul, 11

"Ladder of Citizen Participation, A," 164
Lakoff, George, 98
land trusts, 101–2
leaders, 114, 205
    developing, 126, 151
    power of, 130, 163–66, 173
    public engagement, skills for, 145–46
League of Women Voters, 119, 210
legislative branch, town meetings as, 2
Leighninger, Matt, 65–66
Levine, Peter, 186
liberals, 92–93
lifestyle choices, 85
Linux operating system, 62
Linzey, Thomas, 51–53
listening, selective, 84–85
lobbying organizations, 6, 50, 55
local, slow democracy meaning of, 113–14
local decision making, 6, 19–37. See also
    school boards
    charrette, 35–36, 88
    devaluation of local knowledge, 27–29
    efficiency and, 24–25
    experts, role of, 25–27, 31–32, 34–37
    history of, 20–22
    privatization and, 9–11
    public housing, 30–37
    reclaiming, 54–56
    role of, 29–30
    shift from (See centralization)
local food sovereignty, 45–48
local government. See also public utilities;
    school boards; specific municipalities
    approval rating, 45

budgeting process (See budgeting)
civic engagement, effect of, xxviii, 142
community inclusion, encouraging (See
    inclusion)
food sovereignty regulations, 45–48
issues appropriate to, 29–30
segregation, role in, 28–29
size of, 26
state government guidance, local
    application of programs, 169–70
waste regulation, 51–53
local knowledge, devaluation of, 27–29
local level, participation at, 107–15. See also
    schools
    Appalachian Trail, 191–202
    environmental education, 107–10
    heartfelt connection, importance of,
        110–11
    leadership, role of, 114
    power to govern, 23
    promise of, 112–14
    as school for democracy, 114–15
    sustainable communities, building, 111–12
local sovereignty, 53–54
logging industry, 167–69
Louv, Richard, 108–10
Luntz, Frank, 94

MacKaye, Benton, 189–92
Maine
    community building process, xxvii, 87–88
    food sovereignty laws, 45–48
majority rule, 29, 158–59, 180
Managing Marcellus, 123
manipulation of citizens, 164
Mansbridge, Jane, 155–56, 180
Martin, Linda, 18
Massachusetts Community Preservation
    Act, 169
master plan update, 73–74, 77, 99
Mathis, William, 11
McBride, Arianna, 88
McCoy, Martha, 97
McKibben, Bill, 204
McKinney, Matthew, 168–69
McKnight, John, 121
media, 4, 84–85, 153
mediation, 186
"Meeting in a Box," xxvi, 126
meetings, 95–96
MEGA-Transect Project, 198
Mendocino County, California, 49–51, 55–56
Metheny, Hawk, 200
Mill Creek public housing, 30–37

Millennials, technology and, 61–62
Minneapolis
    Franklin-Portland Gateway housing, 35–36
    Internet forum, 138–39
Montana, 167
Montgomery County, Maryland, schools
    dialogue and deliberation, 148–50

Nalbandian, John, 146
Nathanson, Nancy, 161
National Charrette Institute, 80
National Coalition for Dialogue and
    Deliberation, 79, 147, 209
National Conference on Citizenship, 141–42
National Issues Forum, 80, 153
National League of Cities, 210
National Park Service, 192–94, 199
national politics, 29–30
National Risk and Culture Studies, First and
    Second, 89
Native Americans, 97, 150
natural gas extraction, 54
"Natural Step" sustainability model, 74
Neighborhood College, 162
network weavers, 62, 65
New York City
    community gardens, 7–9
    participatory budgeting, xxvi, 172
Nierras, Rose Marie, 186
North Hero, Vermont, 179
Northwest Area Foundation, 150
Noucas, Jim, 67, 70–73, 78, 99
nuclear power, xviii, 93
Nuclear Regulatory Commission, xviii
Nutrient Management Act, 51–52

Occupy Wall Street, 63, 130–31
Oliveira, Jose Benedito, 186
open-source software, 61–62
Oregon Citizens' Initiative Review, 160–61
Orton Family Foundation Heart and Soul
    Community Planning, 87–88, 210–11
Osbourne, Susan, 48

Palmer, Parker J., 111, 203–4
Pariser, Eli, 85
participatory budgeting. See budgeting
partnership, 165
Pennsylvania, 51–54
    fracking, deliberative theater addressing, 123
    local sovereignty ordinances, 53–54
    Mill Creek public housing, 30–37
    waste regulation, 51–53
personal connection, importance of, 108, 110–11

Philadelphia Mill Creek public housing, 30–37
Pittsburgh, 54
placation, 165
polarization, 111, 131, 143, 161, 186
police, 118–19
political groups, 136
political left, localism and, 23, 27–29
political participation, 6–7, 20
political parties, 4
political quadrants, 89–97
Pollan, Michael, 5, 23
Polletta, Francesca, 158
Porth, Abby Michelson, 133
Portland, Oregon, parks and recreation
    department, 166–67
Porto Alegre, Brazil, 171–72
Portsmouth, New Hampshire, 66–77, 99, 154–55
    Middle School study circles, 71–73
    school redistricting, xix, xxvi–xxvii, 67–70,
        154, 155
    sustainability plan, 74–75, 154
Portsmouth Listens, 73–77, 99, 154
poverty, xxvii, 150–51, 186
power, xxvi, 2, 23, 81, 163–73, 207. See also
    decision making
    advocacy and, 186, 188
    Appalachian Trail, 199–200
    connection to power, clarity of, 172–73
    democratic impact statement, 167
    given by power, 169–70
    juries, 182
    outside existing power structures, 167–69
    participatory budgeting, 171–72
    within power, 170–71
    spectrum of citizen participation, 164–67
    town meetings, 173, 179, 180–82
Pratt, Kristen, 170–71
privatization, 8–11, 40–41
pro-choice/pro-life dialogue, 133–35
project design, 77–78
Project for Public Spaces, 137
Public Conversations Project, 68, 79, 133–35
public good, government for, 11
public hearings, 143–45, 164, 193
public housing, 31–37
public meetings, history of, 20–23, 26
public spaces, 137–38
public utilities, xviii, 38–44, 48–49, 186, 204
Putnam, Robert, 136–37

race relations, 28–29, 73, 148–50
Randolph, New Hampshire, community
    forest, 101–2
Raymond, Eric, 62

recruitment of participants, 117–18
religious traditions, 97
representative democracy, viii–ix, 114–15
residential patterns, 85
resource list, 209–11
Robert's Rules of Order, 158–59
Rocamora, Joel, 186
Rough, Jim, 159–60
rural towns, 6, 12–18
Rushkoff, Douglas, 63
RWE AG, 41
Ryan, Mary, 21

Samsø, Denmark, 102–4
San Lorenzo Valley Water District, 41
Sanders, Lynn, 122
school boards, 12–13, 17–18, 68–70
Schooler, Larry, 125–28
schools. *See also* students
  as community builders, 12, 18, 101
  consolidation of districts, xiv–xv, 13–19, 186
  democracy, training in, 12–13
  local control of, 11–18
  race relations, dialogue and deliberation
    on, 148–50
  redistricting students, xix, xxvi–xxvii,
    67–70, 154, 155
  renovation, 74
  segregated, 28–29
  students, listening to, 71–73
Scopes Trial, 27–28
segregation
  political opinions, based on, 85
  schools, 28–29
selective listening, 84–85
self-organized strategies, 63, 65
Shuford, Elliot, 161
Simmons, Cindy, 182
slow democracy
  as alternative, xxv–xxvii
  local, meaning of, 113–14
  from local action to, 56–57
  need for, 3–7
  overview of, xxi–xxiv
  politics of, xxix–xxx
  principles of, 80–81 (*See also* deliberation;
    inclusion; power)
  rules for, 205–8
Slow Food movement, xxi–xxiv, 112
sludge dumping, 52–54
Smith, Roger, 169–70
Sobel, David, 108
social capital, 135–37, 140, 180
software, open-source, 61–62

solutions. *See* decision making
South Dakota Horizons antipoverty
  program, 150–51
Southampton Township, Pennsylvania, 53
Speak Week, 126
SpeakUpAustin.org, 127
St. Paul, Minnesota, Internet forum, 138–39
St. Peter, Bob, 46–47
21st Century Town Meeting, 184
Stallman, Richard, 61–62
Startzell, David, 193–94, 198, 199–201
state government
  agricultural regulations, 46–48
  approval rating, 45
  civic engagement, effect of, 142
  decision making by, 6, 109–10
  genetically engineered crops
    moratoriums, 51
  issues appropriate to, 29–30
  public good and, 11
  school consolidation and, 13–18
  segregation, role in, 28–29
  size of, 26
  state guidance, local application of
    programs, 169–70
steering committee, members of, 120–21, 206
story circles, 89
storytelling, 122–24, 130
students. *See also* schools
  Austin Corps, 126
  Hampton Youth Civic Engagement, 161–62
  Portsmouth Middle School study circles,
    71–73
  Trail to Every Classroom program
    (Appalachian Trail), 197–98
study circles, 68–79, 97, 130, 149, 153
Suez Environnement, 39–40
sustainability
  Appalachian Trail Community program,
    196–97
  deliberations on, 154
  energy, 102–4
  local communities, role of, 111–12
  Portsmouth, New Hampshire, plan,
    74–75, 154
Sustainable Portsmouth, 75

Tabor, Jim, 73
Tallman, Myrna, 181
Tammany Hall, 21–22
Taylor, Frederick Winslow, 24–25, 37
Tea Party, 63
therapy, citizen participation as, 164
time. *See also* efficiency

citizens willing to invest, 110, 131, 164
to make connections, importance of,
109, 111
planning for use of, 152, 156
public hearings, timing of, 144–45
public participation, taken by,
xxviii–xxix, 205
Tocqueville, Alexis de, 12, 20–21, 23, 26, 29, 177
Torvalds, Linus, 62
town hall meetings, 1–2, 5
town meetings, xiv–xv, 2, 26, 47, 165, 173,
177–82, 184–85
Trail to Every Classroom program
(Appalachian Trail), 197–98
training, 145
Appalachian Trail Community, 196–97
Chicago Conservation Corps, 170–71
CityWorks Academy, 126
facilitators, 157, 162, 206
Youth Civic Engagement, 161–62
Transition Town movement, 23, 63–64, 113
transportation, deliberations on, 154
21st Century Town Meeting, 80

unanimity, 96
Underhill, Pamela, 194, 199
understanding, building. See dialogue
unemployment, strong community
participation and, 141
Unicoi County, Tennessee, 195–97
unions, 121–22
unitary democracy, 155, 180
United States Congress, 3, 29
United States Forest Service, 167
United States government. See United
States Congress
United States Public Housing
Administration, 31
United States Supreme Court
Brown v. Board of Education, 28
Citizens United Decision, 4
United Water, 39–40, 42
unity and freedom, xxix–xxx
University of New Hampshire Public
Conversations Project, 68, 79, 133–35

urban planning, 137
urban renewal, 30–37, 164
USA Springs, 54

Veolia Environnement, 40
Veolia Water, 40
Vermont, xiv–xviii, 51
civil-union law, xvii
Front Porch Forum, 139–40
renewable-energy bill, 204
town meetings, xiv–xv, 178–81
Yankee nuclear plant, xviii
Victor, Idaho, 124
visioning process, 87–89
Volk, Trudi, 109
vote mobs, 125
voting, 146–47
on ballot initiatives, 160–61
candidate forums, 75
by jurors, 183
political participation by voters, 6–7, 136
right to vote, 23
vouching, cultural, 99–102

Walmart, battle to exclude, xxvii, 87
Walsh, Katherine Cramer, 156
waste-management regulations, 52–53
water supply
bottled water, mining for, 54
local control of, 38–44, 186
Weisbord, Marvin, 65
Weiser, Philip J., 182
Who Decides group, 42–44
Whyte, William "Holly," 137–38
wiki websites, 62–63
winning, democracy and, xxvii–xxviii
Winter Park, Florida, 48
women, town meeting participation by, 179
Wood-Lewis, Michael, 139–40
World Café technique, 75, 80, 132

Xcel Energy, 48–49

Year of Civil Discourse, 132–33
Youth Civic Engagement, 161–62

about the authors

Susan Clark is a writer and facilitator focusing on community sustainability and citizen participation and an award-winning radio commentator and former talk-show cohost. She is coauthor of *All Those in Favor: Rediscovering the Secrets of Town Meeting and Community*. Her work has included serving as communications director of the Vermont Natural Resources Council, coordinating a rural grants program, and directing a community activists' network for the northeastern United States and Canada. She has taught community development at the college level for ten years. Clark's democratic activism has earned her broad recognition, including the 2010 Vermont Secretary of State's Enduring Democracy Award. She serves as town moderator of Middlesex, Vermont.

Mark Bushnell

Woden Teachout is an historian and cultural critic interested in the relationship between history, politics, and civic engagement. She holds a PhD in the history of American civilization from Harvard University and has taught at a number of colleges and universities including Harvard, Middlebury College, and Goddard College. She is currently a professor at Union Institute & University. Teachout is the author of the critically acclaimed *Capture the Flag: A Political History of American Patriotism* (Basic Books, 2009), which explored the development of American political culture. In addition to her scholarly work, she has been involved with politics on the state and local levels as a campaign manager, legislative committee assistant, citizen lobbyist, and community organizer. Her advocacy revolves around education, health, and children's issues.

Mark Bushnell

about the foreword author

Frank M. Bryan is the author of several books on democracy, including *Real Democracy: The New England Town Meeting and How It Works* and *The Vermont Papers: Recreating Democracy on a Human Scale*. He is the John G. McCullough Professor of Political Science at the University of Vermont.

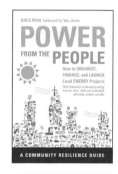
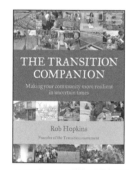

the politics and practice of sustainable living

CHELSEA GREEN PUBLISHING

DON'T THINK OF AN ELEPHANT!
Know Your Values and Frame the Debate
GEORGE LAKOFF
9781931498715
Paperback • $10.00

BYE BYE, MISS AMERICAN EMPIRE
*Neighborhood Patriots, Backcountry Rebels,
and Their Underdog Crusades to Redraw
America's Political Map*
BILL KAUFFMAN
9781933392806
Paperback • $17.95

GET UP, STAND UP
*Uniting Populists, Energizing the Defeated,
and Battling the Corporate Elite*
BRUCE E. LEVINE
9781603582988
PAPERBACK • $17.95

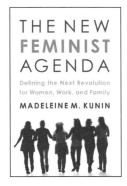

THE NEW FEMINIST AGENDA
*Defining the Next Revolution for
Women, Work, and Family*
MADELEINE M. KUNIN
9781603584258
Hardcover • $26.95
9781603582919
Paperback • $17.95

the politics and practice of sustainable living